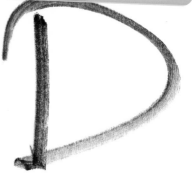

ALSO BY ANDREW C. ISENBERG

Mining California: An Ecological History

The Destruction of the Bison: An Environmental History, 1750–1920

AS EDITOR

The Nature of Cities: Culture, Landscape, and Urban Space

WYATT EARP

WYATT EARP

A VIGILANTE LIFE

ANDREW C. ISENBERG

〰 HILL AND WANG

A DIVISION OF FARRAR, STRAUS AND GIROUX

NEW YORK

Hill and Wang
A division of Farrar, Straus and Giroux
18 West 18th Street, New York 10011

Library of Congress Cataloging-in-Publication Data
Isenberg, Andrew C. (Andrew Christian)
    Wyatt Earp : a vigilante life / Andrew C. Isenberg. — First edition.
        pages   cm
    Includes bibliographical references and index.
    ISBN 978-0-8090-9500-1 (alkaline paper)
    1. Earp, Wyatt, 1848–1929.   2. Peace officers—Southwest, New—
Biography.   3. United States marshals—Southwest, New—Biography.
4. Vigilantes—Southwest, New—Biography.   5. Frontier and pioneer
life—Southwest, New.   6. Southwest, New—Biography.   7. Tombstone
(Ariz.)—Biography.   I. Title.

F786.E18 I84 2013
978'.02092—dc23
[B]

                                                          2012048162

Designed by Jonathan D. Lippincott

Farrar, Straus and Giroux books may be purchased for educational, business, or
promotional use. For information on bulk purchases, please contact the Macmillan
Corporate and Premium Sales Department at 1-800-221-7945, extension 5442, or
write to specialmarkets@macmillan.com.

www.fsgbooks.com
www.twitter.com/fsgbooks • www.facebook.com/fsgbooks

1   3   5   7   9   10   8   6   4   2

For Kai, Elena, and Noah

Do not remember the sins of my youth, or my transgressions. —Psalm 25:7

Revenge may be wicked, but it's natural.
—William Makepeace Thackeray, *Vanity Fair*

Most folk heroes start out as criminals.
—*Slap Shot*

CONTENTS

A photographic insert follows page 112.

★ WYATT EARP'S WEST ★

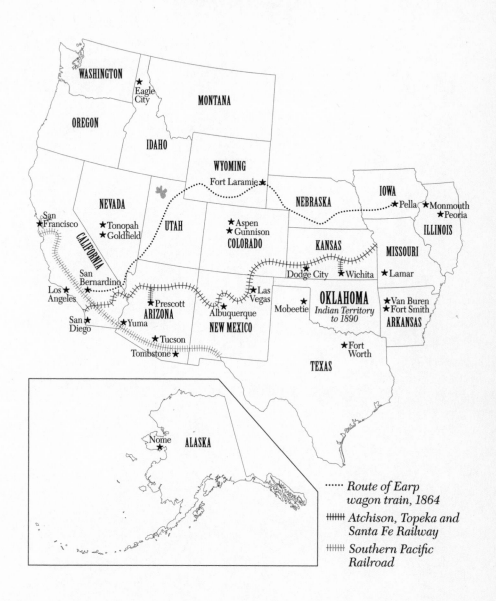

WASHINGTON

★ Eagle City

MONTANA

OREGON

IDAHO

WYOMING

Fort Laramie ★

NEVADA

★ Tonopah
★ Goldfield

UTAH

San Francisco ★

CALIFORNIA

San Bernardino

Los Angeles ★

San Diego ★

★ Yuma

★ Prescott

ARIZONA

★ Tucson

Tombstone ★

★ Las Vegas

Albuquerque

NEW MEXICO

★ Aspen
★ Gunnison

COLORADO

Dodge City

NEBRASKA

KANSAS

★ Wichita

Mobeetie ★

OKLAHOMA
Indian Territory to 1890

★ Fort Worth

TEXAS

IOWA

★ Pella

MISSOURI

★ Lamar

ILLINOIS

★ Monmouth
★ Peoria

★ Van Buren
★ Fort Smith

ARKANSAS

Nome ★

ALASKA

····· Route of Earp wagon train, 1864

╫╫╫ Atchison, Topeka and Santa Fe Railway

╫╫╫ Southern Pacific Railroad

★ THE EARP FAMILY ★

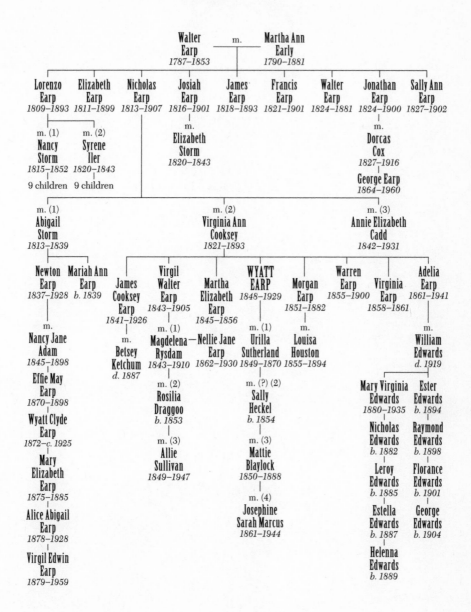

WYATT EARP

LEX TALIONIS

On the night of March 20, 1882, at a train station in Tucson, Arizona Territory, Wyatt Earp, a deputy United States marshal, shot Frank Stilwell, an accused stage-robber and murderer. Wyatt aimed to kill, firing his shotgun into Stilwell's chest at such close range that powder burns encircled the gaping wound. The shotgun blast alone was a mortal wound, but when a railroad worker discovered Stilwell's body the next morning, he found that Stilwell had been shot multiple times. Members of Earp's posse, which included his youngest brother, Warren, and his closest friend, the professional gambler John Henry "Doc" Holliday, had opened fire with their own weapons to make sure of Stilwell's death. The gunfight was one-sided: Stilwell's pistol had not been fired.[1]

By most accounts, Stilwell was a villain. As a deputy sheriff in Cochise County, Arizona, which included the silver boomtown of Tombstone, he was one of several corrupt lawmen who shielded cattle rustlers and stage-robbers from justice. He was in Tucson, seventy-five miles northwest of Tombstone, to face prosecution for having participated in a stage robbery himself. He was at the train station awaiting the arrival of a cowboy who would provide him with an alibi in court—the cowboy was likely prepared to commit perjury. Wyatt had long known Stilwell was a blackguard, but he had another, more important reason to confront him at the train station in Tucson. Two nights earlier, in Tombstone, gunmen had murdered Wyatt's younger brother Morgan. Witnesses had identified Stilwell as one of Morgan's killers, and a coroner's jury in Tombstone had indicted him for the crime.

As Stilwell's wounds suggested, Wyatt, despite his commission as a deputy U.S. marshal, made no attempt to arrest the accused murderer and bring him before a judge. Wyatt's experiences with Arizona's legal system over the previous half year had soured him on courtroom justice. In October 1881, as a deputy police officer in Tombstone serving under his brother Virgil, the town police chief, Wyatt had participated in a gunfight that had left three cowboys dead. (The shoot-out, memorialized as the Gunfight at the O.K. Corral, actually took place in an empty lot behind the corral.) Following the shoot-out, Virgil, Wyatt, and Wyatt's fellow deputies Morgan and Holliday were accused of murder and endured a monthlong courtroom ordeal. Wyatt spent much of that month in a Tombstone jail cell.[2] In late December, confederates of the dead cowboys shotgunned Virgil on a deserted Tombstone street; Virgil survived, but lost the use of his left arm. A cowboy, Ike Clanton, was charged with attempted murder, but in court, seven witnesses swore that Ike had been with them in a mining camp outside Tombstone on the night of the attack.[3] Wyatt feared that if Stilwell was brought to court to face charges for Morgan's murder—which like the shooting of Virgil was in retaliation for the October gunfight—Stilwell's friends would testify falsely to provide him an alibi.

Accused of murdering Stilwell and, in the days that followed, two other cowboys he suspected of involvement in Morgan's death, Wyatt fled Arizona. Despite the ignominy of his exit from Tombstone, his role as a vigilante became a crucial part of his eventual status in American popular culture as an icon of law and order, the violent agent of justice on a lawless frontier. On the surface, it seems unlikely, or at least ironic, that a vigilante killer would become a symbol of rectitude. Yet Wyatt's story appealed to Americans who like him saw justice not in fickle courtrooms, but in the character of stalwarts who were willing to break the law—even to commit murder.

A host of books, films, and television programs propelled Wyatt into his status as the iconic vigilante lawman.[4] In 1931, a biography, *Wyatt Earp: Frontier Marshal*, by Stuart N. Lake, cast Wyatt as an Old West version of an FBI agent and his Tombstone enemies as an organized-crime ring. Like Eliot Ness or Melvin Purvis, Lake implied, Wyatt rightly resorted to extralegal justice because of the brutality of his enemies and the corruption of local police and judges. During the early years of the Cold War, the icon of the resolute lawman became a symbol of resistance to communism. Such resistance was so violent, in Western films such as 1957's *Gunfight at the O.K. Corral*, which starred Burt Lancaster as Wyatt, that the lawman inevitably remained outside of the civil society he protected.[5] In late 2001, when President George W. Bush vowed to get Osama bin Laden "dead or alive," he summoned up the Earp icon of the frontier lawman willing to go outside of the law in the pursuit of justice. On September 19, 2001, a columnist for the *Hartford Courant* referred to the "dead or alive" vow as "Wyatt Earp rhetoric."[6] In 2010, one year before the Justice Department indicted his office for discriminating against Mexican Americans, Sheriff Joe Arpaio of Maricopa County, Arizona, created an armed "immigration posse" to inderdict suspected illegal aliens. One of the posse's members was a Phoenix man, Wyatt Earp, who was not only the namesake of the 1880s Arizona lawman but claimed to be his nephew. Across three-quarters of a century, in battles against organized crime, Soviet communism, Islamist terrorism, and illegal immigration, Americans have invoked the Earp icon to rationalize the extralegal pursuit of justice.

Yet the Wyatt Earp of the nineteenth-century American West was not the film icon familiar to modern Americans. While the Hollywood version is stubbornly, consistently duty-bound, in actuality Wyatt led a life of restlessness, inconstancy, impulsive law-breaking, and shifting identities. Beginning in his late teens, he rarely lived more than a year or two in one place. For much of his life, he was both hunter and hunted: he was a lawman in Missouri, Kansas, and Arizona; he was also a fugitive in Colorado and saw the inside of jail cells in Arkansas, Illinois, Arizona, and California. He was the grand-son of a Methodist preacher and struck most of the educated, genteel, religiously minded people who knew him as a paragon of probity; he also spent most of his life working in brothels, saloons, and gam-bling halls. When he was not wearing a badge, he was variously a thief, brothel bouncer, professional gambler, and confidence man who specialized in selling gold bricks that were nothing more than rocks painted yellow.

His hasty exit from Arizona in 1882 was not the first time that an impulsive criminal act had forced him to become a fugitive. In 1871, he broke out of jail in Arkansas after being arrested for horse theft. In 1872, he left Peoria, Illinois, following a string of arrests for consorting with prostitutes. In 1876, officials in Wichita, Kansas, declared him a vagrant and banished him after he assaulted a can-didate for town marshal on the eve of a municipal election. In each case, Wyatt left behind his scandals, moved to a fresh town where he was largely or entirely unknown, and reinvented himself. In the narrowly localized society of the 1870s, a man such as Wyatt who was willing to pull up stakes and remake his reputation in a new town could outrun his past.

These reinventions often meant abandoning old partners—men and women—for new ones. In Wichita, he left behind his police partner, Jimmy Cairns, with whom he had shared a bed. When he fled Arizona, he abandoned Mattie Blaylock, a woman with whom he had lived for years. Indeed, Wyatt changed partners nearly as often as he changed occupations and addresses. He had three wives over the course of his life; a fourth woman, a prostitute at a brothel where Wyatt worked, once claimed to be his wife. He maintained close relationships with two men; in addition to Cairns, his friend-ship with Holliday was so close that it was described by one contem-porary as romantic.

Self-invention has a long history in America. In the eighteenth and nineteenth centuries, self-invention was closely related to the powerful American belief in the possibilities of moral betterment and upward social mobility. Benjamin Franklin was the prototype for this kind of self-made man; in his autobiography Franklin depicted himself, not entirely without justification, as a runaway servant who rose to wealth and prominence through hard work and virtuous self-denial. In the latter part of the nineteenth century, an ex–divinity student, Horatio Alger, Jr., heralded the American creed of rags-to-respectability mobility through a series of stories aimed at boys and girls. Alger's protagonists were bootblacks and pickpockets who, after experiencing a conversion to the Whiggish creed of upward mobility, righted themselves to become churchgoing entrepreneurs.[7]

Wyatt's version of self-invention differed from that of Franklin and Alger. Socially, his family was downwardly mobile. He had been born into an extended family of churchgoing, Whiggish strivers who adhered to values of hard work. Yet when Wyatt was still a boy, his father, Nicholas, disappointed by a series of financial and legal set-backs, lost his faith in the promise of upward mobility. By the time Wyatt was in his teens, his father had become an inveterate liar who invented for himself the achievements that had eluded him in life. Like his father, Wyatt embraced the prerogative of self-invention, and like him, he eschewed the self-denial that Franklin and Alger maintained was essential to upward mobility. As an adult, Wyatt convincingly acted the part of the upright lawman, but was never willing to sacrifice gambling, prostitutes, confidence games, or petty crimes to become one completely.

The role of the solitary, dutiful lawman was thus one of many identities the protean Wyatt took on and cast off in his life. So, too, was the role of vigilante. His resort to vigilantism in 1882 was not the act of a man unwaveringly committed to justice in a frontier ter-ritory where the courts were corrupt, but the impulsive vengeance of a man who had long disdained authority. He donned and shucked off roles readily, whipsawing between lawman and lawbreaker, and pursued his changing ambitions recklessly, with little thought to the cost to himself, and still less thought to the cost, even the deadly cost, to others.

Yet Hollywood vindicated the vigilante, turning Wyatt into an icon of law and order. His plastic identity and penchant for reinvention freely lent itself to Hollywood mythmaking. Consumed in his last years with justifying his resort to deadly violence in Arizona, he told and retold stories of his life as a law officer in Tombstone and in the Kansas cow towns of Wichita and Dodge City in the 1870s. His tales were as inconsistent and changeable as his life itself: he edited out his missteps and embarrassments, inflated his accomplishments, and appropriated the deeds of others as his own. He spent the last two decades of his life living primarily in Los Angeles and becoming a fixture at Hollywood studios. Befriending Western silent-film actors and directors, he presented himself to them as a lawman singularly committed to justice.

One of those actors, William S. Hart, convinced Wyatt that a memoir, presented either in book form or serialized in a popular magazine such as the *Saturday Evening Post*, should be the basis for a film script. In the late 1910s, Wyatt collaborated on such a memoir with Forrestine Hooker, the author of somewhat formulaic children's stories and the daughter-in-law of an Arizona rancher whom Wyatt had known. Although Hooker's manuscript presented Wyatt in a flattering light, he was dissatisfied with it, or perhaps was not yet ready to settle on a definitive account of a life he had so often reinvented. He steered the manuscript into a desk drawer to be forgotten and did what he was long practiced at doing: he began again with a new narrative. His new collaborator was John Flood, a young friend who regarded Wyatt with unqualified admiration. Yet fidelity proved a poor substitute for ability: Flood struggled with the task of writing Wyatt's biography for two years, eventually producing a convoluted manuscript that was rejected by all of the publishers to whom Hart sent it.

After a decade of false starts, Wyatt settled on Lake, a former journalist and aspiring screenwriter, to write his biography. Yet even as Wyatt reminisced to Lake during the spring of 1928, in what turned out to be the last year of his life, he carefully edited his past. He had long hidden his youthful arrests even from some of his own family. He repeated to Lake many of the same stories he had told his family—for instance, that he had spent the early 1870s hunting bison in the southern plains, when in fact he was compiling a criminal record in Arkansas and Illinois. Wyatt did not intend to arouse Lake's suspicions by mentioning that as recently as 1911 officers of the Los Angeles police's bunco squad had arrested him for running a crooked faro game. Yet he need not have worried. Lake, eager to make his literary reputation by casting himself as Boswell to Wyatt's Samuel Johnson, polished Wyatt's tales to a high shine. The icon conjured by Wyatt and Lake quickly made its way onto the screen, just as Wyatt had hoped, dominating the American memory of Wyatt for a half century. Unlike those Horatio Alger strivers who invented a better future for themselves, Wyatt invented for himself a better past. Though Wyatt, who died in 1929, did not live to see it, Hollywood's embrace of him as a paragon of law and order was the realization of his last and undoubtedly his greatest confidence game, his surest revenge, and his most complete reinvention.

2

THE SONS OF ISHMAEL

In 1845, an extended family of Kentucky migrants—a married couple in their late fifties, their adult sons, and their sons' wives and young children—brought their wagons to a halt in the town of Monmouth in Warren County, Illinois. A few of the town's residents may have referred to the newcomers, led by the family patriarch, Walter Earp, as "butternuts"—a derisive term for Upper South yeomen who dyed their homespun clothes light brown with butternut juices. Yet few residents of Monmouth probably took much notice of the new arrivals. The appearance of another family of Kentuckians was unremarkable. Like many Midwestern towns in the mid-nineteenth century, Monmouth was both a destination and a jumping-off point for western migrants. Indeed, most of the long-term inhabitants of the town had come to Monmouth from elsewhere. The town was originally founded on lands granted to veterans of the War of 1812, and most of its roughly seven hundred residents had been born outside Illinois.[1]

When most people think of antebellum towns such as Monmouth, the image that comes to mind is of one of the many Currier & Ives illustrations of small-town and rural America: regular, neatly plowed fields; fenced pastures; tidy gardens; sturdy homes; and tree-lined lanes. The image bespeaks agrarian serenity, prosperity, and permanence; an age of innocence that preceded the rise of industry and the carnage of the Civil War. Yet to create the kind of bucolic landscape depicted by Currier & Ives that was simultaneously productive and soothingly pastoral required an investment of years if not generations of money and labor. In reality, few nineteenth-century American farms and towns were so orderly and idyllic— and few antebellum American farmers or townspeople so prosperous and permanent in their habitations.[2]

Antebellum Americans were a restive lot. In the nineteenth century, only about half of Americans stayed in one place long enough to be counted by two consecutive decennial census-takers. Some migrations were local, but a fair number—such as the Earps' move to Illinois—were interstate. One study of veterans of the War of 1812 found that by the 1850s, one-third had migrated out of the state of their birth. Altogether, in 1850, nearly one-quarter of Americans lived outside their state of birth.[3] Pressure to migrate was inexorable: relatively cheap western land, large rural families, and increasingly expensive farmland in the settled East conspired to induce many rural families to move west. As antebellum American agriculture turned away from subsistence and toward commercial production, economic pressures to migrate intensified. Successful farmers close to urban markets consolidated the landholdings of their less successful neighbors, while large numbers of rural Americans migrated to cities and towns and into wage work. Mineral rushes to the Far West following discoveries of gold in California in 1848 and in Colorado in 1858 prompted explosive spasms of migration. Finally, between 1861 and 1865, tens of thousands of Upper South and Midwestern farmers migrated to the West to escape the maelstrom of the Civil War.[4] Over several decades, the Earps felt all of these pressures, and from the mid-1840s through the end of the Civil War, the Earps were buffeted from the Upper South to the Midwest to the Far West.

The Earps' wanderings reveal a reality at odds with the Currier & Ives image of antebellum America as an American Canaan, a promised land of patriarchal order. Nicholas Earp, the second son of Walter Earp, and the father of Wyatt, exemplified antebellum

Americans' anxious transience. Nicholas was an impatient and contrarian striver, equally willing to pull up stakes and move in search of new opportunities as he was to challenge local customs. He was drawn to local offices—town constable and deputy provost marshal, for instance—that enabled him to exercise authority over his neighbors. Yet he chafed when those neighbors sought to constrain his behavior; he regarded local laws banning the sale of liquor or mandating the repayment of debts as nuisances to be circumvented—especially when the liquor and the debts were his own. A bully and braggart prone to angry outbursts, he channeled his restlessness into enlistment in the U.S. Army during the Mexican-American War (though he did not serve out his term of enlistment) and migration to California (though he was at odds with his fellow California emigrants long before they reached their destination). If Currier & Ives depicted an American Canaan, then the peripatetic, combative Nicholas was less like Canaan's patriarch Abraham than he was like Abraham's son, Ishmael, who is described in Genesis as "a wild ass of a man, his hand against every man and every man's hand against him." Ishmael, like Nicholas, was cast out of Canaan to wander in the wilderness. Ishmael's sons, like those of Nicholas, were condemned to a migratory existence on the periphery of the promised land.[5]

The migration of Walter and Martha Earp and their children to Monmouth was typical of thousands of border-state farm families in the early and middle nineteenth century. Like most migrants, the Earps were from the broad middle sector of the agrarian economy; the wealthiest landowners had little incentive to move, and the poorest could not afford to go. Migration was costly—in the 1840s, to leave Kentucky or North Carolina and settle in the Illinois or Iowa prairies, and then subsist until the first harvest, cost about $1,000.[6]

Usually, farm families such as the Earps undertook to migrate west to enlarge their landholdings. Migrants leaving North Carolina or Kentucky usually sold small or midsize farms and acquired larger landholdings in the West, where land was cheaper. Yet the simple goal of enlarging landholdings contained deeper complexities.

In the agrarian economy of nineteenth-century America, the family was a workforce. Both husband and wife labored on a typical midcentury farm from sunrise to sundown. Men such as Walter Earp were largely responsible for fieldwork. They cleared forests, plowed, planted, and harvested. Women such as Martha Earp maintained the vegetable gardens that fed the family and attended to the hens and the cows. They spun cloth and sewed clothes (and probably dyed them in butternut juices). They handled tasks such as cooking and laundry—chores made considerably more difficult by the necessity of fetching water and cutting and hauling firewood. Children, too, were pressed into service at an early age. As a child, Nicholas Earp and his eight siblings would have hauled water and wood and have been sent into the fields, gardens, and pastures to weed, herd, and milk. As they became older, they would have taken on more strenuous duties. Indeed, the labor of children was essential to the success of antebellum farms.[7] Most of the farm's production went to the family's subsistence, but backwoods Kentucky yeomen also produced enough surplus to purchase a wide variety of commodities: sugar, tea, coffee, and porcelain among them.[8]

Rural couples married relatively young (Walter and Martha Earp were twenty-two and nineteen, respectively, when they married in 1809), and large families were imperative. One of a farm wife's most important responsibilities was the bearing of children, who would compose the family's corps of laborers. About half of rural wives had given birth by the end of their first year of marriage; virtually all had done so by the end of the third year of marriage. The average farm wife bore seven children in her lifetime; those children were spaced, on average, twenty-nine months apart. Thus, a typical farm wife such as Martha Earp could expect to spend most of the two decades following her marriage either pregnant or nursing. Indeed, Martha Earp bore nine children in the first eighteen years of her marriage: Lorenzo (1809), Elizabeth (1811), Nicholas

(1813), Josiah (1816), James (1818), Francis (1821), the twins Walter and Jonathan (1824), and Sally Ann (1827).

Children in such rural households generally lived with and labored for their parents well into adulthood, with sons continuing to abide in their parents' household after marrying and beginning families of their own. Nicholas Earp, for instance, was thirty-two years old, married with four children of his own, when he accompanied his parents from Kentucky to Illinois. Most sons stayed close to their parents not completely out of filial loyalty. The patriarchs in such rural households held on to the ownership of family lands (or capital) until the end of their lives. Sons could not hope to inherit part of the family patrimony unless they remained in their parents' household and continued to work the family lands.[9]

To ensure that their sons stayed and labored for their parents into their adulthood, farm patriarchs needed extensive landholdings. If they wanted their sons to remain part of the family workforce, they had to possess enough land so that those sons could anticipate inheriting sizable farms themselves. Few fathers in the antebellum American backcountry controlled enough land to allow more than two or three sons to inherit. The others had to strike out on their own. To perpetuate the system of patriarchal control over land and labor, farm families migrated west to increase their landholdings. The pressure to aggregate lands drove thousands of these "patrimonial families" across North America in the nineteenth century.[10]

By the 1840s a definite pattern of rural migration had been established: if a couple were to strike out on their own, they usually did so shortly after marriage, or perhaps after the birth of their first child, when they were not yet deeply rooted in a community. For instance, four years after they were married, Walter and Martha Earp left North Carolina with their three children and settled in Logan County, Kentucky. If a typical rural family moved again, they would do so in their late thirties or early forties, with several more children in tow, looking to acquire a large enough piece of land to support their brood into adulthood. Indeed, this is exactly what the Earps did: Walter and Martha migrated to Ohio County, Kentucky, where they farmed for twenty years.

The Earps appeared well settled in Ohio County. Walter Earp supplemented what the family produced on the farm by teaching school (typically, rural schools met for only a short period of the year and teachers were paid per pupil—children received their practical education at home and in the field).[11] Walter and Martha became fixtures of the local Methodist church. The denomination, heavily centered in the southern states at the outset of the nineteenth century, grew from only a few thousand congregants west of the Appalachians in 1800 to 175,000 by 1830. A decade later, Methodism was the second-largest denomination in the United States. Methodism's rise in the trans-Appalachian West owed itself to itinerant preachers—the so-called circuit riders—who ministered to backcountry Americans, rallying converts at enthusiastic camp meetings, and to local ministers recruited from the laity, who rendered the faith in its simplest terms and in the local idiom.[12] Walter not only became one of those local preachers, but he and Martha opened their home to passing circuit riders. They named their sons after circuit riders and other prominent Methodist leaders: Nicholas Porter, Lorenzo Dow, James O'Kelly, and Francis Asbury.

Martha Earp bore six more children after the family's move to Ohio County. Her eldest children reached adulthood and married: Lorenzo married Nancy Storm in 1834. Nicholas married Nancy's sister Abigail in 1836. To complete the union of the two families, Josiah Earp married a third sister, Elizabeth, in 1837. For three brothers from one family to marry three sisters from another was unusual although not unheard of. It was a way for yeomen to pool limited resources: to consolidate landholdings and share farm implements.[13] It was also an indication of the limited horizons of rural life in the antebellum backcountry. Between spasms of migration in which they would lurch forward hundreds of miles, rural families such as the Earps might live within the bounds of only a few miles, coming into regular contact with only a handful of other families.

Death was also a near-constant presence in such rural families. About 20 percent of children died before reaching their midteens. Childbearing posed a particular health risk to women: about one in every two hundred women died during or as a result of delivery.[14] Nancy Earp, the wife of Nicholas's older brother, Lorenzo, died in 1852 on the day she gave birth to her ninth child. Nancy's sister Abigail died within three years of her marriage to Nicholas, shortly after giving birth to the couple's second child, a daughter, Mariah Ann. The motherless baby died within a few months. Both Lorenzo and Nicholas swiftly remarried; the economic realities of rural life in antebellum America insured that few young widows or widowers remained unmarried for long. Within a year of Abigail's death, Nicholas married Virginia Ann Cooksey. The couple had three children in Kentucky: James Cooksey, born in 1841; Virgil Walter, born in 1843; and Martha Elizabeth, born in 1845.

For most midcentury rural families, two migrations—one when the parents were in early adulthood and one in middle age—were typical. Yet, when they were in their late fifties, Walter and Martha Earp uprooted a third time and moved to Monmouth. Few yeomen owned enough land to provide for seven sons. Had Walter and Martha stayed in Kentucky, they would probably have seen most of their sons—now grown, married, and with children of their own—leave the family homestead. Yet the Earps did not replicate their earlier move from North Carolina to Kentucky by migrating to an underpopulated rural area, where they might have purchased a large farm—a patrimony that might have held the family together for another generation. Instead, they migrated to a town in the center of a thriving commercial agricultural area. In Monmouth, the Earps would combine farming with wage labor: they worked as coopers, teamsters, drovers, clerks, gardeners, express drivers, and liverymen.[15] The strategy they adopted was typical of the movement of people in midcentury America: while hundreds of thousands of Americans moved from farms in the East to larger farms in the West, an even larger number of farmers moved from the countryside to the city, where wage labor beckoned. In contrast to the romantic notion of the western frontier as a "safety valve" that drew off excess wage workers into farming, cities were the safety valves for the countryside, as landless rural Americans migrated into towns to become wage laborers.[16]

Yet as the Earps' migration to Illinois shows, antebellum Americans did not make sudden decisions to quit farming and become urban wage laborers. At the societal level, the transformation in which the Earps were enmeshed was a broad change from rural, patrimonial families to urban, proletarian ones. At the family level, rural Americans eased into the shift by half steps. Many families, like the Earps, sought to continue to farm as some of their members worked for wages. Although Walter Earp's adult sons established separate households in Monmouth and shifted rapidly into wage work, they supplemented their wages by raising crops on rented land.

It could well be that the politics and economics of slavery contributed to the Earps' move from Kentucky to Illinois. One year before the Earps removed to Illinois, the Methodist Church noisily and publicly divided over the question of slavery; for a devout Methodist such as Walter Earp to leave the new Methodist Episcopal Church, South, in favor of the Northern General Conference, signaled his stance on the slavery question.[17]

There were sound economic reasons to leave a slave state, too. In the decades before the Civil War, large numbers of non-slaveholders from the southern border states migrated to the free states and territories of the West and the North. They had been pushed out by planters, who beginning in the 1830s moved in large numbers into the Upper South. Plantations were self-sufficient enterprises that produced not only cash crops but all of their own foodstuffs; skilled slaves worked as carpenters, blacksmiths, wheelwrights, and teamsters. In an economy increasingly dominated by large planters, there was no room for the barter of goods, skills, and services that typified the economy of yeomen farm families. Abraham Lincoln, whose own family had left Kentucky for Indiana in the 1830s, a decade ahead of the Earps, summed up the problem in 1854, during the debate over whether Kansas and Nebraska would be admitted to the Union as free or slave states: "Slave states are places for poor white people to remove from, not to remove to."[18] The Earps were politically active in Monmouth in the antislavery cause: shortly after arriving in Monmouth, Walter Earp joined the Whig opposition to the Mexican War—largely seen in the North as a slaveholders' war to expand slavery; in 1856, Nicholas was one of the founders of Monmouth's Frémont Club, a forerunner of the antislavery Republican Party.[19]

In Illinois, Whigs-cum-Republicans were less opposed to the institution of slavery in the South than to the extension of slavery to the West. The western territories, Whig politicians such as Lincoln believed, should be reserved for small farmers; the availability of land in the West would provide a means for individual betterment. Indeed, antislavery was subsidiary to the central Whig political tenet, upward mobility. The Whigs conceived of western lands, wage labor, and commerce as parts of an integrated system that provided a host of opportunities for social betterment. Lincoln summed up the Whig worldview in 1859, saying, "The prudent, penniless beginner in the world labors for wages awhile, saves a surplus with which to buy tools or land, for himself; then labors on his own account another while, and at length hires another new beginner to help him."[20] It was this sort of upward mobility that the Earps hoped to enjoy in Illinois.

Yet Warren County in the mid-1840s—with its nearly seven thousand residents, virtually all of whom were, like the Earps, native-born, white, literate Protestants—was no promised land of upward mobility. If Walter Earp's sons faced limited options as small farmers in the increasingly planter-dominated southern upcountry, the mechanization and commercialization of agriculture in the Illinois prairie similarly limited their possibilities. By the time the Earps arrived in Monmouth, Cyrus McCormick's factory in Chicago was producing one thousand mechanical reapers each year for Midwestern wheat farmers. Farmers who bought a reaper usually also bought a steam-powered thresher, a machine that removed grain from the dry stalk. Agricultural machinery contributed to the transformation of the Midwest into the breadbasket of the nation.

By the middle of the nineteenth century, the Midwest produced half of the United States' corn and one-third of its wheat; almost all of the Midwest's exports of wheat and two-thirds of its corn went to feed the residents of Northeastern cities. These new machines and others like them rendered obsolete small-scale farms that rural families worked by hand.

To increase production, commercial farmers expanded their landholdings. Throughout Illinois's increasingly commercialized rural landscape, farmland was concentrated in fewer hands. One consequence of land consolidation was a rise in tenancy. Although we tend to think of tenancy and sharecropping as artifacts of the post–Civil War cotton South, they were aspects of the frontier in both North and South long before the war. Squatting, sharecropping, and tenancy were common in Warren County, which was part of the Illinois "Military Tract," an area of 3.5 million acres between the Illinois and Mississippi Rivers set aside for 160-acre land bounties awarded to veterans of the War of 1812. Most veterans had no intention of settling on the lands, however, and sold the property to eastern speculators without ever seeing it. New York and Philadelphia investors thus came to control tens of thousands of acres in the Military Tract. With so much land held by so few, some settlers simply "squatted" on the speculators' lands without title—the Monmouth court dealt with trespassing cases frequently. Others paid rent or a share of their crop: the standard in the mid-1840s in the Military Tract was one-third of the crop or fifty cents an acre.[21] Many of the landless signed on as seasonal laborers for the large estate owners.

Western Illinois may not have been the farmer's utopia of free land and boundless opportunity that bygone generations of historians made the frontier out to be, but as thousands of migrants from the Upper South such as the Earps discovered, there was far more opportunity in the commercializing North than among the growing number of planters in Kentucky. While the long-term effect of land concentration was to close off opportunities for the landless, in the short term wage labor provided welcome opportunities for families such as the Earps to earn cash: hired farmhands in Warren County worked ten-hour days for about $10 a month. In the winter, Nicholas found further work in Warren County's commercial-agricultural economy: he worked as a cooper, building barrels to be packed with pork for shipment by steamboat to urban markets—salt pork was a staple of the American diet at midcentury, and pork packing was a leading Midwestern industry.[22]

Nicholas bought a moderate-size house in Monmouth in September 1845 for $450. It is unlikely that he earned the cash he used to buy the home working as a cooper or a farmhand in Monmouth; he had only recently arrived in Illinois at the time he purchased the house; it would have taken him years to accumulate $450. He may well have worked for wages in Kentucky and brought some savings with him to Illinois, but $450 was a considerable sum. Rather, most of the money to purchase the home likely represented Nicholas's share of the sale of the Earp family farm in Kentucky. Nicholas also acquired the rights to three other town lots with $150 in promissory notes.[23]

Yet Nicholas was not content with a workingman's wage and a modest home, or perhaps he was restless in sedate Monmouth. His moment came in mid-1847, when the United States had been at war with Mexico for a year. Nicholas's employer, Wyatt Berry Stapp, had resolved to recruit a volunteer cavalry company from Monmouth. Nicholas signed on to help organize the one hundred men of the so-called Monmouth Dragoons. The organizers of volunteer units, who staged grand parties, treated recruits to drinks, and sometimes offered cash in return for enlistment, were almost universally elected to leadership positions by the recruits. Stapp, with Nicholas's help, staged a large Fourth of July picnic in Monmouth to attract volunteers. Raising a volunteer regiment was exactly the sort of work at which Nicholas, a burly, gregarious man who enjoyed his liquor, excelled. The Monmouth Dragoons were organized within a month. Stapp became the unit's commander and Nicholas a third sergeant.

In going to war, Nicholas went against his family's political leanings. Walter Earp had signed a Whig declaration against the war in January 1847, which helped him win election as one of Monmouth's three justices of the peace later that year. While Nicholas's enlistment was perhaps a prodigal son's act of rebellion against his father, economics likely factored as much as politics or patriarchy in Earp's decision to enlist. The same impulse toward social advancement that had impelled the Earps to Monmouth may well have drawn Nicholas into the volunteer unit. Soldiers earned a decent wage—$8 a month for a private, $13 a month for a sergeant; moreover, volunteers who served for one year were promised a 160-acre land bounty. For these reasons recruiters of volunteer units did well in southern and western Illinois, where rates of tenancy were high.[24]

The Monmouth Dragoons left for Quincy, Illinois, in August 1847. From there, they were transported down the Mississippi River to New Orleans, and then directly to Veracruz, Mexico, to join General Winfield Scott's bloody assault on Mexico City. According to Nicholas, in his 1877 application for a military pension, the Dragoons primarily accompanied supply trains between Veracruz and interior positions, protecting them from attack by Mexican forces. Guerrillas attacked a convoy guarded by the Monmouth Dragoons in November 1847, resulting in the death of one of the Monmouth volunteers. Nineteen other men of the unit died of disease before the war ended. Sixteen were discharged early—including Sergeant Earp, on December 24, 1847. Nicholas, who later claimed that he was discharged because he had been kicked in the groin by a mule, returned to Monmouth in February 1848. For his half year of service, Nicholas received neither a military pension nor the coveted 160-acre bounty. Instead, the army compensated him for his alleged injury with an extra three months' pay.[25]

The disappointing end to his Mexican adventure seemed to both embitter and embolden Nicholas, now the father of five following the birth, on March 19, 1848, of his fourth son, whom he named Wyatt Berry Stapp Earp, in honor of the commander of the Monmouth Dragoons. After his sojourn in Mexico, Nicholas became more willing to migrate to new communities (even if it meant leaving the extended Earp family behind) and to experiment with different ways of making a living (even if it meant defying local laws). Over the next dozen years, he moved his family to Iowa, back to Monmouth, to Iowa again, to California, and then to Missouri. He tried his hand at farming, police work, and, most improbably, bootlegging in stead-fastly pro-temperance Monmouth. Between 1848 and 1868—during which time Wyatt grew to adulthood—Nicholas and his children spent no longer than seven years in one place. They did not belong to the communities in which they lived so much as they perched on the edge of them, constantly poised to move once more.

A year after the birth of Wyatt, Nicholas abruptly sold his house in Monmouth (for only $300, or $150 less than he had paid for the property in 1845) and headed west with his wife and children. He apparently told the clerk of the Monmouth court, who canceled the sale of the lots Nicholas had purchased with promissory notes, that he was joining the gold rush to California. Instead, he landed in Pella, Iowa, 150 miles west-northwest of Monmouth. Pella had been founded in 1847 on eighteen thousand acres between the Des Moines and Skunk Rivers by the Amsterdam nonconforming minister Hendrik Pieter Scholte and eight hundred of his followers.[26] The immigrants had purchased the land directly from the federal government, or, in some cases, from veterans who had received bounties in the territory. Dutch was the dominant language of the community, but a small number of native-born Americans such as the Earps settled in Pella: the Dutch needed what antebellum settlers called "set-up men": hired hands who built homes, cleared land, and broke sod.[27] A set-up man who remained in Pella might have further employment. As more of Scholte's followers migrated to Iowa from Holland, not only would there be new work, but the value of property promised to rise. For a man such as Nicholas, Pella seemed to promise more opportunity than Monmouth, where by the late 1840s the social order had already become fixed.[28] Yet, as one of the few native-born and English-speaking families in Pella, the Earps found themselves strangers in their own land. The years the Earps spent in Pella—Wyatt's formative early childhood—doubtless contributed to the Earps' aloofness toward the communities in which they lived.

The records are sketchy, but initially in Iowa the Earps were either tenant farmers or squatters (or, as squatters preferred to be called, preemptors). Although Nicholas appears in the 1850 census in Pella as a cooper and a farmer, he did not register the ownership of any land.[29] Squatting was common on the agricultural frontier: thousands of settlers like Nicholas could not afford to pay the minimum government price of $1.25 per acre. Instead, they settled on unoccupied land—especially public land owned by the government or land that had been purchased by an absentee speculator. Eventually they would be confronted by the government or the legitimate owner, but in that case, backcountry custom dictated that the government would extend the right to purchase their claim, or the title holder would compensate them for their "improvements"—a house, a stable, a cleared field.[30] Despite the historical ubiquity of squatters, few liked to remember themselves as impoverished trespassers. In *Wyatt Earp: Frontier Marshal*, Stuart Lake recorded Wyatt as saying of his father, "He never rented, always owned; and he never sold a farm that was not greatly improved over the condition in which it had been acquired."[31] The second part of Wyatt's assertion rings true: the telltale use of the squatter's term *improved*.

Whether he began his sojourn in Iowa as a squatter or not, by 1855 Nicholas had acquired title to a 160-acre farm seven miles northeast of Pella. How he managed to secure title to the land is not entirely clear. The land was not a bounty in exchange for his military service—he had not served long enough to qualify. Starting a farm was expensive. Even at the minimum government purchase price of $1.25 an acre, 160 acres would cost $200; fencing, clearing, and a home would push the start-up cost of a new farm up toward $1,000—although a frugal settler might skimp on the extent of the fencing and the quality and comfort of the home. Even if he stinted on materials, $1,000 was likely more than Nicholas could afford: he had sold his house in Illinois for a loss and defaulted on the promissory notes he had signed on empty lots in Monmouth.

Nicholas managed on so little capital by renting a house in Pella—a large, two-story brick building—thus reducing the costs of his farm to little more than the price of the acreage. He may have acquired the farmland directly from Pella's founder and leader. The land Nicholas owned had previously been purchased, for $1.25 per acre, by "Henry Peter Schotte"—surely an anglicization of Hendrik Pieter Scholte—on February 22, 1855.

Despite his apparent success in Pella, in March 1856 Nicholas resolved to return to Monmouth. After seven years in Iowa (and the birth of two more sons: Morgan in 1851 and Warren in 1855), he sold his 160 acres in a complicated three-way exchange. Officially, Nicholas sold his land to Aquillin Noe of Monmouth, for $2,050. Nicholas never saw any cash from the deal, however. At the same time that he sold his property in Iowa, Nicholas purchased from Noe a house and two empty city lots in Monmouth for the same amount, $2,050. As soon as he had acquired Nicholas's 160 acres in Iowa, Noe sold the land to another Monmouth farmer, Hiram Webster, for $1,600. Webster, in turn, sold forty-four acres outside Monmouth to Noe.[32] Thus, despite the large figures, almost no cash changed hands in the deal. The practical result of the exchange was that after seven years in Iowa, the Earps moved back to Monmouth, Webster moved to the Earp farm in Iowa, and Noe acquired Webster's Monmouth land. On paper, Nicholas returned as a success, having traded in his Iowa lands for $2,000 worth of property in Monmouth. In reality, Earp found himself in 1856 back in Monmouth with more or less what he had owned when he had left in 1849: a house and two other lots. He was as cash-poor upon his return as he had ever been.

Nicholas, now forty-three years old, returned to Monmouth as an agricultural depression, the so-called Panic of 1857, was beginning.[33] Yet the Nicholas Earp who returned from Iowa did not seek work as a hired hand as he once had. He seems to have resolved upon his return to Illinois to try again to break out of the ranks of the wage laborer, much as he had tried to change his luck a decade earlier when he had volunteered for the Monmouth Dragoons. Yet by 1856 he was no longer a young striver, but a middle-aged idler looking for a softer way of making a living: he returned to Monmouth to seek elected office.

Public office was a prospect unimaginable in Pella, where he was a member of the native-born, English-speaking minority. Some native-born Americans won election in Pella—Israel Curtis, for instance, served as the Marion County district attorney and in the Iowa legislature. But in 1855, Scholte had arranged to have two hundred male immigrants from the Netherlands swear their allegiance to the United States en masse to bolster Pella's bloc of Dutch voters. Shortly after Nicholas's return to Illinois, he helped to found Monmouth's Frémont Club, in support of John Frémont, the new Republican Party's presidential nominee. The next year, Nicholas was elected as one of Monmouth's three town constables. He followed his father (twice elected justice of the peace) and his brothers Walter (elected town constable in 1851) and Francis (elected Monmouth's city marshal in 1853) into public office.

According to Stuart Lake, midcentury Monmouth was as lawless as Dodge City or Tombstone would be, and as public officials Walter Earp and his sons were heroic defenders of law and order. "Western Illinois," Lake wrote, "was raw frontier, overrun by border ruffians, renegades, and stock-thieves who made life hazardous for the peaceably inclined. Insistence that Warren County could rid itself of undesirables, if the law-and-order faction would show as much spirit as the outlaws, was speedily exemplified by Walter and Nicholas Earp." The elder Earp, according to Lake, "was elected judge of the Illinois Circuit Court," while Nicholas "was commissioned deputy sheriff to serve without pay."[34]

Lake was wrong not only in the specifics but in the general context. Midcentury Warren County was not a lawless frontier but a sedate place populated by religiously minded merchants and farmers. Walter Earp was not a judge of the circuit court but a local justice of the peace, and his son Nicholas was not a volunteer deputy sheriff but an elected town constable. Walter died in 1853, three years before Nicholas returned to Monmouth and stood for election, so the two never served simultaneously. As for Monmouth's law-and-order faction, Nicholas Earp was a target of their wrath more than he was their hero and protector.

Wyatt was eight years old when his father joined two of Wyatt's uncles as an elected law officer. Yet one should not imagine that the impression Wyatt formed of police work was of a selfless protection of law and order in the community. Like many nineteenth-century politicians, the Earps regarded public office as squatters regarded the public lands: as an economic opportunity. The sociologist Max Weber called such officials "booty politicians." These officials, Weber wrote, sought to use their control of political offices, especially in local governments, to profit individually through municipal fines, taxes, or property seizures.[35]

By the early 1850s, Nicholas's brothers Walter and Francis had together with their father perfected a system of using their elected offices to extort money from vulnerable citizens of Monmouth. Either Walter or Francis would buy promissory notes of debtors unable to meet their obligations. Walter and Francis never paid the face value of the notes; rather, creditors offered them the notes at a discount, in effect writing off the notes as bad debt. The sons then filed suit in the court of their father, the justice of the peace, to compel the signatory of the note to pay its full value. Constable Earp would deliver the defendant before Justice of the Peace Earp, who would order the defendant to pay the debt (to another Earp) as well as court costs.[36]

Using their public offices to profit from debt collection does not seem to have hurt the Earps' standing in the town, probably because they carefully targeted only the most unpopular deadbeats. They were reelected to their positions; when Walter died in office in January 1853, the *Monmouth Atlas* wrote that he "was highly esteemed for his upright and Christian deportment, which he carried into his daily business transactions."[37] Walter's death brought an end to the debt-collection system, however, so Nicholas—who had himself skipped out on his debts when he had moved to Pella in 1849—could not participate in the scheme when he returned to Monmouth.

Instead, Nicholas, while serving as town constable, turned to a new trade—whiskey dealer. The market for whiskey in Monmouth was robust. In the antebellum period, the average American man

consumed a staggering quantity of alcohol. According to one historian, in the 1830s, the per capita consumption of distilled spirits in
the United States was about four gallons per year. Most of that consumption was by men; the 3 million men in the United States in the
1830s consumed 60 million gallons of distilled spirits, especially
whiskey, or an average of half a pint a day. Most of that total was ac-
counted for by about half the adult males in the United States, who
consumed two-thirds of all distilled spirits.[38]

In many ways, the rise of whiskey consumption was a side effect
of the rise of commercial agriculture, and in general what antebellum American historians call the "market revolution."[39] In the early
years of the nineteenth century, whiskey production was centered
west of the Appalachians. Significant numbers of farmers in the region turned to distilling as a way to profitably dispose of their surplus crops: grain shipped to market might be sold for twenty-five
cents a bushel (if it did not rot en route), but that barely covered ship-
ping costs. By contrast, whiskey made from that same bushel of
grain would not spoil and could sell for a dollar.[40]

Yet another side effect of the market revolution was the emergence of the temperance movement: in a commercial economy that
depended upon hard work and self-discipline, sobriety was a sign of
a person's self-control, industriousness, and ambitions for upward
mobility. The rise of whiskey consumption was thus accompanied
by the rise of the temperance movement among Protestant moral
reformers horrified by Americans' consumption of vast amounts of
liquor.[41] In 1851, in the first statewide law of its kind, reformers in
Maine succeeded in outlawing the sale of alcoholic beverages. By
1855, temperance advocates had successfully lobbied for passage
of the "Maine Law" in the other New England states and in the tier
of northern states and territories that contained a large number of
Yankee emigrants: New York, Ohio, Indiana, Michigan, Minnesota,
Iowa, and Illinois.[42]

In those northern states, temperance battles were fought along
class lines. Whiggish, middle-class businessmen demanded sobriety
of their employees. Workers stubbornly adhered to older traditions

inherited from rural America, before the imposition of the time discipline of the modern workplace, when work and drink flowed together.[43] Nicholas's turn to whiskey dealing signaled, perhaps, that his Whiggish aspirations to social status had collapsed. Whigs were generally strong advocates of temperance. By becoming a whiskey dealer, Nicholas was throwing in his lot with the laborers who contested the new discipline of the workplace.

The battles over temperance also paralleled divisions over slavery. In the Midwest, migrants from New England generally supported temperance, while migrants from the South such as the Earps opposed it. Illinois, where emigrants from the North and South mingled, was a battleground: between 1851 and 1855, the state legislature banned alcohol; the state supreme court overturned the ban; and then a state referendum narrowly upheld the court ruling.

Nicholas's Methodism nominally complicated his stand on whiskey. In 1848, following the Methodist Church's split over slavery, the northern branch had taken the opportunity to reassert a Wesleyan prohibition on the use and sale of liquor.[44] Yet those Methodist ties had bound Walter Earp more closely than his second son. Nicholas's father had been a Methodist preacher; Nicholas's younger brother Jonathan would likewise become a Methodist minister; and Nicholas's older brother, Lorenzo, was a deacon. But Nicholas and his family were not regular churchgoers, and his wife, Virginia, was impatient of public displays of piety such as temperance advocacy.[45]

In Monmouth, Presbyterian moral reformers—particularly David Alexander Wallace, who in 1856 became the first president of Monmouth College—engineered a local prohibition of alcohol. Wallace organized a vigilance committee to root out violators of the law. As town constables the Earp brothers Walter and Nicholas were obliged to enforce the prohibition ordinance. Yet outlawing alcohol created a profitable black market in whiskey—one the Earps were quick to enter. The Earps' bootlegging did not escape the notice of the vigilance committee; in early 1858, the Earp brothers were charged in the Warren County circuit court with violating the prohibition ordinance.[46]

Walter did not appear in court to contest the charge. Instead, he sold his home to Nicholas and promptly left town. Nicholas, however, refused to bend to the dictates of the moral reformers. Knowing that there was an avid market for alcohol in Monmouth despite the teetotalers' zeal, Nicholas ran for reelection while he was waiting for his case to come to trial. Nicholas finished third in the field of candidates, thus winning reelection as one of the three town constables. His fate in court was another matter, however. In March 1859, a jury found him guilty of two counts of violating the prohibition law. Nicholas appealed, but in April his appeal was denied and he was fined $20 for each count. The judge also ordered Nicholas's arrest on two new charges of selling liquor. Nicholas pleaded guilty to those charges in October. Before the end of the year, to avoid having his property seized to pay his fines and legal bills, Nicholas had sold his house in Monmouth and returned to Pella.[47]

What the eleven-year-old Wyatt made of his father's legal ordeal is anyone's guess. The episode probably furthered the family's chilly standoffishness toward the communities in which they lived. Perhaps his father's brush with the courts encouraged in the boy a disdain for the law—which might explain Wyatt's own string of arrests when he reached his early twenties. Perhaps Wyatt reflected on the potential profits and pitfalls of booty politics. He may well have adopted his father's contempt for high-minded reformers (coupled, perhaps, with a wariness of the power such reformers wielded). There were certainly lessons to be learned from Nicholas's troubles, not least of all lessons about the money to be made at the edges of a community's moral standards and the power of vigilance committees.

The Earps—a family of nine by the spring of 1861 following the birth of Adelia, the last surviving child born to Nicholas and Virginia—had a brief second stint in Pella. Within a year of their return to Iowa, the Civil War scattered the family. Newton, Nicholas's eldest son, volunteered for a cavalry unit organized in Iowa.

James and Virgil, Nicholas's second and third sons, returned to Monmouth to join infantry regiments recruited there.

The cause of Union probably had little to do with the Earp brothers' enlistment, and antislavery even less so. Illinoisans and Iowans were staunch free-soilers, meaning that they wanted western lands reserved for nonslaveholding white settlers. Whether to allow slavery in the western territories was one of the leading causes of sectional tensions, but free-soilers did not necessarily support the abolition of slavery. Indeed, Midwesterners feared that if slavery was abolished, free blacks would migrate north. In 1851, the Iowa legislature voted to forbid free blacks from settling in the state. Illinois passed a similar statute in 1853. While a vague sectional patriotism and a provincial resentment against elite slaveholders—the so-called slavocracy—might have fueled the desire for enlistment, politics likely played little role. More important was that most of the young men in the community were enlisting. By joining a volunteer regiment, one avoided the stigmas of cowardice and conscription, could elect one's own officers, and could serve with friends and compatriots. Another inducement, as it was for Nicholas in 1847, was the pay: $13 a month for a private (although recruits would discover that the pay often arrived months late).[48]

Because volunteer units were organized much as they had been during the Mexican-American War, with wealthy and prominent local men recruiting volunteers locally, many units had idiosyncratic characteristics. In 1860, nearly 3.5 million northerners had been born abroad, and consequently nearly one-fifth of Union soldiers were foreign-born.[49] Some companies were composed entirely of one ethnic group. If the Earps had joined a unit recruited at Pella, they would likely have served in a Dutch-speaking company. Rather than serve in units of Dutch immigrants, the three Earps who served in the Civil War joined units organized elsewhere.

James was the first of the Earps to leave home after the start of the war. In May 1861, one month after the shelling of Fort Sumter, and a month shy of his twentieth birthday, James returned from Iowa to Illinois to join the Seventeenth Illinois Infantry. The regiment was organized in Peoria, but James's unit—Company F—was formed in Monmouth's Warren County, so James likely returned to Monmouth to serve in a company with Illinois friends.

Following cursory physical exams by a local surgeon, the issuing of uniforms, and the formality of voting the men responsible for recruiting the unit as officers, the Seventeenth moved south to Alton, Illinois, for training.[50] In the summer of 1861, after only a brief stay at Alton, the Seventeenth was ordered to Missouri, a slave state that had not seceded from the Union. However, Missouri's pro-Confederate governor, Claiborne Jackson, who had fought in Kansas in the 1850s against free-state "jayhawkers," was seeking to deliver the state into the Confederacy. The commander of the Union forces in Missouri was John C. Frémont, the former western explorer as well as the Republican Party's presidential nominee in 1856. Frémont—who would enter the Earps' lives again in the 1880s as the governor of Arizona Territory—proved unequal to the task of mastering Missouri's chaos (as he proved in the early 1880s unequal to the task of combating lawlessness in Arizona). By the end of September, Confederate forces controlled half the state and were advancing on the lead mines near Fredericktown—an important source of material for bullets. At Fredericktown on October 21, 1861, the Seventeenth was one of the units arrayed against the Confederate forces of General Jeff Thompson, in a battle that helped determine control of southern Missouri. The Seventeenth charged the Confederate lines and routed them, capturing some artillery pieces and prisoners while suffering seven killed and sixty wounded.

One of the wounded was Private James Earp, who was shot in the left shoulder. His company had been ordered out as skirmishers at the beginning of the battle to draw enemy fire. He fell wounded in the first volley of shots. His wound was first reported by his commanding officers as not serious, but was upgraded to serious within a week.[51] James spent the rest of 1861 convalescing at a military hospital in Ironton, Missouri, not far from Fredericktown. He was sent home on sick leave in December 1861 and formally discharged in March 1863. The wound may have saved his life, as the Seventeenth went on to greater glory and even heavier casualties. After Fredericktown, the Seventeenth was ordered to join General John A. McClernand's Army of West Tennessee. At Shiloh in April 1862, the Seventeenth again distinguished itself by charging the Confederate positions on the last day of the battle. Yet in two days at Shiloh, the Seventeenth suffered 130 casualties. The decimated unit was thereafter assigned largely to garrison duty.

In November 1861, a little over a month after James was wounded at Fredericktown, Newton, twenty-four years old, the eldest of Nicholas's six sons, made his way to Camp Harlan near Mount Pleasant, about ninety miles east-southeast of Pella, to enlist in the Fourth Iowa Cavalry. Newton's unit participated in the siege of Vicksburg from mid-May 1863 until the surrender of the city's forces on July 4, and followed in the wake of General William Sherman's army's march to Atlanta. Employed primarily to forage, patrol, and conduct reconnaissance, cavalry units usually suffered fewer casualties than infantry units—during the entire war, only four officers and fifty-one men of the Fourth Iowa Cavalry were killed in action—although nearly two hundred men in the unit died of disease. Newton served until the end of the war; he was mustered out at Atlanta on August 10, 1865, and discharged two weeks later at Davenport, Iowa.

In August 1862, Virgil, like his brother James, returned to Monmouth and enlisted in the Eighty-Third Illinois Infantry. Like James, he joined a unit that included men he knew, including his cousin Francis Earp.[52] The Eighty-Third served almost exclusively in Tennessee, where it sought to suppress Confederate guerrillas, including those commanded by Nathan Bedford Forrest, later a founder of the Ku Klux Klan. Up to the last weeks of the war, and even after Appomattox, the Eighty-Third skirmished with guerrillas and fought sappers who sabotaged trains entering and leaving Nashville.[53] It was at Nashville that Virgil was mustered out as a private on June 26, 1865; he was discharged in Chicago on July 5.

Thirteen years old when the war began, Wyatt found himself working on the family's plot of farmland outside Pella. According to Wyatt's own telling, he was entirely responsible for the crop—his father left the farmwork to him while serving as a local deputy provost marshal. "Father was too busy recruiting and drilling troops to do anything about the cornfield," Lake quotes Wyatt as saying.[54] Yet Civil War deputy provost marshals did not recruit and drill regular troops. Their primary responsibilities were to arrest—and sometimes execute—deserters, and, after 1863, to enforce compliance with the Conscription Act. Deputy provost marshals were assisted in their duties by men—derisively referred to as the Home Guard— who did not serve in the conflict but ensured that others did. Welch Nossaman, a Pella native and a friend of James and Virgil's, recalled, "Nick Earp got up a company of Home Guards in Civil War times in Pella. He trained and drilled them there."[55] In the later years of the war, when both desertion and resistance to conscription were common, deputy provost marshals and the Home Guard were widely feared.[56]

One season of working in the cornfield was enough for Wyatt. By his own account, in the spring of 1862, at the age of fourteen, he ran away to Ottumwa—forty-five miles from Pella—to join the army. There, according to the story he recounted to both Flood and Lake, he encountered none other than his own father. The deputy provost marshal, in a departure from his usual duty of rounding up deserters, returned the would-be volunteer to his home.[57]

The story might well be true. Wyatt certainly had a lifelong aversion to farmwork, and that a fourteen-year-old boy might be captivated by a romantic notion of a soldier's life and try to join his older brothers in service is entirely plausible. Before Congress decreed in 1864 that volunteers had to be at least sixteen years old to enlist, boys as young as twelve (and in one notable instance, a boy of nine) served as cavalry buglers and infantry drummers. But teenage volunteers were rare—even if Wyatt had not encountered his father, it is unlikely that army officials would have permitted him to serve. Over a million volunteers served in the Union Army, but fewer than one-tenth of 1 percent were under the age of eighteen. Only 457 (0.00045 percent) were, like Wyatt in 1862, below the age of fifteen.[58]

Earp told his biographers only two stories from his childhood: this one of his abortive effort to join the army at age fourteen, and a rather more dubious story about his having single-handedly turned back an Indian raid during his family's emigration to California in 1864. The story appeared in accounts by both Flood and Lake that had as their focus the actions of Earp as an Arizona lawman. As Flood and Lake told it, the story aligned the actions of the teenager in the 1860s with the fearsome reputation of the man in the 1880s. It also exculpated Wyatt for emigrating west with his family a year before the end of the war, which raised suspicions among contemporaries about his dodging the draft. Flood and Lake asserted, to the contrary, that even at a young age Wyatt was willing to risk his life for a good cause.[59] Bat Masterson, a fellow law officer in Kansas in the 1870s, in a short, admiring, and largely invented biographical sketch of Wyatt written in 1907, went still further by simply asserting that Wyatt "served in an Iowa regiment the last three years of the Civil War, though he was only a boy at the time."[60]

By the time the war ended, the Earps were far from the conflict. In 1864, the family—Nicholas and Virginia, along with sixteen-year-old Wyatt, his younger brothers Morgan and Warren, his sister Adelia, and his older brother James, who had been invalided out of the army a year earlier—trekked overland to southern California.

While southern Iowa was far from the worst fighting, the Earps were not unaffected by the war. Across the state border in Montgomery County, Missouri, Union troops fired on the house of Jonathan Earp, one of Nicholas's younger brothers, because they believed he was harboring Confederate soldiers.[61] Southern Iowa was a refuge both for Confederate irregulars (including Jesse James and his followers) and runaway slaves. Sarah Nossaman, one of the earliest residents of Pella, called the war years "strenuous," as southern Iowa "was the camping grounds of the renegades and outlaws, some of the citizens even giving them shelter and food and a great many negroes were railroaded from the south to the north through this community."[62]

The politics of slavery may have impelled the Earps to leave Iowa, as it may have influenced their decision to move from Kentucky to Illinois in 1845. According to Lake, Nicholas "had been a slave owner himself," who withdrew his support for the Union cause from a principled objection to the Emancipation Proclamation.[63] More likely, Nicholas was a free-soiler who opposed the extension of slavery to the West (in order to reserve those lands for white settlers such as himself) and supported the laws in both Iowa and Illinois prohibiting free blacks from settling in those states. He may have been alarmed by the runaways passing through southern Iowa, and by the prospect that in the wake of emancipation thousands more free blacks might migrate to the North. Flood was perhaps closer to the truth: he interpreted Nicholas's objection to emancipation as an affront to the right of the "dominant race" to determine the status of blacks on a state-by-state basis.[64] Whatever the true reason for their decision, the Earps took up with a small wagon train of Iowans bound for southern California in the spring of 1864, joining thousands of border-state families from the Midwest and Upper South who fled to the Far West during the conflict to escape the real and imagined dangers of the war.[65]

By 1864, thousands of emigrant wagons had etched deep ruts along the Platte River and through South Pass; it took relatively little skill to find the way west. Yet good sense dictated that a wagon train have a leader. On the strength of Nicholas's military experience, the company of Iowa emigrants chose him as wagon master. Nicholas's six months' service in a cavalry unit in the Mexican-American War and his command of the Pella Home Guard would have been enough to recommend him for leadership of the train, but during his time in Pella, Nicholas had apparently elaborated on his service record: he claimed to have served in the 1832 Black Hawk War (a claim he repeated in 1877 in his application for a military pension).[66] This assertion might have seemed plausible to the Iowans—the Earps had after all arrived in Pella from Monmouth, the scene of some of the violence in the Black Hawk War. Yet Nicholas's claim was almost certainly false: in 1832 the nineteen-year-old Nicholas was still in Ohio County, Kentucky, five hundred miles from the fighting. The claim nonetheless bolstered Earp's case for leadership among a party of emigrants apprehensive of Indian attacks.

Between the 1840s and the 1870s, a half million Americans migrated to the Far West. Most of the emigrants were, like the Earps, from the rural Midwest or Upper South (three-quarters came directly from Indiana, Illinois, Iowa, or Missouri; almost all of the rest came from bordering states). Most of the emigrants were, like the Earps, bound for California (two-thirds went to California; the rest went in roughly equal numbers to Oregon and Utah). However commonplace the overland experience had become, emigrants regarded the overland migration as a life-defining moment. Thousands of Americans who had never before kept a journal nor would ever again recorded the experience of the migration, making overland emigration one of the best-documented aspects of nineteenth-century western history.[67]

One such diarist was Sarah Jane Rousseau, who with her husband, the physician James Rousseau, and their three children, belonged to the Pella emigrant company. Her journal provides the most extended depiction of Nicholas that has survived. Over the course of the migration, Rousseau's opinion of Nicholas changed from respect to disappointment to contempt. The length of the journey was partly to blame for her falling estimation of the wagon master. The progress of the Iowa train was excruciatingly slow. In the 1850s, the average travel time from Council Bluffs, Iowa, to California was 113 days. The Pella party took nearly twice that long to reach their destination. The convoy left Knoxville, not far from Pella, on May 14; reached Council Bluffs eighteen days later on May 29; Fort Laramie on July 7; Fort Bridger on August 10; Salt Lake City on August 22; Las Vegas on November 20; and San Bernardino on December 17—altogether, a journey of two hundred days from Council Bluffs. While spirits were high when the trip began, after seven months together on the overland trail, many had short tempers.[68]

Encounters with Indians—both real and imagined—dominated Rousseau's impression of the migration. By June 18, when the train was two weeks and 275 miles west of Council Bluffs, Rousseau had begun to scan the horizon for Indians, who, she imagined, "hide behind the bluffs." She wrote, "We are now in Sioux Indian country. We feel afraid to go out of sight of our wagon train." Rousseau attributed almost every difficulty on the trail to the Indians, including the scarcity of game. "The Indians are driving the buffalo and all game off," she wrote on June 24. It is true that by 1864 emigrants found little game along the Platte River trail—almost the only wildlife the train encountered was a pair of antelope that crossed the trail (after whom Nicholas and some other men loosed some shots without result). The cause of the scarcity along the Platte River was not the Indians, however, but the emigrants themselves, who since the mid-1840s had herded half a million cattle and sheep, and cut virtually all of the timber, along both sides of the river, denuding it of forage and forest cover and effectively destroying the river valley as a habitat for bison and other wildlife.[69]

Rousseau's apprehensions of an Indian attack were typical of emigrants, who heightened their own anxieties by telling one another exaggerated tales of Indian depredations. Virtually every season, a rumor of a deadly Indian attack traveled up and down the trail. Such rumors contributed to the number of "go-backs" or "turnarounds," who abandoned their journey and returned to the East without reaching their destination. Go-backs constituted perhaps 10 percent of all those who embarked from Council Bluffs. Rumors of Indian violence were far more common, however, than actual conflict. Between 1840 and 1860, only 362 emigrants died at the hands of Indians—a tiny fraction of the hundreds of thousands who traveled across the West. (During that same period, emigrants killed 426 Indians.) The Great Plains were largely free of Indian-emigrant violence; 90 percent of deadly Indian attacks occurred west of South Pass.[70]

Cooperation between emigrants and Indians was more common than conflict. Indians assisted emigrants in numerous ways: in return for payment, they acted as guides, mail carriers, woodcutters, and retrievers of stray stock. The Sioux acquired a reputation as reliable aides at river crossings on the Platte and Laramie Rivers. Even the Iowans, suspicious as they were of all Indians, eventually contracted with the natives for help: forced to lay over in Utah for a month waiting for the weather to cool so that they could cross the Mojave Desert to southern California, the Iowans hired a local Indian to care for their livestock while they waited to resume their journey.[71]

On the Great Plains, the Indians' fortunes had been in eclipse since the 1830s: a smallpox epidemic, sporadic violence with the U.S. Army, and most disastrously the decline of the bison population owing to drought, commercial hunting, and emigrants' degradation of the Platte River habitat had left many Indians of the plains destitute.[72] While Indians rarely attacked migrants, they regularly sought to profit from the passage of the migrants through their territory. Indians of the plains frequently approached trains seeking to acquire goods by trade, supplication, or theft. Rousseau rebuffed the first Indians she encountered: four Pawnees who asked for matches and soap outside Council Bluffs. Yet a month later, perhaps more accustomed to the presence of Indians along the trail, the Rousseaus traded a cup of sugar and some meat for a bison robe and a pair of moccasins.[73]

During the journey across the plains, Nicholas, however coarse and prone to angry outbursts, had Rousseau's confidence because he was a vigorous advocate of vigilance against Indian raids. While the train was camped near Fort Laramie, the emigrants trusted the guarding of their stock to the soldiers of the fort. According to Rousseau, when Nicholas checked on the train's animals one night, he found that rather than keeping a watch against Indian raiders, the soldiers had "got up a dance." Nicholas "told the guards they must quit their dancing and be on duty. One of the soldiers told him to mind his own business and ordered him off. It made him awful mad and he was for killing. He used very profane language and he could hardly be appeased. But he cooled down after a while and all was quiet."[74]

Nicholas and Rousseau, wary of the many Indians camped around Fort Laramie, were too inexperienced to know that a theft immediately outside the fort was unlikely; typically, raiders attacked trains only after they were a few days' journey from the post. From the Indians' perspective, such attacks were merely tolls charged to emigrants crossing through native territory. Soldiers at posts such as Fort Laramie were powerless to do much to put a stop to such raiding; they had only enough men to police the near vicinity of the post.[75]

Indeed, fifty miles west of Fort Laramie and five days after Earp's altercation with the guards, Indians raided the Iowa train and made off with ten horses—four of which belonged to the Rousseaus. Responsibility for the loss of the horses can be laid, at least partly, at the feet of the wagon master: finding no pasturage for the horses on the side of the river on which they had been traveling, Earp ordered the horses to be brought to the opposite bank to allow them to graze. With the river separating the horses from the wagons and most of the emigrants, the raiders were easily able to make off with the mounts. Several of the men set off in pursuit of the raiders, but—as might be expected—they were unable to overtake expert Indian horsemen operating in territory they knew intimately.[76]

Two days later, on July 14, raiders struck the train again. Rousseau and Nicholas, in a long letter he wrote to a friend in Pella, tell similar accounts of the second raid. Because it was only two days after the first attack, the men of the wagon train were keeping a close eye on the stock. "We were very watchful and as soon as we camped we put the stock out to feed with plenty of guards watching," Rousseau wrote. Nicholas agreed: "[W]e had our gards [sic] properly posted and pickets out for it was no trouble to get the men all to do their duty." Moreover, having learned something from the raid two nights previous, Nicholas made sure that the stock were put out to graze close by the wagons. In case of another attack, the camp circle could serve as a makeshift corral.[77]

According to both Rousseau and Nicholas, a few hours after

they had made camp, a group of raiders on horseback charged the emigrants' stock in an effort to drive off the animals. Nicholas wrote, "I ordered the horses to be brought inside the corell [*sic*] by the gards [*sic*] that was garding [*sic*] them the women all turned out to help get the horses into the corell while we who was not on gard gethered [*sic*] our guns and rushed to meet the Indians." James Rousseau, Nicholas and James Earp, and two other men took off in pursuit of the raiders, one of whom they identified as a white man. (Considerable numbers of white bandits preyed on overland emigrants—a fair number of depredations blamed on Indians were in fact committed by these white outlaws.)[78]

The consistent accounts of Rousseau and Nicholas stand in stark contrast to Wyatt's recollections of the raid. In both Flood's manuscript and Lake's book, Wyatt tells that he was standing guard over the stock when he saw a file of a dozen Indians on horseback approaching the camp. Flood wrote, "All unconscious of the danger, the women and children were moving in and out about the camp; there was no one to sound an alarm. The boy saw, in an instant, what was about to happen, and . . . he fired into the air." Allegedly, the shot alerted the camp to danger, but the Indians spurred their horses forward. According to both Lake and Flood, young Wyatt single-handedly turned the bandits aside by driving the entire stock of the emigrant train—mules, oxen, and horses—*toward* the raiders. Flood wrote in his inimitable prose:

> Before the dozen braves from the river could close in, a sound of turmoil from the opposite bank of the stream was upon them like the rushing of the wind. On it came, turning to thunder now as it struck into the cottonwood trees, and the herd of the emigrant train burst out of the timber onto the river, the horns of the oxen and the manes of the horses flashing wickedly through the geyser-like wall of water as they plunged to the bed of the stream, with the boy Earp riding like mad and urging them from behind. Like an avalanche, they crossed the stretch of sand, whirling and toss-

ing the Indians before them into the circle of wagons toward an open corral.[79]

Lake's account is remarkably similar; after firing into the air to warn the camp, "the boy put his pony on the run for the animals grazing farthest from the ford." In short order, he had the emigrant herd moving toward the raiders. Lake wrote that the "Sioux had small choice. To save themselves from the hoofs and horns of the frenzied herd they scattered from the narrow trail."[80]

Wyatt reminisced to both Flood (extensively) and Lake (intermittently). Lake also had a copy of Flood's unpublished manuscript at hand while he was writing his own version of Wyatt's life. There are thus limited possibilities for the source of the improbable story of young Wyatt driving away the Indians who attacked the train—a story at odds not only with his father's account but also with that of Jane Rousseau. It could not have originated with Lake because the story is in Flood's earlier manuscript. It is possible, though unlikely, that Flood invented the tale; rather, Wyatt was probably the source. Either he told it to Flood, and Lake took the story from Flood's manuscript, or Earp told the story to both Flood and Lake.

Wyatt grew up in a culture of dime-novel Westerns that advanced far-fetched tales of western exploits. His father—who not only said he had fought in the Black Hawk War but at other times claimed to have scouted for Daniel Boone (who died when Nicholas was seven years old!)—was a poor model for veracity.[81] By the time Wyatt told this story to Flood and Lake, he was actively attempting to create a memoir that might be made into a Western film—a genre that, like the dime novel, was not noted for its fidelity to facts.

The Iowa emigrants' journey continued for another five months after the Indian attacks, and Rousseau's regard for Nicholas fell steadily. On July 31, at South Pass, the Earps' team proved unable to pull their wagon up a steep ascent. "Mr. Nicholas Earp got angry with the whole wagon train because they passed him by," wrote Rousseau. "He took it as an insult and talked pretty hard to all. Some thought he had taken a little too much liquor. He used very profane language and told the whole train he would give up his Captaincy." Nicholas's tirade delayed the train for an hour and caused one family, the Clarks, to leave the group.[82]

Following the incident at South Pass, the train began to disintegrate, as emigrants no longer camped as a group for protection but spread out along the trail, sometimes camping miles apart. While the train divided ostensibly to allow for their stock to graze on the thin forage, the emigrants—desperately weary of the sight of each other—doubtless welcomed the relative privacy. Although nominally still wagon master, Nicholas pitched his camp ten miles or more from other emigrants and sometimes took leave of the group inexplicably. At the same time, some of the Iowans continued to offer one another aid: because of the ineffectiveness of the Earps' team, the Rousseaus loaned them the use of some of their horses and oxen. Yet when Nicholas returned to the Rousseaus a borrowed mare in such poor condition that it soon died, Mrs. Rousseau questioned whether he was deserving of her generosity.[83]

As the train slowly made its way through Utah and Nevada, Nicholas became increasingly churlish. He quarreled with the Indian whom the emigrants had hired to care for their famished stock. According to Rousseau, "Mr. Earp came pretty near getting us all in trouble with his temper, swearing and cutting up. The chief got dreadfully mad at him and swore at Mr. Earp. I was very much afraid the Indians would get mad at us." A few weeks later, Nicholas quarreled with the Rousseaus: Nicholas had borrowed oxen and horses from the Rousseaus, and in return he had promised to transport some of their belongings. But on October 23, he refused to haul James Rousseau's heavy medical books any farther. "The arrangement was for him to take them through to California," wrote Rousseau. "It seems we can't place any confidence in what he says." Eventually, Nicholas gave in and hauled the books for another month, but when the train reached Las Vegas, he bullied the Rousseaus into leaving the books there while he continued on with their team. A few days after that confrontation, Nicholas, having already ridden one of the Rousseaus' mares into the ground, refused to double-team his wagon on a steep ascent and instead pushed the Rousseaus' animals to the breaking point. "It appeared to me he didn't care if he killed our horses or not," wrote Rousseau.[84]

Nicholas took out his anger on children as well as livestock—or at least threatened to do so. On November 24, while they were passing through Nevada, Nicholas "had another rippet with his son Warren fighting Jimmy Hatten. And then Mr. Earp raged about all the children, using very profane language and swearing that if the children's parents did not whip or correct their children he would whip every last one of them." The Earp boys were no doubt accustomed to their father's outbursts. Indeed, physical coercion was a routine way for fathers to discipline children in the mid-nineteenth century.[85] But not all children were accustomed to it. The next day, Charlie Copley, a boy Wyatt's age who had been traveling with the Earps, left the Earps' wagon to make the rest of the journey to California with the Rousseaus. Nicholas, Rousseau concluded, "shows every day what kind of man he really is."[86]

On December 17, 1864, the Iowa train finally reached San Bernardino, a farming community where a large number of Mormons had settled in the 1840s. In short order, Nicholas rented a farm ten miles outside town, and the Earps moved into their new home on Christmas Day. According to a long letter he wrote in April 1865 to Charlie's father, James, in Iowa, he planted only about sixty acres of grain crops: twelve acres of wheat, eighteen of barley, and between twenty and thirty acres of corn. With the corn going largely to feed livestock, these relatively few acres of grain would not generate much of a surplus for sale; it seemed intended merely for subsistence production. The commercial potential of the farm was in its orchard and vineyard: ten acres of peaches and apples and thirty-five acres of grapes that the farm's previous residents had planted. Yet Nicholas seemed content to make use of the farm's fruit largely for the family's subsistence. He wrote to James Copley, "Oh don't you wish you and many others of my friends was here to help me eat apples, peaches and grapes this fall & drink wine."[87]

Twenty years after Walter Earp led his family out of rural Kentucky to town life in Illinois, his second son had come full circle and returned to the backcountry-yeoman tradition of subsistence production. It is impossible to say when things changed for Nicholas. At some point between 1845 and 1865—a period that included his disappointing stint in the army, his unrewarding sojourn in Pella, and his arrests for bootlegging in Monmouth—wage work, town life, and the promise of upward mobility lost its allure for him. By 1865, he was content with his rented farm and his homemade wine.[88]

Nicholas may have returned to the yeoman tradition, but not to its legacy of patriarchal order. Like Ishmael, Nicholas challenged patriarchal authority more than he deferred to it. He rejected his father's strict Methodism, and although he accompanied his father to Monmouth in 1845, he left for Mexico in 1847 and for Iowa in 1849, returning only after his father died. He sought authority, but the power he wielded came not from family and tradition but through politics (as town constable), the market (as a bootlegger), and most of all through his own gruff, swaggering, bellicose persona (as a cavalry sergeant, deputy provost marshal, and wagon master). To his sons, he was a forceful and perhaps even fearful presence, but he was not a traditional rural patriarch who commanded the labor of his adult children. Nicholas himself abided in his father's household until his midthirties, just long enough to claim a share of the cash from the sale of the family farm in Kentucky. But Nicholas, whose years of wandering brought only steadily downward social mobility, had no such patrimony that would keep his adult sons nearby. His sons left home at their first opportunity. Yet even then he cast a long shadow over them. Like him, they would lead lives of transience, conflict, and self-invention.

3

YOUTH HATH FAULTY WAND'RED

Just past his twenty-fourth birthday, Wyatt had already acquired enough familiarity with jailhouses to appreciate the modern comforts of the municipal jail in Peoria, Illinois, located in the back of the newly constructed, two-story brick city hall. Having spent a year as a town constable in Missouri, where he had been forced to improvise cells from hotel rooms and empty buildings, Wyatt certainly recognized the convenience of a permanent city jail. As a former inmate of a decrepit jail in Arkansas where he had briefly awaited trial on a charge of horse theft, Wyatt no doubt noted the cleanliness and airiness of the new Peoria jail. Indeed, the Illinois jail was so agreeable that having been found guilty of consorting with prostitutes in one of Peoria's most infamous bordellos in May 1872, both Wyatt and his brother Morgan preferred to spend a few weeks in confinement rather than pay fines of $44.50.[1]

Prisoners in nineteenth-century America were encouraged to reflect on their waywardness in the hope of repentance. The jailers' message of repentance resonated with the Methodist hymns of Wyatt's youth, such as "O, That I Could Repent," and "Yes, from This Instant Now, I Will."[2] If Wyatt used any of the time he spent in the Peoria city jail in the spring of 1872 in such contemplation, the exercise did not produce any immediate results: in September, the Peoria police arrested him once more on the charge of consorting with prostitutes—his third such arrest that year. Reporting on the arrest, a local newspaper referred to Wyatt as "the Peoria bummer," using a term that had entered American slang in the 1850s via German immigrants' *Bummler,* or "loafer."[3] Thus at age twenty-four, after little more than a year in Peoria, Wyatt had succeeded in establishing a local reputation as a layabout. There was little to recommend him as a future popular icon of law and order.

In the last forty years, researchers into Earp's past have discovered that Wyatt's early adulthood—about which relatively little is known—was as misspent as that of the literary archetype of the wayward young man, Shakespeare's Prince Hal, who is introduced in *Henry IV, Part I* as an irresponsible swindler and thief entirely under the sway of the ne'er-do-well knight Falstaff. Called to account, Hal begs the forgiveness of his father, King Henry IV, asking "for some things true wherein my youth hath faulty wand'red and irregular, find pardon on my true submission." Like Hal, Wyatt "wand'red" as a youth. He ran afoul of the law three times between 1870 and 1872, when he was between the ages of twenty-two and twenty-four:

Lamar, Missouri, 1870–71. Following the death of his wife, Urilla, to whom he had been married for only eleven months, Wyatt, who had served for a year as Lamar's constable, decided to leave town. He left, in early 1871, under a cloud of accusations that he had stolen public funds.

Indian Territory, 1871. Shortly after leaving Lamar, Wyatt was arrested for horse theft in Indian Territory—the modern state of Oklahoma. Wyatt was apprehended as he was fleeing toward Kansas, conveyed to a dank holding cell in Arkansas, and indicted for horse theft. Yet he never stood trial—he and six other prisoners escaped by clawing their way out of their cell.

Peoria, Illinois, 1872. From Arkansas, Wyatt joined his older brother Virgil in Peoria. Virgil worked in Peoria's rough waterfront and distillery district as a bartender in a saloon that fronted a brothel. Wyatt likewise found work as an enforcer in one of Peoria's bordellos. Over the course of 1872, Wyatt was arrested three times in Peoria because of his association with the sex trade.

Readers will find no mention of these events in Stuart Lake's biography of Wyatt, a study that admits no flaws in Earp's character. Early drafts of the manuscript tended yet more in this direction; after reading a draft of six chapters, Lake's editor at Houghton Mifflin wrote to him in August 1929 that "we think you are in some danger of dwelling too insistently on the justification and eulogy of your character."[4] Even in the finished manuscript, Lake presents the boy Earp as merely a youthful version of the mature frontier marshal; of Earp at age sixteen, Lake wrote, "His inherent steadiness of mind and habit already was indicated by [his] habitually earnest expression."[5] One scholar characterized such biographies as the type in which "we meet heroes described in terms of their essential, ideal qualities. It is almost as if they had no past; even their childhood is described only in terms of omens of the future 'peak' of their life"[6]—one thinks, for instance, of Lake's apocryphal tale of the teenaged Wyatt fighting off an Indian attack on his family's wagon train.

Lake opted for apology and hagiography in part because he did not know the extent of the young Wyatt's waywardness. Not until 1963, a year after Lake's death, did the author Ed Bartholomew bring to light the evidence of Wyatt's 1871 indictment for horse theft in Indian Territory.[7] Likewise, while Lake knew that Earp's brother James ran a brothel in Wichita, the arrest of Wyatt and Morgan for consorting with prostitutes in Illinois in 1872 came to light only many years after Lake's death, when a genealogist stumbled across a newspaper account of one of Wyatt's arrests.

Even if Lake had known more about Wyatt's misspent youth, literary conventions discouraged him from adopting a narrative of sin and redemption. Although Lake's biography of Wyatt was published in 1931, in many respects it belongs to the Victorian era, when biographies were, as the literary scholar Robert Partin put it, "instruments of moral instruction." As simple morality tales, such biographies discouraged the idea that a youth of vice and crime might be followed by a life of rectitude; they adhered rather to the idea that youthful sins, however inconsequential, would lead only to yet more unspeakable moral squalor in adulthood. The didacticism of Victorian biography had begun to change following the First World War, but Lake's biography of Wyatt remained squarely in the Victorian tradition of an examination of an exemplary life: Lake's tentative title for his first chapter was "For the Benefit of a Newer Generation."[8]

Finally, if Lake's version of Wyatt seems to render him as a kind of dime-novel Western hero, or silent-film cowboy, that is because such a wooden persona was exactly what Lake sought to create. Not until John Ford's 1939 film *Stagecoach* did the Western genre admit the possibility of a morally ambiguous hero. Writing a decade earlier, Lake adhered to contemporary norms and aimed for the broadest readership possible. He had no interest in overturning or complicating the reading public's image of a law-and-order marshal on the frontier. Rather, he cast Earp as vividly (and profitably) as possible in that role. "It has all the exciting qualities of a dime novel," one reviewer wrote of Lake's book in the *New York Herald Tribune*, "and the curious virtue that it might be used as a Sunday School text or a Hollywood scenario."[9]

But the Wyatt who emerged in *Frontier Marshal* was not simply a product of Lake's imagination. Wyatt took an active part in steering Lake toward a heroic interpretation of his youth and early adulthood. Lake did not know of Wyatt's arrests and dissolute youth because Wyatt actively sought to conceal the truth. While it is unlikely that Wyatt was familiar with the literary conventions governing biographies, he wanted to contradict the negative portrayal of him in the press. He understood that if he was to justify his resort to vigilantism in 1882, he needed to present himself as a man who had but for that single instance spent his lifetime on the right side of the law.

Wyatt Earp marked his seventeenth birthday on March 19, 1865, on the family farm outside San Bernardino. As he approached adulthood, he grew to an imposing size. Bat Masterson described him as "weighing in the neighborhood of one hundred and sixty pounds, all of it muscle. He stood six feet in height."[10] In stature, he resembled his father as well as his brothers Virgil and Morgan, all roughly six feet tall.[11] The Earps towered over most other men in mid-nineteenth-century America, when the average man was five feet eight inches tall—about two inches shorter than the modern American average.[12]

Tall and muscular, the Earp brothers were not only physically imposing but, as contemporaries such as Masterson noted, handsome: dark blond with high foreheads and deep-set blue eyes. An 1869 photograph of Wyatt shows a twenty-one-year-old man with a thin mustache and a wisp of hair on his chin, gazing intensely at the camera.

Though Wyatt may have grown to his adult height as he reached his seventeenth birthday, like many rural Americans in the mid-nineteenth century, he lacked much experience beyond the family farm. That could hardly be considered a deficiency in nineteenth-century America: most farm boys grew up to be farmers; their rural upbringing sufficed as their practical education. The Earps' seven-month-long overland emigration in 1864 had marked Wyatt's only real experience outside the farm towns where he was raised. He had little chance to learn more of the world in sparsely populated San Bernardino. Had he been a few years older, he might have served in the Civil War together with his brothers and half brother. But his age and the family's migration to California in 1864 combined to keep him clear of the conflict. Three thousand miles from Virginia, the Earp farm in southern California was a safe distance from the closing battles of the Civil War, which came to an end three weeks after Wyatt's birthday.

While Wyatt lacked worldliness, his older brothers Newton, James, and Virgil certainly did not. Wyatt found himself part of an interstitial generation of American men who came of age just as the war ended. Men of this generation, too young for enlistment, found themselves looking up to older men, and in particular their older brothers, who had served in the conflict and become models of masculine virtue in a postwar period that put new emphasis on martial qualities.[13] The novelist Henry James, two of whose older brothers served in the Civil War, envied his brothers for the "romantic chances" the war had offered them to "master" the ways of physical courage.[14] Wyatt likewise strove to emulate his older brothers, particularly Virgil, who was closest to him in age. The desire to be like Virgil never quite left Wyatt. Late in life, in reminiscing about his past, he was prone to present some of Virgil's deeds as his own.

Like Henry James and many other men who were not quite old enough to serve in the war, Wyatt could rely on his veteran older brothers to teach him some of what they had learned as soldiers as he took his first stumbling steps toward adulthood. After the war's end, Virgil rejoined the Earp family in California and over the next few years took Wyatt along with him to work as a freighter and, reportedly, as a laborer in railroad camps. Wyatt told Flood that by 1867 he was hauling freight between San Bernardino and Salt Lake City, probably in the company of Virgil.[15] In the mining camps and frontier army posts of the mountain and desert West, Wyatt likely had his first exposure to saloons, brothels, and gambling halls.

Under Virgil's tutelage, Wyatt became an eager student of the soldier's arts of drinking, fistfighting, and shooting. However avid a student of the martial arts, initially, at least, Wyatt was not particularly adept. According to Lake, by the early 1870s Wyatt was a master with both a rifle and a pistol and frequently won target shooting matches against professional hunters.[16] Yet, like everyone else who masters firearms, Wyatt had to learn the skill, and early on he was frequently bested. As riflemen and pistoleers, his elder brothers easily outclassed him. Welch Nossaman, a friend of James and Virgil's from Pella, recalled that "Jim and Virg were handy with six-shooters. We used to go down to our place four miles south of Pella, hunting squirrels and rabbits and turkeys, and they could do as well with their gats as I could with a rifle."[17] The older brothers refined their skills in the army. Wyatt's sister Adelia recalled that when the brothers were together for family events, they would engage in shooting contests. "Newton and Virgil would always win. They were very good shots, trained by the army."[18]

Fistfighting was a tradition in the yeoman backcountry. It was also common in both armies in the Civil War, as regiments staged bouts to keep up morale.[19] Though Wyatt eventually became, as Lake wrote, a "skillful boxer," this aptitude was hard-won, and the process of learning how to use his fists was marked by defeat.[20] One of Wyatt's first serious fistfights occurred in the late 1860s, while he and Virgil were working as freighters in Wyoming. The brothers found themselves in a conflict with three other workers. The three eventually clubbed Virgil into unconsciousness, but according to his sister, Virgil "did a lot of damage" before they finished him. Wyatt, by contrast, "lasted about half a minute! Even in that time he took a terrible beating. Next day, all battered and cut and limping, he decided he had better learn to fight proper."[21] Eventually Wyatt became a formidable fighter—he was, by all accounts, not only tall and muscular but quick.

Though Wyatt learned how to shoot and fight, the bootlegger's son struggled to learn how to drink, according to Adelia. He took his first drink of whiskey in his late teens in a Prescott, Arizona, saloon. He promptly passed out, and when he awoke, he was still, according to his sister, in a "terrible state . . . sick, headache, perspiring and trembling all over." On Virgil's advice Wyatt took another shot of whiskey to cure his hangover, but "got just as bad as before."[22] When he had recovered, he swore off alcohol completely—a pledge he kept for most of his adult life. Later in Wyatt's life, upstanding community members in Kansas and Arizona would remember that unlike many other lawmen and cowboys, he was a teetotaler. While Adelia's account of Wyatt's susceptibility to liquor may well be exaggerated, if there is any truth to it, Wyatt's hypersensitivity to liquor may have been a form of alcohol intolerance, caused by a rare genetic inability to metabolize alcohol completely and break down its toxicity.[23]

As Wyatt studied drinking and fighting at the feet of his older brothers, Nicholas remained as restless as ever. The Earps did not stay long in San Bernardino. Less than four years after they had settled on their rented farm outside town, Nicholas uprooted the family again and moved to Lamar, Missouri, the seat of Barton County in the southwestern part of the state. Like Nicholas's earlier homes in Kentucky, Illinois, and Iowa, the southwest corner of Missouri was dominated by small farms. Although Missouri had been a slave state, there had been no large plantations in Barton County and only a handful of slaves. In 1860, most of Missouri's 114,000 slaves and 24,000 slaveholders (of a total population of 1.2 million) were clustered in a tier of counties in the Missouri River valley.[24] By contrast, nonslaveholding yeomen farmers populated Lamar and its surroundings.[25]

If Lamar was somewhat less impoverished and remote than San Bernardino, it was not by much, especially in the immediate postwar years. When the Earps arrived, Lamar was still little more than a hamlet, and certainly not a thriving center of commercial agriculture such as Monmouth or Pella; in contrast to those places, Barton County's population was smaller and its farms were fewer and less valuable.[26] Unlike Monmouth, the town had no rail link to larger cities. Local amusements were rare: hunting in the Lamar environs or watching Lamar's baseball team, the Panthers, occasionally take on a team from another town, such as the Carthage Tornadoes.[27] Wyatt's sister Adelia recalled Lamar as "a dull, dusty place."[28]

The Earps had good reasons to settle in this seemingly unpromising place. As Lamar rebuilt after the war, it offered economic opportunities. The town was certainly prostrate at the war's end: in 1862 and again in 1864, the Confederate guerrilla William Quantrill had raided the town, which was garrisoned by the local Seventh Missouri Provisional Cavalry. During another raid in 1863, most of the buildings in the center of Lamar, including the courthouse, were burned.[29] Businesses in Lamar when the Earps arrived were "very mediocre," according to Wyatt's cousin George Earp. Nicholas quickly established his family in the reconstructed town. Though he was listed in the census of 1870 as a "grocer," according to his nephew, Nicholas ran the only restaurant in town. The Earps made frequent forays to Fort Scott, Kansas, fifty miles northwest of Lamar, to acquire food for resale. Whether the Earps' business was a grocery or a restaurant or both, one assumes that customers could purchase alcohol there from the former Illinois bootlegger, and that the authorities in Lamar were friendlier to dramshops than the tee-totalers of Monmouth had been. Indeed, in early 1871, the local newspaper reported that "rot-gut whiskey [was] . . . liberally dispensed in some parts of the town."[30]

Entrepreneurs in Lamar had ambitions: when Lamar's founders plotted out the town in 1856, they left room for an enormous courthouse square; the courthouse itself (rebuilt after the war) was an impressive two-story wooden structure worthy of a regional commercial capital city. Some of Barton County's farmers sought to expand southwest Missouri's commercial agriculture to match the pretensions of the courthouse. By 1871, ambitious farmers in the county had founded an agricultural society to promote scientific farming. Together with Lamar merchants, they lobbied for a rail line to carry their produce to wider markets. Newly arrived in town, Nicholas played the role of commercial booster. In July 1870, he was one of thirty-six Lamar men who met to select a delegation to go to Carthage, Missouri, to lobby representatives of the Tebo and Neosho Railroad to route their line through Lamar.[31]

Lamar was a likelier place than San Bernardino for the Earps—scattered since the beginning of the war in 1861—to reassemble as a family. Newton, who was mustered out of the Fourth Iowa Cavalry at the war's end, rejoined his father's family in Lamar by mid-1870. One of Nicholas's younger brothers, Jonathan, who had first moved to Montgomery County, Missouri, in 1857, moved his family to Barton County in 1869 and established a farm in the northeast corner of the county. It may have been Jonathan who persuaded Nicholas to move his family to Missouri. Unlike his older brother, Jonathan adhered to the staunch Methodist traditions of his father; he was a schoolteacher who eventually became a minister, ordained by the West St. Louis conference of the Methodist Episcopal Church in 1872. There were other differences between the two Earp families. According to Jonathan's son George, "While Wyatt and others of Uncle Nick's family lived in Lamar, my father was a farmer and I and my brothers grew up on a farm as typical 'Hill-Billy' boys of the Ozarks." Yet the transformation of Wyatt—twenty-one years old when the family resettled in Lamar—from farm boy to a townsman was hardly complete. He frequently visited his uncle's farm and his "Hill-Billy" cousins to hunt—just as his older brothers James and Virgil had once hunted on the Nossaman farm south of Pella. According to George, "There were many wild deer and turkey on the timbered portions of our farm and Wyatt often came to our farm to shoot deer and turkey."[32]

Lamar more so than San Bernardino offered the possibility for a reunited Earp family to engage in the kind of "booty politics" that had once supported them in Monmouth. Because Nicholas lacked a large landholding or other forms of wealth, the family tradition of booty politics was all the patrimony that he could leave to his sons. Both Nicholas and Wyatt won office in Lamar. As northerners who resettled in the South (even a southern state such as Missouri that had nominally remained loyal to the Union) and sought political office, they might have expected to be derisively referred to by local residents as "carpetbaggers." Indeed, in the immediate postwar years, Missouri politics were characterized by profound tensions between Democrats unreconciled to the Confederate defeat and Radical Republicans determined to reap the political benefits of Union victory.[33] The Earps seem not to have felt such resentment, probably because they had no interest in Reconstruction politics. Rather, Nicholas seemed eager simply to reconstruct the booty-politics system of debt collection that his brothers and father had run in Monmouth.

Nicholas found work in Lamar as town constable shortly after arriving there. By mid-November 1869, he had not only moved on to a higher office but had brought Wyatt into the Earp family tradition of office-holding. On November 17, Nicholas resigned his position as constable to accept appointment as Lamar's justice of the peace. To fill the vacant position of town constable, the Lamar municipal authorities appointed twenty-one-year-old Wyatt.[34] On

March 3, 1870, when the town of Lamar was officially incorporated, both appointments were reaffirmed.[35] At the time of his appointment, Wyatt had no experience in peacekeeping or public service. Indeed, he had nothing to recommend him for the position other than his physical stature and his father's endorsement.

The office did not require much experience, as there was little crime in Lamar. The local newspaper editorialized in March 1871 that "our town and county is civil and quiet" though "some three or four homicides have occurred in the county," and in another instance "a boy stole a horse and was sent to the penitentiary." Indeed, the newspaper made clear that "our courts are particularly down on horse-stealing."[36] Crime was so infrequent that Lamar had no jail. When Wyatt arrested two local drunkards and a vagrant in June 1870, he confined them, according to the local newspaper, in "a stone building which he has appropriated for just such customers." The building had a hole in the roof, however, and all three men escaped before morning.[37]

Nicholas's ascent to justice of the peace and his installation of Wyatt as town constable afforded the Earps opportunities to collect payments from the township and county governments for services rendered. Most such opportunities were decidedly unglamorous: in March 1870 the Lamar trustees decreed that the town constable should be responsible for impounding stray hogs (twenty-five cents each) and killing stray dogs (seventy-five cents each).[38] The two drunks Wyatt arrested in June (who escaped the makeshift jail but did not leave town) he brought before his father, who fined the men $5 each. (The vagrant left town before appearing before the justice of the peace.)[39] On May 3, 1870, Nicholas earned $1 and Wyatt $6 in jury fees; on December 21, Nicholas received $6 and Wyatt $14 from the county court for services rendered in a case before the court; on March 17, 1871, the county court determined that Wyatt was owed $38.50 for services rendered in another case.[40]

Initially appointed to their positions by the town trustees, both Nicholas and Wyatt were compelled to stand for election to their posts in November 1870. Wyatt's main opponent in the race for town constable was his half brother, Newton, who on the strength of his service in the Iowa cavalry received the Republican Party's endorsement. Wyatt defeated his brother 137–108. If the Earps imagined that by running both Wyatt and Newton for the post of constable they would be able to maintain their hold on city offices, their hopes were dashed when Nicholas lost the election for justice of the peace, finishing third in a close four-way race: of 530 votes cast, the first- and fourth-place finishers were separated by only 29 votes.[41]

Before this setback, however, as the Earps gathered in Lamar, Wyatt married a local woman, Urilla Sutherland, the daughter of William and Permelia Sutherland, who operated the Exchange Hotel in Lamar. Nicholas, as the local justice of the peace, officiated at the marriage, which took place on January 10, 1870.[42] Lake referred to Urilla as Wyatt's "girl bride" to suggest the innocence of the union; in fact, she was almost twenty-one at the time of the marriage.[43]

Wyatt and Urilla married at a moment when the meanings of marriage, family, and sexuality were in flux. For Nicholas and Virginia Earp's generation, the all-enveloping agrarian world they had inhabited defined these things. Large families were the norm in the agricultural Upper South and Midwest; children lent a hand on farms from an early age. But the Earps' move to Lamar reflected a broader shift in American society, which became increasingly urban over the nineteenth century. Family size declined along with the waning of American rural society. In 1800, the average American woman bore seven children; by the end of the century, that average had fallen by half.[44] As a townsman—though the village of Lamar barely qualified as a town—Wyatt was part of the first generation of Americans for whom sex and marriage were not simply about producing a brood of children who would comprise the family farm's workforce. For Wyatt's generation, marriage and sexuality were cut loose from these rural moorings and set adrift in an urban, commercialized world. In this modern world, young adults such as Wyatt would have to reinvent their meanings.

Like the Earps' shift from farming into wage work in Monmouth a generation earlier, the transformations of their attitudes toward marriage, family, and sexuality were halting and complicated. Between 1861 and 1870, three of the Earp brothers—Newton, Virgil, and Wyatt—married. Only one of the brothers' marriages endured for more than a year.

Virgil had been the first of Wyatt's brothers to leave his father's household and marry. In September 1861, while the Earps were in their second stint in Pella, Virgil eloped to Knoxville, Iowa, with Magdelena "Ellen" Rysdam (or "Rijsdam"), the daughter of Dutch immigrants. Their ages (both were eighteen) and the ethnic and religious differences between them (native-born Methodist and immigrant Dutch confessional) forced the elopement. The young couple married under assumed names: "Walter" Earp and Ellen "Donahoo." By early 1862, Ellen was pregnant.

In the late summer of 1862, whether the romance between Ellen and Virgil had soured, or their parents' disapproval of the marriage had finally borne down upon them, or they had simply run out of money, Virgil, still only nineteen years old, had determined to enlist in the army. Perhaps the prospect of fatherhood unnerved him—he would not have been the first young man to enlist to escape parental obligations. As his older brother James had done in the first weeks of the war, Virgil returned to Monmouth to enlist, signing his enlistment papers in August, around the time that his wife gave birth to a daughter in Iowa. Two weeks after the girl's birth, he was in uniform in Illinois.

Virgil's enlistment in the army only a year after the elopement and just as his young wife delivered a child suggests that he was looking for a way out of the hasty marriage. When the war ended, he apparently returned to Iowa and learned that his wife and daughter were gone. Whether he was told the truth—that Ellen had migrated with her parents to Oregon in 1864 and married a fellow Dutch immigrant, John van Roosen—or whether he was told that his wife and daughter had died is unclear. Ellen had apparently been told that Virgil had been killed in the war.[45] Neither seemed eager to probe too deeply into the truth of the matter. In an era when divorce was difficult to obtain, spousal abandonment was a common way out of an unhappy marriage.[46]

In contrast to Virgil, four years in the army seem to have inspired rather than inhibited Newton Earp's marriage plans. Newton was discharged from the Fourth Iowa Cavalry on August 24, 1865, in Davenport, Iowa; by mid-September, he was in the town of Philadelphia in Marion County, Missouri, to marry Nancy Jane Adam. The rapidity with which Newton entered into marriage after his discharge from the army and the ceremony's proximity to Monmouth suggests that Nancy was a hometown sweetheart from Newton's days in Illinois. Indeed, the 1850 census counted John Adam, a farmer, in Warren County, together with his wife, Christina; son, Thomas; and daughter, Nancy J., then aged five—which would make her twenty years old in 1865.[47] Adelia Earp recalled that Newton's new wife and mother-in-law "had strong moral character and were very religious." According to Adelia, Nicholas Earp and his younger children "were all trying to be good Christians but we never did match up to Newton's family."[48] Newton and Nancy eventually had five children: Effie May (1870), Wyatt Clyde (1872), Mary Elizabeth (1875), Alice Abigail (1878), and Virgil Edwin (1880).

In the years after the Civil War, Newton and Virgil, the two Earp brothers who had served until the war's end, offered a study in contrasts. Newton settled down into a respectable and apparently faithful family life. Following Virgil and Ellen's mutual abandonment of each other, Virgil eventually landed in Peoria, Illinois, living in Bunker Hill, the town's red-light district, where several of Peoria's gin mills were clustered. He worked in a saloon owned by William Vansteel, a Danish immigrant and a fellow veteran of an Illinois infantry unit.

Sometime in the first half of 1870, Virgil took a hiatus from his job bartending in Peoria and traveled to Lamar. There, in late May, justice of the peace Nicholas Earp officiated at the marriage between Virgil and a seventeen-year-old immigrant from France, Rosilia Draggoo.[49] Virgil likely brought the young woman with him from Peoria: one-quarter of Peoria County's residents in 1870 had been born abroad, and several of the saloonkeepers and their wives in the Peoria district where Virgil lived were French immigrants. She remained in Lamar long enough to appear, as "Rosa Earp," in the 1870 census as Virgil's wife and a member of the extended Earp household. Immediately after the census, however, Rosilia disappeared from any public records. Virgil stayed in Lamar at least until late 1870, but by 1872, he was back in Peoria, living again in Bunker Hill and working at Vansteel's saloon.[50]

Wyatt, a few months short of his twenty-second birthday, was presented with the contrasting examples of his brothers Newton and Virgil. On the one hand, his half brother Newton had quickly settled down in marriage. On the other hand, his brother Virgil led a highly mobile existence of impulsive unions and equally impulsive abandonments. Since the end of the war, Virgil had been Wyatt's mentor as Wyatt tried to find his way to adulthood, and one might expect that Wyatt emulated him. Yet, in early 1870 at the time of his marriage to Urilla, Wyatt seemed ready to adhere to Newton's example.

Wyatt's marriage to Urilla endured for less than one year. Married in January, by November Wyatt was a widower. According to Wyatt's cousin George Earp, Urilla died of typhoid fever.[51] Whether Urilla suffered from typhoid is impossible to say with certainty: diagnoses of such diseases were inexact in the mid-nineteenth century; with its characteristic high fever and red rash, typhoid fever shared some symptoms with malaria and scarlet fever, among other illnesses. Yet the diagnosis might have been accurate: transmitted through contaminated water supplies, typhoid fever was most common in large cities, but virtually every county in the United States in 1870—including those in northern Arkansas, eastern Kansas, and southwestern Missouri—reported some cases in the federal mortality census of 1870. The timing of Urilla's death—ten months or so after her marriage—has led some Earp chroniclers to assert that she died in childbirth.[52] There is no real evidence for that supposition, but the death of Urilla did mean a quick end to Wyatt's apparent effort to create a family life in a Midwestern small town.

Shortly after Urilla's death, Wyatt abandoned Lamar and his elected post there, amid accusations of financial misconduct. On March 14, 1871, the town of Lamar accused Wyatt of pocketing over $200 in taxes he had collected, as part of his work as town constable, for the construction of a local schoolhouse.[53]

It was Wyatt's misfortune that in 1871, Barton County taxpayers harbored deep suspicions of official corruption, particularly in regard to the school tax. Ironically, Nicholas had helped fan the flames of that suspicion. In April 1870, Nicholas had been one of thirteen Lamar men to post an announcement in the *South-West Missourian* protesting county taxes—in particular whether a tax collector had turned over moneys to the county and whether the county's sale of certain lands had been legitimate—and urging a public meeting to take further measures. The officials were ultimately vindicated, but throughout 1871, the *South-West Missourian* editorialized repeatedly, wondering why a significant amount of money had been collected to build a public school while construction was not yet under way.[54]

On March 31, a Barton County farmer, James Cromwell, filed another suit against Wyatt. According to Cromwell, Wyatt had kept some of the money from the sale of a mowing machine worth $75 that Cromwell had surrendered to fulfill a court order.[55]

It is impossible to judge whether Wyatt was falsely accused because he left town without facing the charges against him. His departure, however, certainly created an impression of guilt, at least to the first charge of stealing $200 in school construction funds. Cromwell's suit, by contrast, may have been opportunistic. Cromwell, delinquent on his property taxes both in 1868 and in 1869, would have been aware that Wyatt had been charged with embezzlement, left town, and would be unable to answer new charges against him.[56] Given these circumstances, Cromwell may well have seized the opportunity to charge Wyatt with stealing from him as a way to avoid paying the court the money he owed. In May 1872, the Barton County Court decided that James Maupin, a bondsman who had stood as Wyatt's suretor when he took office as constable, had to pay Cromwell $6.50.

The full truth will likely never be known, but the bare facts are these: Wyatt left town in early 1871, at the same time that the town council decreed that $200 was missing from the public till. It is entirely plausible that the newly reelected town constable made the impulsive decision to leave town in grief over the death of his wife. Whether he followed another impulse to abscond with public moneys is impossible to say—but also impossible to dismiss. Wyatt lived in an era in which municipal corruption was commonplace. Moreover, he had been raised in a family whose members not only practiced booty politics but who flouted local laws (such as those governing liquor sales, the repayment of debts, and bigamy) when it suited them.

Within months of Wyatt's departure, Nicholas, Virginia, and the youngest Earp children had also left Lamar. Years before, Nicholas had defaulted on his promissory notes when he had left Monmouth; sometime between October 1871 and June 1872 he once again left town without repaying his debts. On January 5, 1871, in the first hint that Nicholas's finances were not in good order, the local newspaper, the *South-West Missourian*, published the names of its subscribers who had not paid their subscriptions, including "Earp the baker man." By the spring, it was apparent that Nicholas's business was failing; he owed hundreds of dollars to his creditors. On May 15, 1871, James Montgomery filed a claim in the Barton County Court alleging that Nicholas owed him $256.41. A week later, D. A. January & Co. filed suit against Nicholas for non-payment of $209.34. On September 7, 1871, the Barton County sheriff posted a notice in the local newspaper announcing that on Friday, October 13, 1871, the county would auction Nicholas's property in Lamar from the steps of the courthouse to satisfy his debt to D. A. January & Co. The following June, James Montgomery once again filed suit for the money Nicholas owed him. Nicholas had long since left Lamar; the writ was directed "to any Sheriff in the State."[57]

Only two weeks after the charges against him were filed in Lamar, Wyatt surfaced across the Missouri border in the Cherokee Nation, a slice of land in the northeastern corner of the Indian Territory, now the state of Oklahoma. Of all the dangerous places in which Wyatt found himself in his turbulent life—including Dodge City and Tombstone—the Indian Territory in 1871 was in many respects the most brutal and corrupt. The resident Cherokees, whom the federal government had forcibly removed to the Indian Territory from Georgia in the 1830s, were divided into bitter factions that frequently exploded into violence. Scores of Cherokees were killed in factional disputes in the decades after removal. Numerous outlaws found refuge in the sparsely populated Indian Territory, a vast region under the tenuous legal authority of the Western District of Arkansas Court. Many of the Western District's 140 notoriously corrupt deputy U.S. marshals had been schooled in the violence of the Civil War—some had been members of Quantrill's irregular force.[58]

The Western District in the late 1860s and early 1870s was not only a haven for outlaws but for a version of the booty politics so familiar to the Earps. In 1866, the principal chief of the Choctaws, who occupied a reservation in the southeastern corner of Indian Territory, complained that the deputy U.S. marshals for the Western District "annoyed and harassed" them by "going about our country with an armed force and arresting numbers of our citizens for offenses alleged to have been committed." The arrests, the Choctaw chief argued, "are without any just cause, the main inducement with the assistant marshals being to make fees thereby."[59] By 1874, the abuses in the Western District prompted a committee of the U.S. House of Representatives to hold hearings. Their findings confirmed the charges of the Choctaws: false arrests and fraudulent accounts were the norm.[60]

There was enough real crime to keep the deputy marshals busy. In its spring 1869 session, the Western District Court tried one Chickasaw and three Cherokee men for three separate murders.[61] In September, two Choctaws—one a veteran of the Confederate army—murdered two men, a Choctaw and an African-American, to steal the goods they were hauling to a store in Indian Territory.[62] Across the border in Arkansas, disputes were also deadly. In May 1869, John Read, who was in Van Buren to serve as a juror in the district court, shot and killed William Bledsoe rather than surrender the horse that Bledsoe had won from him in a wager.[63] In August of the same year, Monroe Srum shot Harris Thomas to prevent Thomas from courting Srum's sister.[64] As in other parts of the Reconstruction-era South, white violence against African-Americans in western Arkansas was rarely punished: three white men who killed an African-American man in 1869 were acquitted because the only testimony against them came from African-American witnesses. White supremacist societies operated with such impunity that the Van Buren baseball team called itself the Ku Klux Klub.[65]

Altogether, the Indian Territory was not a place for anyone looking to stay out of trouble, and it took only a short time for trouble to find Wyatt. A bill of information filed on April 1, 1871, by Jacob Owen, a deputy U.S. marshal of the Western District, accused Wyatt and two other men of stealing two horses. "Wyatt S. Earp, Ed Kennedy, [and] John Shown," Owen wrote, "on the 28th day of March AD 1871 in the Indian country in said District did feloniously willfully steal take and carry away two horses each of the value of one hundred dollars, the property goods and chattels of one William Keys."[66]

Anna Shown contended that Wyatt and Kennedy duped her husband into stealing the horses. She told Owen that they "got my husband drunk near Ft. Gibson, I.T., about the 28th of March 1871. They then went and got Mr. Jim Keys horses, and put my husband on one and he lead [sic] the other, and told him to ride fifty miles toward Kansas," where they would meet him. Shown rode north with the stolen horses to the thieves' appointed meeting place fifty miles north of Fort Gibson; his wife accompanied Wyatt and Kennedy there in a hack. Once reunited, the four hitched the stolen horses to the hack and continued their flight toward Kansas, driving the horses at night and resting by day to avoid detection. Keys, however, followed their trail and overtook them after three days.

According to Anna Shown, "Earp and Kennedy told Keys that my husband stole the horses. They also said that if Shown (my husband) turned states evidence then they would kill him."[67]

Six days after Keys overtook and apprehended the thieves, a posse including Owen took Wyatt, Kennedy, and Shown into custody.[68] Owen returned with the prisoners to the Western District courthouse in Van Buren, a building set on a square overrun with unfenced swine—the local newspaper waggishly referred to the courthouse square as "our public pasture."[69] On April 14, Wyatt, Kennedy, and Shown were arraigned before the U.S. commissioner for the Western District, James Churchill, who set bail at $500 each. Unable to make bail, Wyatt was confined in the district jail in Van Buren.[70] Conviction seemed likely.

Horse theft was a felony (and together with counterfeiting, one of the most common felonies on the nineteenth-century frontier), but contrary to popular belief, it was not a capital crime in the American West in 1871. The last time a court in the United States ordered anyone hanged for stealing horses was in California in 1851. If Wyatt had been convicted of horse theft, he would likely have been sentenced to five years in the federal penitentiary in Little Rock. That was the sentence handed down to three horse thieves in the Western District Court in December 1869.[71] A horse thief on the "middle border" where Missouri, Kansas, Arkansas, and the Indian Territory converged had more to fear from vigilantes than from the authorities. In the fall of 1870, in Butler County, Kansas— less than one hundred miles from Fort Gibson—a vigilance committee of nearly eight hundred men lynched eight suspected horse thieves.[72]

While the authorities did not hang horse thieves, a sentence of five years in prison was a sobering prospect. If convicted, Wyatt would have spent some of that time in the Western District courthouse jail before being transferred to Little Rock to finish his term. Though Wyatt may not have known it, between his arraignment and his scheduled trial, the Western District of Arkansas Court was scheduled to move from Van Buren a few miles west, across the

Arkansas River, to the abandoned army post of Fort Smith. A Western District marshal had transformed two rooms in the basement of the new Fort Smith courthouse into a jail. A Van Buren newspaper reporter described the Fort Smith jail shortly after its opening as a "Hole in the Wall" that was "gloomy and dark and rank."[73] As described by Anna Dawes, who visited Fort Smith with her father, Senator Henry Dawes, in 1885, the jail consisted of two dark, low rooms, with as many as fifty men per room. Light and ventilation entered each room through eight grated windows that opened into the areas beneath the ground-floor verandas. A single chamber pot—placed in the unused fireplace in the hope that the stench would be carried up through the chimney—served all of the inmates of a room. Prisoners slept on the floor and were given few opportunities to wash. Anna Dawes described the jail as "dirty beyond description" and "a piece of mediaeval barbarity."[74]

Wyatt did not stay in Arkansas long enough to experience the basement dungeon in Fort Smith. Just as the three men he had confined in Lamar a year earlier had escaped from their makeshift jail, Wyatt escaped from the prison in Van Buren. He and six other men made a bold daylight escape on May 3, roughly two weeks after his arraignment and only days before the court moved to Fort Smith.

Wyatt was among ten men confined to a cell in the upper story of the soon-to-be-defunct Van Buren jailhouse. His cellmates included John Shown, the man he had allegedly duped into horse theft; two accused murderers who faced hanging; and two brothers, Henry and Jerry Perry, charged with counterfeiting and the attempted murder of Benjamin Shoemaker, a Western District deputy marshal. Wyatt, Shown, the Perry brothers, and the two accused murderers pried off the rafters in one corner of the cell, hoisted themselves into the low attic, and crawled across the rafters to a small, grated window that provided ventilation. They enlarged the window opening by removing some stones from the building's exterior wall and, tying blankets from their cell into a rope, lowered themselves twenty feet to the ground. After crawling under the fence surrounding the jailhouse, they were free.[75]

On May 8, the court issued a writ ordering the Western District marshal to force Wyatt and Shown to appear for trial in November. A week later, Kennedy, Shown, and Wyatt (the latter two in absentia) were indicted for horse theft in Fort Smith. On June 5, Kennedy was tried and acquitted of the crime. The acquittal may have been a direct result of the jailbreak: if Anna Shown had fled Arkansas along with her husband, then she would not have been present to testify. The acquittal was not entirely unusual: the most complete study of prosecutions on the frontier indicates that only about half of all indictments led to convictions.[76] In the Western District, where the authorities arrested numerous people on trumped-up charges, the conviction rate was even lower: in its November 1871 term, 28 criminal cases (including Wyatt's case) were carried over from the May term and added to 238 new indictments. Of those 266, prosecutors secured only 51 convictions. There were 45 acquittals and 77 continuances.[77]

Certain stalwart defenders of Wyatt's legacy claim that the man who was arrested for horse theft in Indian Territory was not the same Wyatt Earp who became a police officer in Kansas and Arizona. Rather, according to one such defender, Earl Chafin, the arrestee was "another Wyatt Earp, a lawless ex-Confederate soldier from Tennessee."[78] Yet geography among other factors suggests that the man arrested for horse theft was, as Chafin put it, "our" Wyatt Earp. Wyatt was in Lamar in late 1870, a few months before and less than one hundred miles away from Fort Gibson, the place where the theft was alleged to have happened.

Wyatt was arrested, but the question remains whether he committed the theft. The deputy marshals of the Western District were notorious for making arrests on specious charges simply to collect fees for their services. As one former deputy marshal testified to Congress in 1874, "We would go out and gobble up everybody that we could get hold of. Marshal Britton told us to arrest any person there was a charge against and bring them to Fort Smith; that we could get warrants when we got here." To exploit the system to the fullest, Britton, the U.S. marshal for the Western District, would exaggerate the number of men in a posse and the number of miles they traveled to claim greater expenses. In return, Britton kept a third of the inflated expenses due his subordinates.[79]

Wyatt may have been in the wrong place at the wrong time and "gobbled up" by Britton's corrupt system. Owen, the deputy marshal who signed the bill of complaint against Wyatt, was one of the deputies who lined his pockets by arresting unoffending Indians and the occasional white vagrant and conveying them to the court in Arkansas. In 1874, Benjamin Shoemaker, one of the deputy U.S. marshals in the Western District, testified that Owen was one of the "confidential men" who routinely committed fraud by exaggerating the number of men in posses. Moreover, according to Shoemaker, Owen was one of the deputies who pressured him into giving false testimony when a federal investigator came to Fort Smith in 1873 to look into the fraud charges.[80] Owen was not called to testify in that congressional inquiry. This was not, however, because he was above suspicion, but because he, together with another of the Western District's "confidential men," was killed in a bloody shoot-out in the Indian Territory in 1872, only a year after Wyatt's flight.[81]

By Wyatt's account, he spent the early 1870s hunting bison in the southern plains. Most bison hunters were Civil War veterans who had learned during the war to handle newly developed, heavy, long-range rifles. Though he was not a veteran, Wyatt's recollections of those days in Lake's *Frontier Marshal* have a certain authenticity, especially his recounting of the habits of the bison and the straitened economics of the bison hunter. Yet certain aspects of his account do not ring true. Wyatt, according to Lake, disdained the large, cumbersome "buffalo guns" that bison hunters used to deliver heavy bullets from hundreds of yards away. Instead, he claimed to have approached on foot to within one hundred yards of the bison and felled his prey with a shotgun. This fanciful account belies Lake's claim that Wyatt was much of a marksman, at least with a buffalo gun. Moreover, it casts doubt on Wyatt's claim to have spent years hunting bison, or at the very least to have had any success at it, as bison are skittish animals. Few hunters could consistently have walked within one hundred yards of a herd of bison without causing the animals to flee. Wyatt may well have taken aim at a few bison during these years—thousands of Americans did so in the 1860s and 1870s. Or perhaps he signed on for a few stints as a hide skinner in a bison-hunting outfit—a role more suited to a young man lacking experience with the heavy buffalo guns. Yet his recollections have the texture not of an experienced hide hunter but of someone who had traveled widely in the southern Great Plains and had heard the yarns of bison hunters.[82]

In early 1871, rather than hunting bison, Wyatt was in the Indian Territory southwest of Lamar. After his escape from Van Buren in May, Wyatt traveled north to join his brother Virgil in Peoria, putting almost six hundred miles between himself and the federal court in Fort Smith. Along the way, he may have stopped in Lamar to collect his brother Morgan. Their sister Adelia recalled that Wyatt was in Lamar in 1871 before he and Morgan "went buffalo hunting."[83] If the Earp brothers spent any time on the bison range, it was not for long. By early 1872, Morgan and Wyatt had joined Virgil in Peoria, Illinois.

In Peoria, Wyatt and Morgan were drawn into the world of the bordello. By the time they landed in Peoria, the Earp brothers had long inhabited a world in which prostitution was a visible part. Like fighting and drinking, frequenting prostitutes was expected of both soldiers and young men with roots in the backcountry.[84] War had familiarized James and Virgil with prostitution. In northern cities where soldiers gathered for transport to the South, prostitution became suddenly more widespread than it had been before the war. Wartime Washington in particular was notorious for commercialized sex. A provost marshal's report in 1862 estimated that the city had more than four hundred brothels and seven thousand prostitutes. Prostitution contributed to the rapid spread of sexually transmitted disease among the troops. The Union Medical Department found that over the course of the conflict one out of every twelve soldiers was infected with a sexually transmitted disease.[85]

Prostitutes established themselves near army posts in occupied cities in the South as well, notably in Louisville, New Orleans, Portsmouth, and Norfolk. One city well-known for prostitution during the war was Nashville, where Virgil Earp was stationed during most of the conflict. In 1863, military authorities attempted to deport 150 prostitutes from the city, but no neighboring communities would accept them. By 1864, at a time when a provost marshal reported nearly four hundred prostitutes in Nashville, military authorities were desperate enough about the spread of venereal disease among the troops that they instituted a system of medical treatment and regulation: a surgeon examined prostitutes weekly and issued a license to those who were healthy; those found to be infected with a sexually transmitted disease were taken to a local hospital—supported by the license fees—for treatment.[86] Nashville became so notorious for prostitution that in the Kansas cow town of Ellsworth in 1872, the red-light district was known as Nauchville.[87]

In the immediate postwar years, James, Virgil, and Wyatt lived and worked in parts of the West where prostitution was highly visible. Mining, ranching, and logging were the dominant industries of the West in the second half of the nineteenth century; each of these industries, like the army posts that also dotted the West, employed large numbers of young men. Prostitutes flocked to such places where a skewed gender ratio created a high demand for sexual labor. In mining towns in California and Nevada when Wyatt was in his teens, for instance, prostitutes comprised between 5 and 10 percent of the female population.[88] It is likely that while working as freighters in the immediate postwar years, Virgil introduced Wyatt not only to fisticuffs, shooting, and drinking, but also to prostitutes.

The rise of prostitution in mid-nineteenth-century America owed itself to more than war and the demographics created by extractive industries; it also reflected a general shifting of standards of nineteenth-century sexual behavior. As the United States became increasingly industrial and urban, fertility rates declined dramatically. Some married couples conceived fewer children because they hewed to the advice of midcentury moralists who preached sexual abstinence. As sex for reproduction declined, however, other Americans began to think of sex as an erotic rather than primarily a procreative activity. The emergence of nineteenth-century nonreproductive sexuality was reflected in the increasing availability of contraception and abortion (as many as one in five pregnancies may have been medically terminated in 1870); homosexuality; and not least of all, the rise of prostitution.[89]

Peoria as Virgil knew it in the 1870s was neither wartime Nashville nor a frontier mining camp. At the same time, it was not the dull, straitlaced place that modern Americans have understood it to be. By 1850, Peoria was both the second-largest manufacturing center in Illinois, after Chicago, and a regional center for the production of agricultural commodities, within a trade network centered in St. Louis. As an urban and transportation center (the first railroad reached Peoria in 1854), the city was a center for Union recruitment (the units that both James and Virgil joined were organized in Peoria). With that recruiting effort came the by-products—gambling, drinking, and prostitution—that attended thousands of young men camped on the outskirts of town.

In the years after the war, Peoria's manufacturing expanded considerably—particularly its leading industry, distilled spirits. In 1865, Peoria had fifteen distilleries; by 1880, Peoria was the largest liquor-producing city in the United States. Indeed, the city's distilleries surpassed the liquor production of the entire state of Kentucky. (That was no mean feat: Kentucky had two hundred distilleries at the time.) Peoria liquor was noted for its potency: a rural newspaper reported in 1866 that "out in Peoria, Illinois, a noted whiskey manufacturing region, they test the quality of the liquor by the distance a man can walk after tasting it. The liquor called 'tangle legs' is said to be made of diluted alcohol, nitric acid, boot legs, and tobacco." A man who took a swig of "tangle legs" was said to be able to walk no farther than four hundred yards before collapsing.[90] Peoria was so synonymous with alcohol that between 1895 and 1918, the city's minor-league baseball club was known as the Distillers.

Arriving in Peoria about a year after the death of Urilla, Wyatt quickly found work in the sex trade. Virgil introduced Wyatt to the brothel keepers of Bunker Hill, as the gin-mill and red-light district where Virgil worked was known. By March 1, 1872, according to the Peoria city directory, Wyatt was living in the house of Jane Haspel—a notorious Peoria madam—just down the street from the saloon where Virgil worked. As the Earp researcher Roger Jay has explained, that is where Wyatt came to know Jane's eighteen-year-old daughter, Sarah "Sally" Haspel. She had grown up in the sordid world of the brothel; Jane had introduced both Sally and her younger sister, Mary, to the life of the prostitute at an early age. By 1872, Sally was working as a prostitute in the Bunker Hill district, both at her mother's brothel and at another a few blocks away known as the McClellan Institute (so called after a former Union Army commanding general, George McClellan, because soldiers made up most of the brothels' customers during the war). Wyatt and Sally eventually became business associates, or companions, or both—an arrangement that endured until the fall of 1872, or perhaps longer.

On February 24, 1872, the Peoria police raided the Haspel bordello, arresting both Wyatt and Morgan. The brothers were charged with consorting with prostitutes and fined $20 each. Although Wyatt was living at the brothel, the amount was consistent with what a prostitute's customer would have been fined. A little over two months later, however, Wyatt and Morgan were arrested again, this time at the McClellan Institute. They were fined $44.55 each—an amount consistent with what a confederate of the prostitutes would be fined, suggesting that the brothers were working at the bordello as enforcers. Unable or unwilling to pay the fine or work it off, they served a light sentence in the Peoria jail.

By June 11, Morgan and Wyatt were visiting their sister Adelia for her eleventh birthday. Adelia was still under the impression that her brothers had been hunting bison in the southern plains. "Wyatt and Morgan went buffalo hunting," Adelia later recalled, "and came back in 1872 with quite a heap of money. They visited us on the farm and on my eleventh birthday they gave me a whole package of pretty clothes. I reckon I was the best-dressed farm girl in Missouri for some time to come."[91] One can only assume that the "pretty clothes" were castoffs from the prostitutes of the McClellan Institute.

By September, Wyatt was back in Peoria, working as a bartender and enforcer on a keelboat brothel moored three miles down the Illinois River from Peoria. On September 7, Peoria police raided the keelboat and arrested Wyatt and the boat's owner, John Walton. The local newspaper reported a few days later that "John Walton, the skipper of the boat and Wyatt Earp, the Peoria bummer, were each fined $43.15."[92]

The paper also reported that among the "good looking" but "depraved" women arrested were "Sarah Earp, alias Sally Heckell, [who] calls herself wife of Wyatt." Sally Heckel was likely Sally Haspel. There is no record of their having legally married, and it is unlikely that they did. In nineteenth-century America, it was not uncommon for marriages to be arranged informally; courts usually recognized cohabitating couples as legally married.[93] More likely, however, the marriage was a fiction. It was common practice for prostitutes to take the name of their pimp, or in this case the bordello's enforcer, and for the two to claim that they were married, or that the woman was a sister, niece, or cousin. Such practice provided some rationale, however slim, for the presence of young women in a house when police came to bordellos. Whether Sally Haspel's claim to be Wyatt's wife was merely a pretense or indicated a real bond, in either case it shows the depth of Wyatt's integration into the Peoria demimonde.

Beyond literary conventions that encouraged Lake to cast Wyatt as a paragon of virtue; beyond the ambition of Lake and Wyatt to see the biography transformed into a film; beyond Wyatt's keen desire for exculpation for his vigilantism in Arizona—the fundamental reason that Lake did not present Wyatt as a frontier Prince Hal who progressed from lawbreaking youth to lawgiving adulthood was that Wyatt did not encourage such an interpretation and, unlike Shakespeare's character, he never repented of his misspent youth. Though he spent much of the time after leaving Peoria as a police officer, he remained ensconced in the world of vice for the next decades. Indeed, by 1872 certain stubborn characteristics had taken hold: an attraction to the underworld of petty crime, an impulse to seize opportunities regardless of the legal consequences, and a disposition to flee when his situation became untenable. Not least, by 1872, Wyatt had developed a willingness, perhaps even an eagerness, to reinvent himself. To the end of his life, these traits remained a part of him.

He shared these traits with his father, who left Monmouth in 1859 disgraced as a bootlegger and a deadbeat only to resurface in Pella, presenting himself as a veteran of the Black Hawk War. Nicholas had not reformed by 1871, when, unable to pay his debts in Lamar, he fled the state. Likewise, Wyatt, at the outset of his life, was able to reinvent himself repeatedly because American culture in the early 1870s was stubbornly local—forming a nation of "island communities," as the historian Robert Wiebe termed it.[94] Wyatt could flee Indian Territory and his felony arrest and land in Peoria without anyone knowing of his past. He could disguise his activities in Peoria by telling his sister that he was hunting bison. When he left Peoria, he could go to Kansas and make himself into a lawman, reinventing himself as thoroughly as Prince Hal, who, in the last act of *Henry IV, Part II*, ascends to the throne and distances himself completely from Falstaff: "I know thee not, old man," he says to his erstwhile friend. Hal's rejection of Falstaff marks the beginning of his reinvention of himself as the upright Henry V, the victor over the French at the Battle of Agincourt.[95] Repentance transformed the wayward Prince Hal into Henry V. But Wyatt could leave home, reinvent himself, and simply shed his past. He had no need of repentance.

★ **4** ★

JERK YOUR GUN

Gunfights were the ultimate tests of manhood in the mythic West. According to Stuart Lake, Wyatt's reputation for armed violence as a law officer in the Kansas cow towns between 1875 and 1879 made him a man among men—a characterization that Lake established in implicitly sexualized terms: Lake armed his protagonist with one of the biggest pistols in the West. The story Lake told was that in 1876 the dime novelist Ned Buntline visited Dodge City—where Wyatt had recently moved and joined the police force. In gratitude to the peace officers of Dodge City—Wyatt, Charlie Bassett, Bill Tilghman, Bat Masterson, and Neal Brown—for providing him with so many colorful tales of the West, Buntline presented each of them with specially ordered .45-caliber Colt pistols with twelve-inch barrels, four inches longer than was standard. Subsequently, as Lake told it, all the officers but Wyatt proved unable to handle the extralong pistols and cut the barrels back to standard length. But Lake wrote that Wyatt told him, "I carried it at my right hip throughout my career as marshal."[1]

Nearly every aspect of this story is demonstrably false. According to the historian William Shillingberg, Ned Buntline never wrote a story about Wyatt, Masterson, or any of the other police officers in Dodge City. In 1876, the officers were largely unknown outside of Kansas. Buntline did not travel to the West in 1876–77; rather he was fishing in the Poconos, writing articles for *American Angler*, and addressing the Republican National Convention in Philadelphia. The Colt Company did not manufacture a pistol with a twelve-inch barrel until 1892. The company named its twelve-inch pistol a Buntline Special only in 1957, the year that an episode on ABC's *Wyatt Earp* television program (for which Lake served as a consultant) featured Buntline presenting Earp with the fictional pistol with its elongated barrel. By the time that episode aired, the Buntline Special had become, thanks to Lake, an inextricable part of the Earp mythology; it was, as Shillingberg put it, his Excalibur.[2]

The Buntline Special was also, of course, an overtly phallic symbol—when it came to asserting Earp's masculinity, Lake was not subtle. According to Lake, Wyatt not only possessed the longest-barreled pistol on the frontier but was "the speediest, deadliest gunfighter of the Old West." So important to Lake was Wyatt's alleged skill at gunplay that he originally wanted to entitle his book *Wyatt Earp: Gunfighter*, until persuaded otherwise by an editor at Houghton Mifflin.[3] According to Lake, Masterson testified, "A hundred men, more or less, with reputations as killers, whom I have known, have started gunplays against him only to look into the muzzle of Wyatt's Colt before they could get their own guns half-drawn." In *Frontier Marshal*, this statement attributed to Masterson immediately follows Lake's tall tale about the Buntline Special. If in arming Earp with an extralarge pistol Lake conflated violence with sex, his anecdote about the gunfights continued the conflation, depicting Earp as having had a hundred or more contests of sexual prowess. Earp proved himself in each of these encounters as more of a man than his opponent—his pistol leveled and ready while theirs were still half holstered. These alleged encounters foreshadowed the gunfight in Tombstone in 1881 where, according to Lake, Wyatt let his antagonist Ike Clanton flee the fight because "he didn't jerk his gun."[4]

Lake maintained that one of those hundred gunplays and Wyatt's most important gunfight before Tombstone occurred in Ellsworth, Kansas, in 1873—as Lake told it, this was Wyatt's entry into the world of the Kansas cow towns. His opponent in that alleged altercation, the renowned gunman and gambler Ben Thompson, like Ike Clanton, failed to jerk his gun. According to Lake, Wyatt happened to be in Ellsworth when Thompson's brother, Bill, shot and killed one of Ellsworth's law officers, Sheriff C. B. Whitney. The assassin fled town while his brother remained behind, patrolling Ellsworth's main plaza with a shotgun, to discourage anyone from pursuit. The mayor promptly appointed Wyatt marshal; Wyatt coolly confronted Thompson and ordered him to drop his shotgun and submit to arrest. The gunman meekly surrendered; Wyatt, according to Lake, consigned Thompson to jail and resigned as marshal after just one hour on the job. The story, however entertaining, is almost certainly untrue. While Bill Thompson indeed shot and killed Sheriff Whitney in August 1873—he was tried for murder in December and acquitted when a cowboy testified that Thompson's weapon had accidentally discharged—there is no evidence that Wyatt was in Ellsworth in 1873.[5]

Lake's story of Wyatt's encounter with Thompson was fanciful, but he was right about one thing: when Wyatt came to the Kansas cow towns (not Ellsworth in 1873 but Wichita a year later), he entered a world populated by young men engaged in an ongoing battle for status and dominance. In Kansas, Wyatt became a police officer and a professional gambler; he jockeyed for preeminence as both, and by 1879, despite some setbacks, achieved it. As a lawman first in Wichita and later in Dodge City, Wyatt was feared for his skills with his fists (and, far less often, with a pistol). As a gambler, he excelled at faro, a popular game of chance in which participants staked not only large sums but also their public standing. Wyatt became so adept at dealing faro that by the end of the 1870s he earned his living at it every winter and spring. When the men of the Kansas cow towns competed with one another either at cards, with their fists, or (infrequently) with pistols, their masculine identity was at stake.

At the same time, for Wyatt, encounters with other men were not mere contests for masculine dominance. In the Kansas cow towns where men outnumbered women by a large margin, he also looked to men for companionship. In Wichita, he befriended his partner on the police force, Jimmy Cairns. In Dodge City, he formed an enduring friendship with John Henry "Doc" Holliday, who would later accompany him to Tombstone, to the streetfight in October 1881, and on his vigilante campaign in 1882.

A code of behavior dominated this men's world of competition and camaraderie: it demanded that men gamble (or risk being seen as afraid to lose); consort with prostitutes (or risk being thought effeminate); and defend any slight to their honor with violence (or risk being branded a coward).[6] These injunctions had limits: in Wichita, Wyatt was dismissed from the police force for a brutal beating he administered to a candidate for city marshal after the candidate had insulted him. One could also take male camaraderie too far, in the eyes of some contemporaries. Bat Masterson, a friend of Wyatt's from Dodge City, intimated that Wyatt's friendship with Holliday was so close that it verged on the romantic. Masterson registered his disapproval in coded terms by likening Wyatt and Holliday to the storied friends from Greek antiquity Damon and Pythias. Indeed, coded language permeated this world. At the green cloth (the faro table), a cheater (or mucker) was disdained—but less so than a piker, who timidly wagered only small amounts. Oblique language was universal when speaking of prostitution, or the white hood. Not least, when a violent dispute had reached its ultimate point, a man was obliged to jerk his gun.[7] Understanding Wyatt's place in Kansas in the mid to late 1870s, a period in which he evolved from the callow bummer he had been in Peoria to a man of local esteem, thus requires some decoding.

Wichita, Kansas, in 1874 was the dust-choked capital of the Kansas cattle trade. Its buildings were hastily constructed, one-story wooden "shacks," according to one longtime resident, with awnings to provide some shade. Wichita is situated on the eastern edge of the dry shortgrass plains, and its surroundings struck many travelers from the East as a barren desert. That impression was especially strong in the summer of 1874, when swarms of grasshoppers—technically the now-extinct Rocky Mountain locusts—swept through the region. According to one traveler, within a day of their arrival the grasshoppers "had eaten everything in the way of vegetation; in some corn fields they even eat up the stalks." The insects had even stripped the leaves from the trees in creek bottoms so that "it looks like winter."[8]

According to the Wichita resident David Leahy, the town in 1874 had about twelve hundred inhabitants, composed largely of "transient cowboys, gamblers, horse thieves, and landseekers."[9] Wilson Purdy, a traveler who came to Wichita that summer, concurred, describing Wichita as "a lively place of gambling and drinking" populated by "Texas cow herders." Having just returned from South America before embarking for Kansas, Purdy described the cowboys as "a Second Edition of the South American Gaucho."[10]

Cowboys and gamblers were not the only residents of the Kansas cow towns, however. Hundreds of cattle buyers headquartered in the cow towns during the cattle season; merchants, physicians, lawyers, and their families populated the towns. These citizens occupied a world apart from the gamblers and the drovers. They built churches, schools, and opera houses; staged lavish weddings and children's birthday parties; and founded temperance societies. They adopted urban American fashions in dress and style and fads such as croquet and roller skating. Genteel culture in the Kansas cow towns was in large part about class distinctions, separating professionals and merchants from laboring cowboys. Class in nineteenth-century America was not only about capital: it was also a function of ceremony. By adhering to a certain code of behavior—the middle class like the cowboys had their own code—a teetotaler and a minister's grandson such as Wyatt who abstained from alcohol and deferred to the moral authority of the clergy might purchase admittance to middle-class society.[11]

Cowboys and middle-class merchants found themselves together in Wichita because the town emerged in the years after the Civil War as a midway point between the cattle ranges of west Texas and the meatpacking plants of Chicago. Before the war, between

3 and 4 million cattle had grazed in Texas, but the west Texas rangelands were remote from markets.[12] After the war, northern industry—lurching spasmodically into the West to satisfy its appetite for minerals, timber, and other natural resources—drew Texas cattle to urban markets. The extension of railroads to Kansas—the Kansas Pacific reached Denver in August 1870, and the Atchison, Topeka, and Santa Fe reached Dodge City, in western Kansas, in September 1872—brought rail transportation to within a few hundred miles of the Texas rangelands.[13] Seeing an opportunity, an Illinois cattle buyer, Joseph McCoy, enticed Texas ranchers to drive their cattle to Abilene, Kansas. The town, which elected McCoy its mayor in 1871, was near to the Chisholm Trail—a trade route to Texas that could serve as a cattle trail—and by 1867 was linked to eastern markets by the Kansas Pacific. From Abilene, the cattle were shipped by rail to feedlots in Iowa, Indiana, and Illinois, where they were fattened on a diet of corn before being shipped to their last destination, the vast stockyards on the south side of Chicago.[14]

Yet on their way to the Kansas railroad, drovers had to stay to the west, away from the farms that were overspreading eastern Kansas and the farmers who objected both to cattle trampling their crops and to the diseased ticks the Texas longhorns carried. In 1870, the population density of most of the counties east of Wichita was over ten people per square mile; west of Wichita, the population density dropped to fewer than two per square mile. As Kansas settlement spread westward over the late 1860s and 1870s, the Texas drovers likewise veered ever more to the west as they herded their cattle to Kansas. Gradually they shifted from Abilene to Ellsworth (which the Kansas Pacific reached in 1867) to Wichita (which a branch line of the Atchison, Topeka, and Santa Fe reached in July 1871) and finally to Dodge City (which the Santa Fe reached in 1872). Each city dominated the cattle trade for only a few years before being supplanted by a rival farther to the west.[15]

In the heyday of the cow towns, thousands of cowboys—many ex-Confederate soldiers as well as a fair number of Tejanos and African-Americans—drove hundreds of thousands of cattle from

Texas to Kansas every summer. At a pace of ten to twelve miles per day, it took approximately three months of monotonous labor to drive a herd from Texas to Kansas. The cowboy's work was seasonal: of the twenty thousand cowboys in the American West in the second half of the nineteenth century, roughly half were out of work for six months or more every year. Unemployed or underemployed cowboys spent the winter doing odd jobs on ranches in return for a bed and meals. Conditions for cowboys were so poor that in 1883, two hundred cowboys in the Texas Panhandle tried to go on strike just weeks before the spring rodeo was scheduled to begin. A cooperative of large ranchers broke the cowboys' organizing effort easily.[16]

While winter and spring in Texas were hard times for cowboys, when they reached the cattle towns of Kansas, the drovers were flush with cash. Having spent months driving cattle from Texas to Wichita, the cowboys received their pay when they reached their destination. Many immediately spent their earnings in Wichita's saloons, gambling halls, and brothels.[17] Compared to the cattle trail and to the shabby exteriors of the cow towns, the cowboys found the interiors of the saloons lavish: carpeted, wood paneled, and gaslit. Bars were ornate and highly polished; walls were covered with prints and mirrors; drinks were served in matching glassware.[18] A helpful bartender might direct the cowboys into a back room where high-stakes gambling took place, or to an adjoining building where prostitutes could be found.

In Wichita in 1874, many of the cowboys who collected their pay and went in search of prostitutes found them at a bordello belonging to Bessie and James Earp. Bessie, a former Illinois prostitute, and James had moved to Wichita within a year of marrying in Illinois in 1873. Their bordello was in operation in Wichita by January 1874, according to city records.[19] As the capital of the Kansas cattle trade, Wichita was an ideal location for a brothel: thousands of cowboys came to the town every summer. Even during the winter months, the usual gender imbalance of the ranching and mining West prevailed; in 1870, Sedgwick County, which included Wichita, had a population of 763 men and 332 women. The demand for commercial sex was high.

One Wichita resident recalled that in 1874 James Earp was a bartender in a local saloon.[20] As a bartender, James was in a position to steer potential patrons to the Earp brothel. Indeed, just as most saloon owners allowed professional gamblers to work in their saloon in return for a percentage of their winnings, most saloons operated in cooperation with a local brothel. In such instances, little distinguished a bartender from a pimp.[21]

Wichita's upstanding citizens tolerated prostitution as they tolerated saloons and gambling in part because they feared that if they outlawed it, cowboys would take their cattle to a more obliging town. An open letter to "Texas Drovers," which the Wichita city council drafted in April 1875, touted the advantages of Wichita over other Kansas cow towns: rail connections, good prices for cattle, and not least of all "houses of amusement of an excellent character."[22] Moreover, prostitution was a source of municipal income. In January 1874 the town collected $1,147 in various fines—about one-quarter of that amount came from fines levied on prostitutes. Among those charged with prostitution in January 1874 was Bessie Earp. She was assessed a fine of $8 and ordered to pay court costs of $2.[23]

Also assessed a fine of $8 and court costs of $2 was a woman who called herself Sallie Earp. That a woman working at the Earp brothel would give herself the Earp surname was, as for Sally Haspel in Peoria, standard procedure for nineteenth-century prostitutes claiming fictive kinship. Women known as Eva, Kate, and Minnie Earp were all charged with prostitution in Wichita in 1874; they were fictive kin, related to the Earps by neither blood nor marriage but simply employees in the Earp brothel.

The woman calling herself Sallie Earp in Wichita may have been Sally Haspel herself. That would suggest that Wyatt may have been in Wichita by January 1874, too. Following his last arrest in Peoria in September 1872, Wyatt had dropped out of sight, or at least out of the public record. He did not surface again until October 1874, when a newspaper noted his presence in Wichita. Jimmy

Cairns, later Wyatt's police partner, recalled, however, that Wyatt came to Wichita in 1873 directly from Missouri. Cairns may have been correct, if for no other reason than when Lake asked Wyatt about it in 1928, Wyatt disputed Cairns's recollection by invoking his familiar cover story: "I arrived in Wichita direct from my Buffalo hunt in seventy four and not from Mo."[24] Whenever Wyatt arrived in Wichita, by 1875 he was living at the Earp bordello. The Kansas state census of 1875 lists Wyatt Earp, age twenty-six; James Earp, age thirty-four; and Bessie Earp, age thirty-two, as residing in the same dwelling. Bessie's occupation was given as "sporting."[25] In all likelihood, Wyatt was working as an enforcer at James and Bessie's brothel—the same work he had done in Peoria.

The Earp bordello stayed in operation in Wichita for over a year, judging by the arrest records. Bessie was arrested almost every month in 1874 on the charge of prostitution—paying a fine or a bribe, or both, to local authorities on each occasion. The names of Bessie and Sallie Earp appear most frequently in the arrest documents. In November and December 1874, and January 1875, only Bessie's and Sallie's names appear; with the cowboy trade finished for the winter, Kate, Minnie, Eva, and any other fictive kin would have been let go for the season.[26]

The last arrest in Wichita of a woman calling herself Earp was in March 1875. That Wyatt joined the police force in Wichita in April of that year hardly seems coincidental: as a police officer, he could protect the Earp bordello from official scrutiny. Yet how is it that a brothel enforcer came to be a police officer? Wyatt told Flood that he arrived in Wichita directly from the southern plains bison range, and that shortly after entering town he stepped between a Texas cowboy, Doc Black, and a sixteen-year-old boy whom Black was victimizing. Wyatt, according to his own account, pummeled Black into submission. Black in turn roused his fellow Texans against Wyatt, and twelve cowboys assembled to lynch him. En route to lynch Wyatt, the mob happened across another man who somehow sparked their wrath, and they resolved to hang him, too; to escape the noose the man sought Wyatt's protection. Wyatt stared down the lynch mob and they withdrew; the mayor, impressed by Wyatt's steadfastness, immediately offered him a position on the police force. Wyatt accepted, vowing, "Right is right and I shall never compromise with evil men."[27]

When Lake wrote to David Leahy to find out if this dramatic tale was true, he learned that Doc Black was not a Texas cowboy but a resident of the east end of Douglas Avenue—Wichita's main boulevard—whose only "billigerant [sic] record" was an intolerance for trespassers. Leahy offered his own equally inaccurate story of how Wyatt became a Wichita police officer: "Bill Smith, the marshal, was desperately in need of a man who had nerve enough to wear a star—for it was a dangerous occupation in those days. He saw Wyatt Earp, a stranger, in the street one day and sizing him up as a man who might be fit he asked him if he would care to take the position."[28] Lake blended both of these versions into yet another fictitious account of Wyatt protecting a "small choreboy" from Black, standing down a lynch mob, and then accepting the deputy marshalship.[29]

In truth, Wyatt came to the attention of the town marshal, Mike Meagher, in October 1874, when Wyatt and a city police officer, John Behrens, tracked down thieves who had stolen a wagon. The wagon was the property of a local merchant, M. R. Moser, who hired Behrens and Earp—who was still working as an enforcer at his brother's brothel—to reclaim the wagon or its value in cash from the thieves who had taken it. According to the *Wichita Eagle*, Behrens and Earp "fear nothing and fear nobody. They made seventy-five miles from sun to sun, across trackless prairies, striking the property and the thieves near the Indian line. To make a long and exciting story short, they just leveled a shotgun and six-shooter upon the scalawags as they lay concealed in some brush, and told them to 'dough over,' which they did, to the amount of $146, one of them remarking that he was not going to die for the price of a wagon."[30]

In one sense, the event was unremarkable: for a hired gunman, recovering stolen property was not too different from working as a brothel bouncer. Yet, just over three years before, Wyatt had been not far from Wichita, driving a team of stolen horses out of Indian Territory. That misadventure had ended with his arrest by a pursuing law officer and—had it not been for his timely jailbreak—might have meant conviction and a sentence of five years or more in a federal penitentiary. Two years before, he had been arrested for consorting with prostitutes, and a local newspaper had disparaged him as a shiftless troublemaker. In Kansas in 1874, however, Wyatt found himself on the side of the law; in contrast to the disgrace his arrests had brought him, his participation in the successful pursuit of the wagon thieves in 1874 brought him public acclaim.

It goes too far to say that this moment was an epiphany for Wyatt. It was another six months before he became a police officer. Moreover, the Wichita police force was composed of men who, like Wyatt, had been (and would remain) on both sides of the law. Mike Meagher, the Wichita marshal who appointed Wyatt, was a gambler and gunman who later became the mayor of Caldwell, Kansas; while mayor he was arrested for the murder of George Flatt, whom Meagher had dismissed as the city marshal; a year later, Meagher was shot and killed in a saloon.[31] Yet at the same time the recovery of the stolen wagon and the public acclaim Wyatt received drew him toward police work. Watching his father and uncle as police officers in Monmouth, and his own brief tenure as constable in sleepy Lamar, had taught him little more about the value of police work than its potential for booty politics. If he was going to try to make a living from his skills with his fists and with firearms, he might just as well work as a brothel enforcer—or steal horses. The account of the reclamation of the stolen property in the *Eagle*, however, showed Wyatt that working on the side of the law could bring another, intangible benefit: public stature.

Yet a police officer must also enforce the law, and Wichita was not sedate Lamar. Anecdotal evidence suggests that Wichita was a perilous place. Purdy wrote that on July 6, 1874, "the Texas herders attempted to take the town or at least they marched through the streets with their revolvers drawn and defied the police. The citizens turned out en masse with rifles shot guns and arms of all kinds." On this occasion, the cowboys' march through town might have been just a raucous extension of an Independence Day celebration. Such trouble, according to Purdy, was constant in Wichita, "but the Texas trade is what keeps the place up so the citizens put up with considerable of their nonsense but they are a hard set to deal with."[32]

According to the historian Robert Dykstra, homicide was a rare event in the cow towns. Between 1870 and 1885, the five largest Kansas cow towns—Abilene, Ellsworth, Wichita, Dodge City, and Caldwell—experienced altogether only forty-five murders. Altogether, Dykstra concluded, the five towns "averaged only one and a half adult homicides per cattle-trading season."[33] Wichita had no homicides in 1875 and 1876, while Wyatt was a police officer there; Dodge City had seven killings between 1876 and 1879, the period in which Wyatt served intermittently as a police officer. Other historians, including Roger McGrath and Clare McKanna, have argued that one must calculate the number of homicides per hundred thousand inhabitants to arrive at a homicide rate that affords comparison. According to this calculus, lightly populated Abilene's three homicides in 1871 gave it a homicide rate of 98.6 per 100,000 inhabitants—far more than New York City's 1871 homicide rate of 5.8 per equivalent population.[34]

The Kansas cow towns were so small, their populations so transient, and the number of seasons in which they operated as cattle-trading centers so few that viable comparisons are virtually impossible.[35] Wichita had one homicide in 1874 and thus ranked statistically as one of the deadliest places in the United States; in 1875 and 1876 it had none and thus ranked as the safest. Such vacillation suggests that neither extreme is accurate. Indeed, the truth lies in between: the cow towns experienced spasms of violence when they were at their height. Most of the victims and perpetrators were cowboys, gamblers, and law officers. Alcohol, youth, boredom, and the ready availability of firearms all contributed to the outbreaks of deadly violence.

So, too, did an "honor" culture that the historian Bertram Wyatt-Brown has linked to the nineteenth-century South. Southern honor, according to Wyatt-Brown, was a masculine ethic that demanded that men demonstrate such behavior as risk-taking (gambling was "almost a social obligation"), virility ("male lust was simply a recognized fact of life"), and above all physical courage (duels and feuds "made violence a part of the social order"). The maintenance and defense of one's reputation was at the heart of the southern ethic of masculine honor. As Wyatt-Brown wrote, it was a "social necessity for men of all ranks to preserve white manhood and personal status in the fraternity of the male tribe." A readiness to use violence to redress perceived offenses characterized white men of the Old South who adhered to the culture of honor. Those characteristics persisted in the postwar era.[36] When Texas cowboys came to the Kansas cow towns, they brought the southern honor culture—and its proclivity for violence—with them.

In Wichita, Wyatt did not have to confront the cowboys alone. According to Leahy, the Wichita police worked in pairs, "something after the manner of the Italian police." Wyatt and his police partner, Jimmy Cairns, Leahy continued, "made the Texas wild ones quite tame."[37] Wyatt made his first notable arrest—of a horse thief—in May 1875. When the suspect fled during questioning, Wyatt fired a warning shot to induce him to submit.[38] Yet most of his arrests were decidedly unglamorous: he took a man found in a "drunken stupor" into custody in December 1875, for instance.[39] And he had his share of public embarrassment: in January 1876, his pistol slipped from his holster while he was sitting in a saloon. The hammer struck the chair and the pistol discharged. The bullet passed through Wyatt's coat before ricocheting off a wall and lodging in the ceiling.[40]

Wyatt's status in Wichita cannot be determined merely from arrest records, however. In the masculine honor culture of the cow towns, men established their reputations through combat. In a 1928 letter to Lake, Wyatt related two instances in which he used force in Wichita—in one case against an army sergeant and in the other against a "Texas gambler." Both men, according to Wyatt, were "friendly with the cowboy element." The sergeant, Wyatt claimed, was "surrounded by a large crowd" and "flourishing a gun and boasting what he would do to Wyatt Earp." Wyatt approached him, "discerned immediately that he was a big bluffer," and disarmed him, "much to the surprise of the crowd." (In Wyatt's accounts, his triumphs frequently occur before a crowd of awed onlookers; the masculine honor code demanded public demonstrations of physical courage.) His altercation with the gambler was likewise public. The gambler was, as Wyatt put it, "intocitated" and drunkenly invited Wyatt to remove his pistol and badge for a fistfight in the rear of a cigar store. "Accepting the challenge at the instant, I placed my star and gun on the top of a cigar case and went into the rear room." In the ensuing fracas, Wyatt quickly pummeled his alcohol-impaired opponent into submission, emerging, once more to an impressed assembly, cool and unruffled.[41]

In a cow town with an overwhelmingly male population, Wyatt found not only fistfights but friendships with other young men. Wyatt's closest friend in Wichita was Jimmy Cairns, his police partner from the time he joined the force in the spring of 1875. Sometime that spring, as Wyatt reinvented himself as a police deputy, he moved out of the Earp bordello and in with Cairns—or Cairns moved into Wyatt's room at the brothel. As Leahy explained, "They were together not only at work but at rest for they slept and roomed together."[42]

Leahy's comment suggests that Wyatt and Cairns shared not only a room but a bed; it was not uncommon for nineteenth-century roommates to do so. Less commonly, such relationships were sexual. In the nineteenth century, wherever men labored in extended isolation from women—on ships at sea, for instance—close male relationships were more common, or at least more apparent, than elsewhere.[43] Historians of sexuality have argued that same-sex relationships were just as common in remote mining and logging camps and on ranches in the nineteenth-century West.[44]

Wyatt could find sex in his brother's brothel, but he found companionship with Cairns. Leahy recalled that "Jimmy Cairns in his quiet way has told me often that Wyatt Earp was the most dependable pal he has ever had during his long career as a border police officer and that he was a clean fellow through and through."[45]

Nineteenth-century America was a homosocial world: outside of the family, men socialized with other men and women with women. Young adults of different genders had little opportunity to socialize unchaperoned. Even after marriage, many adults found their closest friendships with others of the same gender. The skewed gender ratios of the cow towns only intensified homosocial friendships.[46]

Cairns was impressed by Wyatt as a physical specimen. In a 1929 interview, Cairns said of Wyatt, "I can see him now as plainly as then. Earp was in the prime of his young manhood, a little over six feet tall, well-proportioned, an athlete, quick as a cat on his feet; erect, hair a bit long, but well combed, a large moustache that drooped down over his mouth, almost hiding it, a big strong chin."[47] Cairns was not the only person to note Wyatt's physical attractiveness. Contemporaries in Kansas, both male and female, invariably described Wyatt as uncommonly handsome. Lake wrote that in interviewing Judge Charles Hatton, who knew Wyatt in Wichita in the 1870s, the judge's wife interrupted to describe Wyatt as "the handsomest, best-mannered young man in Wichita."[48]

By the spring of 1876, Wyatt had, it seems, mastered Wichita. He was admired for his good looks and feared for his raw nerve and skill with his fists. He enjoyed not only the camaraderie of the saloons and the pleasures of his brother's brothel, but the esteem of respected members of society such as Mrs. Hatton. He had found friendship with Cairns. Then, suddenly, he left Wichita for Dodge City. Wyatt told Flood that he left because duty called him. "The conditions at Dodge became so bad that the Mayor of that city wrote him a letter," Flood wrote. The mayor's request was "supplemented with the plea of the many friends of Earp who were living there."[49]

Yet Wyatt did not leave Wichita of his own accord; he left because the world he had created there fell apart rapidly in April and May 1876. Ironically, Wyatt's penchant for violence, and his impulse to defend any slight to his reputation with his fists, both vaulted him to prominence in Wichita and led to his downfall. In April 1876, Mike Meagher, who had appointed Wyatt to the police force, was standing for reelection. Wyatt's position on the force—and in a larger sense his reputation in town as a lawman rather than merely as a brothel enforcer—depended on Meagher's reelection; a new city marshal would appoint deputies loyal to him. On Sunday, April 2, on the eve of the election, while canvassing for votes, Wyatt was drawn into a one-sided fistfight with Bill Smith, Meagher's opponent in the election. During the campaign, Smith said that Meagher intended to appoint Wyatt's brothers to the force—an apparent reference to James's brothel and to Wyatt's protection of the brothel while serving on the police force. Wyatt, Smith implied, was nothing more than a jumped-up pimp. Smith knew both that his words would be relayed to Wyatt, and that such a provocation could be met only with violence, according to the prevailing masculine honor code of the cow towns. Wyatt thus sought out Smith and beat him severely. According to the *Beacon*, Wyatt had "fight on the brain" and went looking for Smith intending to "mutilate and disable" him. Wyatt was arrested, fined $30 for disturbing the peace, and summarily dismissed from the police force.[50]

Meagher was reelected, but the public dismay at Wyatt's brutality compelled the city council to decline to reinstate him, even though, as the *Beacon* wrote, "He has made an excellent officer, and hitherto his conduct has been unexceptionable." Wyatt had done nothing but act according to the dictates of the cow town honor code. While few in Wichita were his match in a fistfight, he was defeated— as his father had been in Monmouth in 1859—by middle-class moralists who controlled the municipal government. Wyatt thus found himself in much the same predicament as in Lamar in early 1871: a year that had begun with great promise had ended in disrepute. Once again, Wyatt, having likely decided to quit the town, impulsively decided to embezzle public funds before leaving. Despite his dismissal from the police force, Wyatt continued to act as a police officer and collect municipal fines. The city council responded by withholding Wyatt's back pay until he turned over to the city the moneys he had illegally collected. On May 10, the city council declared "the Earps" (Wyatt and probably also James and Bessie) vagrants and ordered them to leave town.[51]

Within weeks of leaving Lamar, Wyatt had found himself in deep trouble: arrested for horse theft in Indian Territory. Five years later, he managed his departure from Wichita gracefully. Just two weeks after being ordered to leave town, on May 24, a Wichita newspaper reported that Wyatt had joined the police force in Dodge City.[52] By 1876, Dodge had already begun to supersede Wichita as the leading cattle-trading center in Kansas. Perhaps family connections lured Wyatt to Dodge: earlier in 1876, his parents and his half brother, Newton, had relocated to Garden City, Kansas, sixty miles northwest of Dodge.[53]

Dodge City, founded as Buffalo City in 1872, was like Wichita a frontier cow town—only more so. As the Santa Fe railroad, gradually extending westward along the Arkansas River, approached Fort Dodge, the post's enterprising commander, Col. Richard Irving Dodge, joined with his officers and a few frontier merchants in creating a townsite company. They filed a claim to a plot of land on the north bank of the Arkansas River five miles from the fort. The town, soon renamed Dodge City, was initially the capital of the southern plains bison-hide trade. An early resident recalled that at the moment the railroad reached the new city, "the streets of Dodge were lined with wagons, bringing in hides and meat and getting supplies from early morning to late at night."[54] In Dodge City's first winter, it shipped roughly four hundred thousand bison hides east.[55]

By 1876, hide hunters had largely exterminated the bison from southwestern Kansas. In the aftermath of the slaughter, the grasslands were strewn with bones. One Kansas settler complained that the bones were "a nuisance to our breaking of the sod."[56] Settlers and ranchers alike collected bones and brought them by the cartload to Dodge to be shipped east by rail for sale to carbon works and fertilizer plants. When Wyatt first arrived in Dodge City, the town was surrounded by enormous barricades of bison bones. One resident of Dodge wrote, "There were great stacks of bones piled up by the railroad tracks—hundreds of tons of them."[57] Another reported a rick of bison bones alongside the railroad tracks a quarter of a mile long and as high as the bones could be thrown.[58]

The cairns of bones marked Dodge City's decline as a center of the commerce in bison products. Yet as Dodge City receded as a collection point for bison hides, it supplanted Wichita as the capital of the Kansas cattle trade. Texas ranchers drove 250,000 head to Dodge in 1876, and 300,000 in 1877. Cattle buyers transformed the remote and unsettled region surrounding Dodge—rendered empty by the work of the bison hunters—into ranches. They let the stringy cattle they had purchased for $8 a head fatten for a year or two before shipping them to market at $25 a head. By 1878, over a hundred thousand cattle grazed in the area around Dodge City.[59]

With its surrounding ranches, nearby army post, and the lingering effects of the hide and bone trades, Dodge City was larger, more libertine, and more lethal than Wichita. Its permanent population in the late 1870s was about twelve hundred; transients, however, doubled that number. It had between fifteen and twenty saloons—"no little ten-by-twelves, but seventy-five to one hundred feet long, glittering with paint and mirrors," according to a Kansas City journalist.[60] Wentin Wilson, a bison hunter who passed through Dodge City in 1876, noted that there "is all kinds of gambling going on; hundreds of dollars changing hands every hour. The women are out on the streets drunk and smoking cigars. This is the hardest place I ever saw in my life."[61]

During Wyatt's tenure, Dodge was a deadlier place than Wichita: in 1878, for instance, Mike Dalton, a rancher, was killed by some of his hands outside Dodge City in February; Ed Masterson, the city marshal, was killed in April; a federal deputy marshal, H. T. McCarty, was killed in a drunken dispute in July; also in July, George Hoy, a cowboy, was killed by police (Wyatt was one of the officers who fired at Hoy); finally, Dora Hand, a saloon entertainer, was killed in October (Wyatt was a member of the posse that arrested her killer, James Kennedy).[62]

Yet like Wichita, Dodge City also had a permanent cohort of merchants and professionals. Robert Wright, the president of the Dodge City townsite company, who, with Charlie Rath, operated Dodge's largest general store, wrote that Dodge City's police ceded the area south of the railroad tracks—a narrow strip between the tracks and the winding Arkansas River—to the saloons, gambling houses, and brothels. The north side, by contrast, they "kept respectable."[63] In 1878, Wright helped found a Presbyterian church in the "respectable" section of town; by 1879, Dodge also had a Methodist church.[64]

As a police officer, Wyatt was to keep order in Dodge City's south side on behalf of the "respectable" north-side merchants and professionals. As the sociologists Cyril Robinson and Richard Scaglion have argued, nineteenth-century police officers such as Wyatt were agents of social control who emerged as class replaced kinship as the dominant structure in modernizing, urbanizing societies. Merchants and professionals in Dodge City, like the bourgeois in cities throughout the industrializing world, created police to ensure their dominance.[65]

By the time he reached Dodge City, Wyatt had learned his lesson about the power of the professional and merchant class: he had had his first such lesson in Monmouth, when he had watched his father tried for violating local liquor laws; he received further tutelage in Peoria when he was arrested multiple times for consorting with prostitutes; and he seemed finally to have grasped it when he ran afoul of municipal authorities in Wichita for brutalizing a political rival. Such awareness would not deter him from gambling, confidence games, or violence, but at the same time, in Dodge, he made sure that the town's authorities knew he was the abstemious grandson of a Methodist minister who adhered to the standards of middle-class propriety. In 1881, in the aftermath of the Tombstone street fight, virtually the entire city government and merchant class of Dodge—including the Ford County probate judge, attorney, sheriff, commissioner, treasurer, tax collector, and the chair of the county board; and the Dodge City mayor, an ex-mayor, four members of the city council, treasurer, and registrar of deeds; and twenty-five other signatories who described themselves variously as merchants, grocers, liquor dealers, hoteliers, and cattle dealers—testified that while in Dodge between 1876 and 1879, Wyatt "occupied a high social position and was regarded and looked upon as a high minded honorable citizen."[66] Perhaps more surprisingly, the law firm of Sutton and Colburn—a partnership of the Dodge City attorney and the Ford County attorney—presented the former horse thief with a pocket-size New Testament that had been printed by the American Bible Society. It was inscribed, "To Wyatt S. Earp, as a slight recognition of his many Christian virtues, and steady following in the footsteps of the meek and lowly Jesus."[67]

While Wyatt sought—and received—the approval of Dodge's governing class, his memoirs dictated to John Flood seethe with resentment against the very people who hired him to keep order. He made a point of telling Flood that while in Dodge he once locked up a city councilman for an unmentioned offense. In another instance, he explained that, after he had arrested James Kennedy for shooting Dora Hand, Kennedy's father, a "man of wealth," hired a lawyer who won an acquittal through "days and months of delays, excuses, subterfuges." Wyatt described a wealthy cattleman, Cad Pearse, as "a success; he had wealth and his cattle extended into many hundred head. . . . He was for the law which ran not contrary to him."[68] In courting the approval of the middle class, Wyatt, chameleonlike, assumed a protective coloration of middle-class propriety. Yet, at a deeper level, he understood that the justice he enforced was not impartial—and he resented it. Police officers such as Wyatt occupied an anomalous position in nineteenth-century America: they had more camaraderie and more in common with the class they policed than with the municipal officials they served.

Whether he shared the values of Dodge City's bourgeoisie or not, as a police officer, Wyatt was obliged to enforce the law. The Dodge City police attempted to maintain order on the south side by banning the carrying of weapons. A city ordinance of 1875 proclaimed, "No person shall in the city of Dodge City carry concealed about his person any pistol, bowie knife, sling shot or other dangerous or deadly weapon except United States, state, county, township, or city officers." In 1876, the city approved a new ordinance stipulating that no one was permitted to carry any of the above weapons "concealed or otherwise about his or her person." The city weapons ordinance was only loosely enforced, however. The *Ford County Globe* editorialized in March 1878—at a time when the rancher Mike Dalton had just been murdered outside town and prior to the killings of Masterson, McCarty, Hoy, and Hand, which would occur before the end of the year—that "some of the 'boys' in direct violation of City Ordinances, carry firearms on our streets, without being called to account for the same. They do it in such an open manner, that it don't seem possible that our City Officers are ignorant of this fact."[69]

Dodge City police were generally casual about the enforcement of the weapons ban because the vast majority of cowboys were harmless laborers interested only in enjoying Dodge's saloons, gambling halls, and brothels after having spent months on the cattle trail. Most "intoxicated and quarrelsome" cowboys did no more than "hurrah" the town—awakening residents by firing pistols into the air after a night of drinking on the city's south side. Dodge's merchants were likewise disinclined to have the police be overzealous in enforcing the firearms ordinance, fearing that it might dissuade cowboys from coming to Dodge to spend their money.[70]

Yet cowboys who drunkenly discharged their pistols were a threat to life, and Dodge's police generally persuaded cowboys to surrender their pistols if they were intoxicated. A month after the *Globe* editorialized about the lax enforcement of the weapons ban, Dodge's marshal, Ed Masterson, the older brother of the Ford County sheriff, Bat Masterson, was shot and killed by a drunken cowboy whom the marshal had tried to disarm. The cowboy, Jack Wagner, had initially submitted to Masterson's authority and surrendered his weapon, which Masterson gave to Wagner's friends to return to him when he had sobered up. Wagner, however, was apparently carrying a second, concealed pistol and approached Masterson and shot him in the abdomen at close range; he was so close to Masterson when he discharged the pistol that the marshal's clothes caught fire. Local newspapers reported that Masterson, mortally wounded, managed to draw his pistol and shoot both Wagner, who died of his wounds, and another cowboy who joined the affray.[71] Ed Masterson, however, died within a half hour of being shot, and it is unlikely that he managed to return fire. The shooter of Wagner and Walker may have been his brother, Bat, who was reportedly nearby when the altercation began.

A few months after Ed Masterson's shooting, Bat and Wyatt shot a cowboy, George Hoy, who was "hurrahing" the town with gunfire. At three o'clock in the morning on July 26, 1878, three or four cowboys, including Hoy, were preparing, after a night of drinking, to leave town and return to their camp south of the city. On their way out of town, they loosed a few gunshots, most into the air, but one into a dance hall. Wyatt and Bat returned fire and pursued the cowboys as they rode toward the bridge leading across the Arkansas River into the rangelands south of Dodge. All but Hoy escaped across the bridge. He fell from his horse just short of the river; a shot from either Wyatt or Bat had struck him in the arm. Hoy, who was under indictment for cattle theft in Texas, and whom the *Dodge City Times* described as "rather an intelligent looking young man," died a month later.[72]

Wyatt and Bat were involved in another shooting before the end of 1878. James Kennedy, the son of a wealthy Texas rancher, Miflin Kennedy, had become obsessed with a popular Dodge City entertainer, Dora Hand. She, however, was the companion of Dodge City's mayor, James "Dog" Kelley. Single women in mining camps or cow towns such as Hand who had no kin but were not—and hoped not to become—professional prostitutes oftentimes attached themselves to prominent protectors, usually police officers or members of the city or county government. The 1880 census indicated that Bat Masterson shared his house with Annie Ladue, a nineteen-year-old "concubine" whose occupation was given as "keeping house." His brother Jim, who also served sporadically on the Dodge City police force, shared his house with Minnie Roberts, a sixteen-year-old "concubine" who kept house. When Wyatt left Dodge City for Tombstone in 1879, he did so in the company of such a companion, Mattie Blaylock. In the 1880 census, she is listed as Mattie Earp,

Wyatt's wife. In Tombstone, Wyatt's future wife, Josephine Marcus, a onetime showgirl like Dora Hand, was the companion of the county sheriff, John Behan.[73]

Kennedy, either in an attempt to kill Kelley or because his obsession with Hand had turned violent, fired from the street into her home one night, killing her. Masterson, as county sheriff, led a posse that likely included Wyatt in pursuit. The posse overtook Kennedy; in a brief gunfight Kennedy was shot in the shoulder. Kennedy was tried and acquitted—Wyatt's contention that his father's wealth played a role in the acquittal may well have been true. Two years after the shooting and Kennedy's arrest, the *Dodge City Times* reprinted a rumor first reported in a Caldwell, Kansas, newspaper that Wyatt, who had left Dodge for Tombstone a year earlier, had been shot and killed by Kennedy in Sand Creek, Colorado. "Earp had shot and wounded Kennedy in the shoulder a year or two since," the *Times* reported, "and meeting at Sand Creek both pulled their revolvers, but Kennedy got his work in first, killing Earp instantly." The *Times* recognized the report as a "fabrication"—the first of what would become countless erroneous tales of Wyatt's exploits as a gunman.[74]

Of the many fabrications about Wyatt, Stuart Lake's were more egregious than anyone else's. In *Frontier Marshal*, he depicted Dodge as a city under siege by organized gangs of cowboys bent on terrorizing Dodge's law-abiding citizens. "From the moment the first cow outfit struck Dodge," Lake wrote, "Texas men bragged that they intended to run the town and would welcome diversion in chances to prove it."[75] Dodge City certainly had its share of violence in 1878, but the homicides were not aimed at overthrowing the established authorities of the cow town; rather, they were impulsive acts born of drunkenness and thwarted affection. As a police officer, Wyatt was not a lone lawgiver among renegades. He was, rather, employed by the moneyed merchants who controlled Dodge to keep the peace so that the city could continue as a collection point for cattle—and moreover so that saloons and brothels could continue to siphon off the cowboys' pay.

·

Participating in the capture of Kennedy was one of Wyatt's last no-table acts as a Dodge City police officer. Indeed, between 1876 and 1879, he was only intermittently a member of the police force in Dodge, spending only the summer and fall—the cattle-drive season—as a policeman. At the end of every fall, he would resign his position on the police force and travel south into Texas (in the winter of 1878, for instance, he was at Fort Clark, Texas), returning to Dodge in the late spring or summer.[76] In Texas, among the cow-boys, Wyatt plied a new trade, one that would sustain him into the twentieth century, long after he had given up police work: he became a professional gambler.

Wyatt may first have learned the card games that professional gamblers played while working with Virgil as a freighter in the Far West after the Civil War. By the time he reached Dodge City, he was adept. In the Kansas cow towns, gambling was as common as prostitution, an artifact of the market revolution that overswept the United States in the nineteenth century. Gambling had been a pastime of the Virginia gentry in the seventeenth and eighteenth centuries—wagering affirmed the gentry's values of personal inde-pendence, competition, and materialism—though the Virginia gentry preferred cockfights and horse races to card games.[77] Professional gambling of the type that prevailed in Kansas, however, emerged in the first half of the nineteenth century along the Mississippi River commercial corridor between New Orleans and St. Louis. Eighteenth-century Virginians had played trick-taking card games popular in England such as whist and piquet. Nineteenth-century professional gamblers on the Mississippi River preferred French games in which the odds favored the dealer: monte, faro, and vingt-et-un.[78]

The most popular game in the Kansas cow towns—the one that Wyatt learned to deal—was faro (a corruption of pharaoh, report-edly derived from French playing cards that once bore the image of a pharaoh). Played with a standard fifty-two-card deck, the action of faro takes place on a playing surface, or layout, usually made of green cloth. A faro layout has printed on its surface the images of the thirteen cards in a suit, from ace to king. The basic rules are simple. Players place bets on one or more of the thirteen cards printed on the layout. The dealer draws from the top of the deck two cards: the losing card and the winning card, which pay the dealer and the players, respectively. If the losing card is, for instance, a three, the dealer collects any bet that has been placed on the three on the layout. The dealer then turns the winning card. A player who has bet on the winning card on the layout wins the full amount of his wager. If the losing and winning cards have the same value—a split—the dealer collects half of what any player has bet on that card. Players then place their bets again, and the dealer again draws losing and winning cards. Play proceeds rapidly: the dealer will play through a deck in fifteen minutes or less.[79]

Upon this simple framework, however, were a multitude of embellishments. One innovation allowed players to copper their bets by placing a penny on the image on the layout on which they had wagered. A player who coppered his wager reversed what was called a straight bet in order to bet with the house—winning on the losing card and losing on the winning card. A player who bet one card and coppered another stood the chance of a whipsaw: collecting money on both the losing and winning cards. A whipsaw could also work in favor of the dealer—the player might lose both bets.

A player might also bet on the high card. The high card bar was at the top of the layout, closest to the dealer. Players who wagered on the high card bet that the winning card would have a higher value than the losing card. Unlike players who placed bets on specific cards on the layout, a player who bet on the high card won or lost on each pair of turns.

Players could bet as many cards as they liked. Chips placed between cards on the layout (splits) meant a full bet on both cards. Bets placed in the middle of four cards were known as squares. A grand square was placed between the ace, two, queen, and king. A jack square was between the three, four, ten, and jack. Still more complicated were corner bets, placed on the corners of cards. A chip placed on the corner of the ace represented a split bet on the

ace and three; a chip on the corner of the two meant a split bet between the two and the four. While many players placed more than
one bet on the layout, snowballers, who spread small bets across the
layout, were scorned.

Because of these complications, in a well-attended game the
layout could become crowded with a complex assortment of wagers.
A dealer often had an assistant, or lookout, who oversaw the place-
ment of bets, collected losing wagers, and paid out winnings. As an
aid to players to keep count of which cards had been played, some
lookouts helpfully updated the count on an abacuslike device known
as a case counter, cue box, or coffin. If a player was oblivious to the
coffin and placed a bet on a dead card—that is, a card that had already been turned four times—the first person to notice the bet,
either the dealer or another player, and call out "dead card" or
"sleeper" was entitled to confiscate the bet.

After discarding the top card of the deck (the soda card) and
playing through twenty-four two-card hands of faro, three cards were
left in the deck. For these final three cards, players bet on the order
in which the cards will be turned. Here, the odds—which to this point
in the game are even except for the small advantage to the dealer on
splits—turn decisively in favor of the dealer. Indeed, for professional
faro dealers, the game centers on these last three cards; the prior
play exists merely to draw players to the table. If the three remaining
cards are of different value, only six sequences are possible. A player
who correctly predicts the order (a one-in-six possibility) receives a
four-to-one payoff. If two of the three remaining cards are the same
value, the situation is a cat hop and the payoff is only two to one
(though the chances of a correct prediction are only one in three). In
the rare instance that all three remaining cards are the same value (a
case), no bets are made and the deck is simply reshuffled.[80]

When the game is played square, the odds favor the dealer—
but only slightly so, which is one of the primary reasons why faro is
infrequently offered in modern casinos, which prefer games in
which the house has a greater advantage. More than odds, the bank
had an advantage over players in a square game simply because the

dealer, with, for instance, a reserve of $500, had one hundred chances to win $5 from a single player.[81] Yet the game was rarely played squarely by professional gamblers. "Who can tell," asked a writer for the *Chicago Tribune*, in a long 1866 report on gambling, how much the dealer's advantage was improved by "the many tricks of 'drawing double,' 'sanded' and 'roped' cards, and other devices of a 'skin' or dishonest game?"[82] Shaving the edges of certain cards, so that the marked cards either bowed in or out slightly (such were known as strippers or humps), was a common trick. A practiced dealer could feel the small difference in the shape of the cards immediately and both engineer splits and ensure that he drew the cards on which players had wagered as losing cards. Even the innovation of shoes—boxes of cards meant to prevent dealers from cheating—could not completely negate the influence of shaved cards, as the boxes were outfitted with springs, levers, and other devices to allow the dealer to produce the cards he wanted in the order he wanted them to appear; slightly misshapen cards were discernible to experienced dealers; and a dexterous dealer could palm cards as he drew them from the shoe.[83]

Simple skill at palming cards was not enough to ensure success as a faro dealer. To cheat effectively, a dealer needed to learn the habits of players—he had to be something of an amateur psychologist. Most players had certain tendencies, either conscious or subconscious: they habitually coppered or bet on a certain card or bet both ends against the middle (placing bets on the highest and lowest cards). A savvy dealer, according to one 1882 exposé, "can tell after the first deal he makes for you in a given play pretty nearly how to shuffle the cards. If in the first deal you get in a good many more bets than you lose the dealer knows that it is his business to shuffle the cards next time so as to break up your system as much as he can." In some cases, especially if a dealer noticed that a player was stuck on a certain card—consistently betting it to win—the dealer would take the card by the ear and draw it, through sleight of hand, as the losing card. A good dealer would let the player win on the favored card once per shuffle to keep the player at the table.[84]

When the deck was reduced to the final several cards, a dealer's skill at sleight of hand became most important in tipping the odds in his favor. When the deck was short, both the players and the dealer were well aware of which cards were most likely to turn up. All bets would be placed on these few cards—either as straight or coppered bets. A skilled dealer could ensure that he turned cards in an order that benefited him. Likewise, when the final three cards were to be turned, or when a player made both straight and coppered bets in an effort to whipsaw the dealer, a dealer's skill came into play.

Because the odds of faro were only slightly in favor of the dealer, a man (or a woman—many women dealt faro professionally) who could make a living dealing faro was, firstly, almost by definition a cheater; and secondly, at the pinnacle of the hierarchy of professional gamblers. Dealers cultivated an air of detachment and imperturbability—the 1866 *Chicago Tribune* report described the typical faro dealer as "calm" and "cold" as well as "one of the acknowledged leaders of the gambling fraternity." An 1886 report in a Denver newspaper noted the characteristics of a successful faro dealer: he or she "must be devoid of nerves," "quick," and can never "get rattled." One notably successful faro dealer had been known to "deal the cards coolly and collectedly while men around him have been frenzied with rage at losing, knives and pistols have been flourished, but that dealer has never been known to have lost his self-possession for a moment, even."[85] The dealer's air of calmness and detachment both befitted his or her status as a leading figure among professional gamblers and, moreover, created the illusion of fairness. Habitual faro players knew that the dealer was trying to cheat them—outsmarting a crooked dealer was one of the attractions of bucking the tiger, as wagering at faro was known. For Wyatt, who already had learned to play the roles of lawman and upright Christian, the detached faro dealer was another mask to wear. The coolness and poise for which Wyatt later became famous in Tombstone was a character trait he developed not only as a police officer but also, perhaps primarily, as a faro dealer.

For a faro dealer, the boundary between card cheat and confidence man was murky. Numerous faro dealers worked with partners who posed as players in order to dupe unsuspecting players. One professional gambler described a scam known as the "green cowboy," in which "a rough-looking fellow, unshaven and long-haired, with a huge Buffalo Bill hat on his head, came up to the table and said he was from Texas, and had never been in this part of the country before," and laid a large bet and won. The cowboy was, in fact, a confederate of the dealer's, there to lure players to think that it would be easy to win.[86]

While making the rounds of the southern plains gambling halls, Wyatt probably participated in such scams, as any successful faro dealer would. According to Jim McIntire—who like Wyatt was a gambler, occasional lawman, and sometimes fugitive from the law—Wyatt ran other scams, too. McIntire wrote that Wyatt and a partner, Dave Mathers, appeared in Mobeetie, Texas, in the fall of 1878 during Wyatt's seasonal faro-dealing junket, running a gold-brick scam on unsuspecting residents. They claimed to have stolen one or more gold bricks—actually ordinary rocks painted yellow—which they reluctantly allowed themselves to part with for much less than their purported value. According to McIntire, he helped run Wyatt and Mathers out of town. He believed that they were later arrested elsewhere in Texas for trying the scam again.[87]

Knowing that Wyatt had supported himself by dealing faro, Lake assured him in 1928 that he would present this part of Wyatt's life fairly. "Times have changed," Lake wrote, asserting that in the frontier West "a faro bank, for example, was just as legitimate a business enterprise as the savings bank down the street, and often the head of one was the bosom friend of the man who ran the other."[88] Indeed, both a faro dealer and an investment banker ran speculative ventures in which players put money at risk. As George Devol wrote in 1892, reflecting on his career as a professional gambler from the mid-1840s to the mid-1880s, "What are the members of the Board of Trade but gamblers? The Board of Trade is just as much a gambling house as a faro bank."[89] In his formulation of the similarity between investing and faro, Devol was closer to the truth than Lake: gambling at cards was not more reputable for its similarity to speculative investment; rather, in the eyes of nineteenth-century Americans, investors were less reputable because of their similarities to those who gambled at cards.

To the extent that nineteenth-century Americans saw gambling as a metaphor for speculative investment, their views represented their ambivalence about raucous, booming American capitalism. The historian Karen Halttunen has noted that midcentury middle-class advice manuals warned young men of the dangers of confidence men such as Devol. Confidence men represented the dark underside of the nineteenth-century marketplace, a bewildering world of consumer items and investment opportunities that were often fraudulent. Eighteenth-century Americans were acquisitive and market-oriented, but most lived geographically narrow lives—when they bought or sold goods and services, they usually dealt with people they knew. The mid-nineteenth-century American population was mobile and increasingly urban—both consequences of the rapid expansion of the market economy. Confidence men capitalized upon the necessity of people in a market economy to deal with strangers—an environment that made fraud and confidence games all the more possible. Herman Melville set his 1857 novel *The Confidence-Man* on a Mississippi steamboat—not only the heart of American gambling but, like an American city, filled with strangers. The novel's con man presents himself in various guises, including a seller of medicinal potions and a vendor of stock in a coal mine, to cheat the steamboat's passengers. The critique of confidence men in advice manuals and in Melville's novel was, as Halttunen argued, at root "a critique of capitalist speculation."[90]

Middle-class advice manuals distinguished between cardplayers and capitalist investors, casting the former as disreputable parasites and the latter as pioneers of industrial progress. Yet professional gamblers such as George Devol and, by the late 1870s, Wyatt Earp saw gambling as their trade. If faro was disreputable, a heartless enterprise that bankrupted the naïve, then it was not much different from nineteenth-century capitalism itself. In this sense, gambling at cards mimicked larger cultural values, just as it had for the Virginia gentry in the eighteenth century.[91] Andrew Jackson epitomized the nineteenth-century culture of gambling. Not only did he wager frequently and heavily, but in 1805 he killed a man in a duel over the disputed terms of a wager on a horse race. Jackson's advice to a nephew summed up the aggressive capitalist ethos of nineteenth-century America: "You must risque to win."[92]

As Jackson's resort to dueling pistols to resolve the wager demonstrated, gambling was an important ingredient of the masculine honor culture of the cow towns: to abstain from gambling was seen as timid and effeminate.[93] Certainly, many cowboys who placed large bets on the faro table could not afford to lose—they were engaged in what the British philosopher Jeremy Bentham called "deep play": contests in which the stakes were so high that it made no sense to engage in them. In his analysis of the cultural significance of certain types of gambling, the anthropologist Clifford Geertz borrowed Bentham's concept of deep play, showing how such irrationally large wagers are not about money per se but about larger cultural values. For the Kansas cowboys, staking a large bet meant engaging in the masculine culture of competition. A large bet, whether won or lost, affirmed their status as risk-takers. As Geertz wrote, the importance of gambling "is not merely that risk is exciting, loss depressing, or triumph gratifying, banal tautologies of affect, but that it is of these emotions, thus exampled, that society is built and individuals put together."[94]

Gambling reflected the prevailing culture of the Kansas cow towns. As freewheeling centers of commerce where alcohol and sex could be purchased, the cow towns epitomized nineteenth-century American capitalism. Like ranchers and cattle buyers, gamblers at the faro table made large wagers on which their livelihood and public standing depended. Speculation and risk in the gambling halls mirrored the economic ethos of the cow towns and of nineteenth-century capitalism generally.

•

By 1878, Wyatt had settled into a pattern: in the summer and fall he was in Dodge, serving on the police force, and likely dealing some faro (other Dodge police officers, including Bat Masterson, Luke Short, and Charlie Bassett, were accomplished dealers as well); every fall, he resigned his position on the police force and followed the cowboys back into Texas. He spent the colder months of the year traveling the north Texas and eastern New Mexico gambling circuit—places such as Fort Clark, Fort Griffin, Fort Worth, and Denison, Texas; and Las Vegas, New Mexico—dealing faro to cowboys, soldiers, and the few remaining bison hunters.

In Texas—perhaps at Fort Griffin or Fort Worth—sometime in early 1878, Wyatt encountered a fellow gambler who would become his closest friend: a slight, tubercular, alcoholic dentist, John Henry "Doc" Holliday. In Earp lore, Holliday, who had been born in Griffin, Georgia, in 1851, the only son of Henry Burroughs Holliday and Alice McKey Holliday, is often depicted as a scion of the southern planter aristocracy. In truth, Henry Burroughs Holliday was a part of the small antebellum southern middle class. Concentrated in cities and towns, the southern middle class, composed of merchants, bankers, lawyers, and professionals, tended to support the Whig Party and its ideology of commercial development and upward social mobility.[95] Unlike wealthy planters, the southern middle class disdained such aristocratic pretensions as dueling and gambling. Instead, they valued hard work, sobriety, piety, and education. The middle class scorned planters as lazy, improvident, and anti-intellectual; because Holliday's middle-class, professionally minded family placed so much value on education, John Henry Holliday received an excellent private education in Georgia, followed by a rigorous course of study in dentistry.[96]

Indeed, the southern middle class had much in common with middle-class northerners—with one notable exception: the antebellum southern middle class reconciled its cultural values and economic ambitions with the institution of slavery.[97] Though not a planter, Henry Holliday owned both land and slaves, which he leased to planters on annual contracts.[98]

The Civil War and its aftermath dominated John Henry Holliday's youth. His father, who like Nicholas Earp had served in the Mexican-American War, was forty-two years old when the Civil War began. Henry Holliday served in the Confederate forces as a quartermaster from December 1861 until August 1862, when he was discharged for "chronic diarrhea and general disability." Like Nicholas Earp, who migrated with his family to California in 1864, Henry Holliday thought it best to remove his family from the potential path of the war. That same year, as General William Sherman's Army of the Tennessee approached north Georgia, Henry Holliday relocated his family from Griffin (forty miles south of Atlanta) to remote Valdosta in Lowndes County, Georgia, on the Florida border.[99]

The years John Henry spent in Valdosta—from 1864 until 1870—were unhappy. In 1866, his mother, Alice, died—probably of tuberculosis. Henry Holliday remarried after only three months—a scandalously brief period of mourning by nineteenth-century standards (or any standard, for that matter). His new wife, Rachel Martin, was only eight years older than his fifteen-year-old son. Following the marriage, Thomas McKey, Alice's younger brother and a much-admired role model for John Henry, sued Henry Holliday to recover custody of Alice's property. If his hasty second marriage made Henry Holliday unpopular with his onetime in-laws, he was further reviled in Valdosta as a scalawag—a southerner who cooperated with the northern occupation forces. After the war, Henry Holliday, a former Whig, became a Republican (the party of the northern occupation), as well as an agent for the Bureau of Refugees, Freedmen, and Abandoned Lands (the postwar agency charged with assisting freed slaves with health care, employment, and education).[100] John Henry resented both his father's remarriage and his politics. By 1868, the teenager was drawn into the popular resistance against the Freedmen's Bureau and the African-American troops who occupied Valdosta. In 1868, boys from the Valdosta Institute, a preparatory school where John Henry was studying, disrupted a political rally for a Republican congressional candidate by detonating a keg of gunpowder under the Valdosta courthouse.

Henry Holliday was one of five citizens of Valdosta who condemned the act. Shortly after the incident, Henry sent his son north to Jonesboro, Georgia, for a long visit with relatives.[101]

In 1870, Henry Holliday sent his only son still farther north, to Philadelphia, to study at the Pennsylvania College of Dental Surgery. Nineteen years old when he arrived in Philadelphia, and two years past the disruption of the political rally in Valdosta, Holliday, though likely reconciled neither to his father's postwar politics nor to his young stepmother, appeared ready to apply himself to a course of professional study and take his place in the southern middle class. He completed the curriculum—six months of training in Philadelphia, a year of practical work back in Georgia, and finally another six months in Philadelphia—successfully. In mid-1872, he received his degree and entered into a partnership with a prominent Atlanta dentist, Arthur C. Ford.[102]

Yet by the end of 1872, Holliday had developed a racking cough; he was shortly afterward diagnosed with consumption, or pulmonary tuberculosis, a disease caused by a bacterial infection of the lungs and characterized by chronic bloody coughs, weight loss, fever, and chest pains. In the nineteenth century, consumption was believed to be an inherited disease. The treatment, such as it was, was removal to a warmer, drier climate. Physicians thus advised Holliday to relocate to the Southwest. In September 1873, he embarked for Dallas, Texas. When he first came to Dallas, he still intended, apparently, to pursue his professional career; in Dallas, he entered into a partnership with John A. Seegar, a Georgian who had studied dentistry in Philadelphia. And at the time he arrived in Dallas, he still adhered to middle-class proprieties: he joined a Methodist church and a local temperance society.[103]

Within months, however, Holliday was drawn into the world of saloons and gambling. Holliday had indulged in such pastimes before coming to Dallas. According to family lore, he had learned numerous card games as a child in Georgia from a slave in the Holliday household, Sophie Walton, who taught Holliday how to skin cards.[104] But not until coming to Texas did he give himself over completely to drinking and cardplaying. His diagnosis of tuberculosis, the disease that had killed his mother at age thirty-seven, likely prompted the change. Anticipating declining health and an early death, Holliday found it difficult to adhere to the middle-class values of sobriety and deferred gratification. Gloomy and seeking, perhaps, to ease the chronic pain of his disease, he began to drink heavily.

Holliday's drinking and increasing involvement with gambling impelled Seegar—a pious Baptist—to dissolve their partnership. One month after the partnership ended, in April 1874, Holliday was arrested for gambling. (Texas police, like their colleagues in Kansas, arrested both prostitutes and gamblers regularly, imposing fees that funded city governments.) His arrest was but the first of many in Texas, as he abandoned, step by step, the middle-class mores of his family. In place of that ethic, he increasingly adopted the code of masculine honor that predominated in the cow town West. That code not only endorsed gambling, but required that Holliday defend any slight to his reputation (such as any suggestion that he had skinned a card) with violence. Knowing that he suffered from a terminal disease, Holliday encouraged his enemies in the belief that he had little reason to back down from a gunfight. In January 1875 he was charged in Dallas with assault with intent to murder, a result of a shooting incident that had occurred on New Year's Eve. No one was injured in that shooting, and Holliday was found not guilty. In July 1877, in Dallas, he fought with another gambler, Henry Kahn. Both men were arrested, charged, and released; later that day, Kahn sought out Holliday and shot him in the shoulder.[105]

Around the time of this shooting, Wyatt encountered Holliday on the Texas gambling circuit. The men, despite their differences, became friends. While Holliday was a frail, well-educated alcoholic, Wyatt was a robust, unschooled teetotaler. Yet they shared important similarities. Both Wyatt and Holliday had been too young to serve in the Civil War. Both had been spirited away from the conflict by their strong-minded fathers in 1864. Both idolized older relatives who had been in the war and thus had the chance to prove their courage. Wyatt looked up to his older brothers, particularly

Virgil. Holliday admired his uncle Thomas McKey, nine years his senior, who had been something of an older brother to him when he had lived in the Holliday household in Griffin between 1856 and the beginning of the war. In Texas in the 1870s, Holliday frequently used the alias T. S. McKey. Both men knew death and despair: Wyatt's wife had died in 1870 after less than a year of marriage; Holliday's mother died of tuberculosis in 1866. Both had abandoned Methodism and the Whiggish aspirations of upward social mobility that their extended families embraced, yet both knew how to make at least an outward demonstration of adherence to middle-class proprieties. Both were capable of impulsive acts of violence.[106]

By the late 1870s, both were shrewd and successful professional gamblers, and habitués of the southern Great Plains circuit of cow town brothels and saloons. By 1878, when Holliday joined Wyatt in Dodge City, they may have had a mutual acquaintance.[107] Doc's companion, Kate Harony, had worked as a prostitute in Wichita in 1874. She may have been the woman who called herself Kate Earp in James and Bessie's brothel. Harony had been born in Hungary in 1850 and had emigrated to Iowa in 1860. Her parents died in 1866; she left home and eventually became a prostitute in St. Louis and, later, Wichita. She left Wichita for Dodge City in 1875 and eventually found her way to Texas. By 1878, she claimed to be Holliday's wife.[108]

Holliday was to most observers an unlikely contestant in the competitive, masculine world of the cow towns. Bat Masterson described Holliday as high-strung and effeminate. "Physically, Doc Holliday was a weakling who couldn't have whipped a healthy fifteen-year-old boy," he wrote. "He was slim of build and sallow of complexion, about five feet ten inches, and weighing no more than 130 pounds." Emotionally, Holliday further reflected nineteenth-century notions of womanhood: he had an "ungovernable temperament" and was "hot-headed and impetuous." Yet the taciturn Wyatt and the emotionally volatile Holliday were "fast friends." Perhaps in Wyatt, Holliday saw something that reminded him of his revered uncle. According to Masterson, Holliday's "whole heart and soul were wrapped up in Wyatt Earp."[109]

Wyatt's 1896 recollections in the *San Francisco Examiner* of his "dear old comrade" affirms the close friendship between the two men that Masterson noted. Although the choice of words belonged to a ghostwriter, Wyatt's affection for Holliday was authentic. Wyatt described Holliday as a "mad, merry scamp with a heart of gold," and as a kind of romantic wanderer: "He was a Virginian [*sic*, he was born in Georgia] but he preferred to be a frontiersman and a vagabond. He was a dentist, but preferred to be a gambler. He was a philosopher, but he preferred to be a wag." Where others such as Masterson saw Holliday as a violent, antisocial personality, Wyatt saw him as a free spirit. Similarly, while Masterson described the physical Holliday as weak and girlish, Wyatt recalled him as "long, lean, ash-blonde."[110]

Just as nineteenth- and early-twentieth-century Americans spoke in coded language about prostitution and gambling, they had coded language to describe sexuality. A seemingly offhand remark by Masterson invoked that bygone code. Noting how Holliday put his life at risk in the service of Wyatt in Arizona in 1881 and 1882, Masterson wrote, "Damon did no more for Pythias than Holliday did for Wyatt Earp."[111]

What did Masterson mean by likening Holliday and Wyatt to Damon and Pythias? The reference was to the fourth-century B.C. friends whose story was set down by Cicero, Petrarch, and Schiller, among others.[112] Their story was well known to Americans through the work of the Irish playwright John Banim, whose five-act *Damon and Pythias*, composed in iambic pentameter, was first performed in London in 1821. Banim's play was performed widely in the nineteenth-century United States by touring stage companies.[113]

Banim's play differs little from earlier versions by Cicero and others: When a tyrant seizes power in a coup, Damon attempts to stab him but is apprehended and sentenced to death. Pythias offers his life as hostage so that Damon can have a few last hours to spend with his wife. As the hour of execution approaches, Damon has not yet returned, yet Pythias insists that Damon must be unavoidably delayed (as, in fact, he is) and welcomes the opportunity to give his life for his friend. At the last moment, Damon returns. The tyrant, impressed by the strength of the friendship between the two men, not only spares Damon but asks both men to remain at his court as advisers.[114]

Banim's *Damon and Pythias* had a profound effect on Justus Rathbone, a schoolteacher and a serially dissatisfied member of American fraternal societies. At various times a member of the Freemasons, Sons of Malta, and Red Men, Rathbone was inspired by Banim's play to name the fraternal society he founded in 1864 the Knights of Pythias. The order celebrated "the chivalry of manhood—the moral virtues which separate the mercenary from the generous friend."[115] The Knights of Pythias were active in the West: members founded a branch of the order in Tombstone in June 1881, four months before the street fight.[116]

What connotations attached to Damon and Pythias in late-nineteenth- and early-twentieth-century America? For Rathbone, it meant the virtue of brotherhood, which he thought might restore harmony to a nation rent by civil war. In other contexts, however, it implied romantic same-sex friendship. The story of Damon and Pythias had a long-standing association in the English-speaking world with homosexuality. A dramatic version by the English poet Richard Edwards, an Oxford chaplain and professor of logic, had its first performance at Queen Elizabeth's court around Christmas 1564. Edwards invented foils for Damon and Pythias: the false friends Aristippus and Carisophus, and a pair of comical lackeys, Will and Jack, whose banter is replete with innuendo implying sex between men.[117]

Likewise, Louisa May Alcott described Lizzie and Rebecca, two of the characters in her 1870 novel *An Old-Fashioned Girl*, as living together and taking care of each other "in true Damon and Pythias style"—an oblique reference to lesbianism. Despite Lizzie's impending marriage, Rebecca intends to continue to live with the new couple. Fanny, the protagonist, finds to her surprise that Rebecca and Lizzie are not "mannish and rough," but she nonetheless concludes that they are a "different race of creatures." Like Alcott's reference, Masterson's allusion to Damon and Pythias was code

with a particular meaning in the bygone homosocial environment
of the nineteenth century. Through this analogy, Masterson meant
(like Rathbone) that Wyatt and Holliday were brothers in arms and
(like Alcott) that theirs was a same-sex friendship that went beyond
the ordinary homosocial bonds of the era. This was, Masterson implied, a "romantic friendship," in the language of the literary critic
Marylynne Diggs.[118]

Wyatt found an identity in the Kansas cow towns, or, to be more pre-
cise, somewhat like Melville's confidence man, he found many identities: a feared police officer, a cool and skilled faro dealer, a "meek"
Christian, and Pythias to Holliday's Damon. Wyatt's Janus-faced,
multiple identities reflected the complexities of the cow towns
themselves. Midway between the Texas rangelands and the Chicago
stockyards, the Kansas cow towns were liminal places where merchants (with their middle-class mores) and cowboys (with their
masculine honor code) commingled. This volatile world, where
competing cultural orders clashed, was a fertile environment for
the imagination of a man already inclined toward self-invention. In
the cow towns, the future vigilante learned that reinvention was
not only a way to shed an embarrassing past, but a way to be simultaneously a confidence man and a police officer, a lawbreaker and a
lawman.

Wyatt's parents, Virginia and Nicholas Earp, in an undated photograph. (Courtesy of the Kansas State Historical Society)

Wyatt in 1869, at about the time that he rejoined his father in Lamar, Missouri.

Wyatt (left) with Bat Masterson in Dodge City, Kansas, in the late 1870s.

(Courtesy of the Arizona Historical Society)

John Henry "Doc" Holliday at the time of his graduation from the
Pennsylvania College of Dental Surgery in Philadelphia in 1872.

Wyatt's older brother Virgil Walter Earp. (Courtesy of the Robert G. McCubbin Collection)

Wyatt's younger brother Morgan Earp. (Courtesy of the Robert G. McCubbin Collection)

The Tombstone volunteer fire company. Wyatt is standing in the back row at the far right. (Courtesy of the Arizona Historical Society)

Dodge City, 1883. Front row, left to right: Charlie Bassett, Wyatt Earp, Frank McLain, Neal Brown; back row, left to right: Bill Harris (Luke Short's partner at the Long Branch Saloon), Luke Short, Bat Masterson. A slightly different version of this photograph, showing W. F. Petillon, a Ford County district court clerk, standing next to Masterson, ran in the July 21, 1883, edition of the *National Police Gazette*. (National Archives and Records Administration)

Wyatt in 1887, at the time he lived in San Diego.

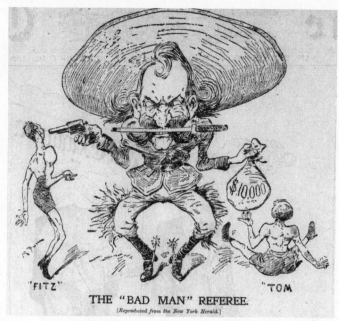

THE "BAD MAN" REFEREE.
[Reproduced from the New York Herald.]

"The 'Bad Man' Referee," *San Francisco Call*,
December 12, 1896.

The Northern, a saloon Wyatt managed in Tonopah, Nevada, in 1902. Wyatt capitalized on his notoriety by putting his name on the sign over the door. The woman on the left may be his wife, Josephine. (Courtesy of the Nevada Historical Society)

Wyatt in Los Angeles in the 1920s. (Courtesy of the Arizona Historical Society)

5

WILD JUSTICE

From 1955 to 1961, *The Life and Legend of Wyatt Earp* anchored the American Broadcasting Company's television programming on Tuesday nights. Over its six-year run, the program followed Earp from Ellsworth, Kansas (where he was imagined to be the city marshal), to Wichita, Dodge City, and finally Tombstone, Arizona. By the program's last season, the hero, played by Hugh O'Brian, was a deputy U.S. marshal confronting an organized gang of Tombstone criminals led by "Old Man" Clanton. On the program, the "Clanton Gang" specialized in stagecoach robberies and cattle rustling. As depicted by the show's lead writer, Frederick Hazlitt Brennan, they were in league with a group of corrupt officials based in Tucson known as the Ten-Percent Ring.[1]

With Earp as a federal law enforcement agent battling an organized-crime ring, the program's final season—which had its climax at the O.K. Corral—closely resembled ABC's Thursday-night program that year *The Untouchables*. Produced, like *Wyatt Earp*, at Desi Arnaz and Lucille Ball's Desilu Studios in Los Angeles, *The Untouchables* starred Robert Stack as Eliot Ness, a Federal Bureau of Investigation agent who squared off against the organized-crime leader Al Capone in Prohibition-era Chicago.

Stuart Lake had helped create the Wyatt Earp television program, and its depiction of Earp as an Eliot Ness of the Old West closely followed his characterization of Earp in *Frontier Marshal*. In the book, Lake depicted Earp as a federal agent opposing an organized-crime syndicate in Tombstone no less powerful than Capone's crime operation in Chicago. Writing at the end of the Prohibition era, when gangsters such as Capone were at the height of their power and celebrity, Lake modeled the cowboys on contemporary organized criminals, describing the Clanton Gang as "three hundred outcasts of frontier society," including "professional killers" and other "fugitives from border justice" who rustled cattle, robbed stages of the silver bullion they carried, and extorted protection money from honest ranchers.[2] In his notes for the book, Lake had given his imagination free rein, inventing a long criminal past for Clanton that had him joining a notorious criminal syndicate in Gold Rush Montana and committing several murders in southern California before moving his operation to Arizona. There, Lake had Clanton controlling a criminal organization that stretched from California to New Mexico.[3]

The hero who confronts such a powerful and unregenerate criminal must possess nearly superhuman abilities. Like the cartoonist Chester Gould, whose enduring detective character, Dick Tracy, appeared in 1931—the same year that Houghton Mifflin published *Frontier Marshal*—Lake modeled his protagonist on a literary figure that the scholar Richard Gid Powers has called the "action detective": the policeman who not only solved crimes through ratiocination but faced down criminals with his fists and his firearm. The literary exemplar of the action detective was Nick Carter, a character created by John Coryell in 1886. Carter neither smoked nor drank and possessed superhuman strength (he could lift a horse and its rider overhead!). He was the protagonist of over one thousand serialized crime stories by Coryell and other writers, comic strips, and a series of films in the 1930s. Lake's version of the action detective, with Earp cast as a lawman with superhuman abilities as a pistoleer, not only drew on the tradition established by Coryell but furthered it.[4] A year after Lake's biography appeared, a radio scriptwriter, Fran Striker, created a fictional Old West action detective, the Lone Ranger. Like Wyatt, the Lone Ranger was a Southwestern lawman who turned to vigilantism after the murder of his brother.

The first rule of detective fiction is that there must be a clear distinction between heroes and villains. John Flood, despite his limitations as a writer, understood this rule well enough. For Wyatt, "the law always remained paramount," Flood wrote.[5] In her unpublished account of Wyatt's role in the violence in Tombstone, Forrestine Hooker likewise adhered to this rule, introducing Wyatt as "an officer who could, and would, enforce the law." The cowboys, by contrast, were "outlaws and rustlers." Hooker was careful to note that "there was never anything of a friendly nature between the Earps" and "that bunch of men."[6]

In southern Arizona in the early 1880s, however, Wyatt was not the stalwart defender of law and order that Lake, Flood, Hooker, and Wyatt himself made him out to be; nor were the cowboys an organized-crime syndicate. In important respects, the cowboys of southern Arizona were much like the Earps. The Clanton family—two of whose members, Ike and Billy, confronted the Earp brothers in the gunfight in Tombstone in October 1881—like the Earps had roots in the Upper South backcountry and knew the privations of yeomanry and tenancy. Both families had migrated to the Far West in the middle of the nineteenth century looking to improve their lot. Both viewed the public sector—whether government lands or elected office—as an opportunity for personal advancement. For Wyatt, Tombstone was another chance to reinvent himself; it presented him with the possibility of moving beyond the faro table to enjoy the fruits of booty politics on a grand scale.

Newman Haynes Clanton, the father of Ike and Billy Clanton, was born in Tennessee in 1816. Married in Missouri in 1840, over the next decades he migrated restlesssly with his family, settling for brief periods in Illinois and Texas until, at the end of the Civil War, he moved with his family to California. The Clantons, in short, were like thousands of other rural families in the Midwest and Upper

South: they were pushed out by better-capitalized farmers who could afford to purchase the latest labor-saving farm machinery, produce cash crops, and acquire the land of their less successful neighbors. Like thousands of other landless farmers, the Clantons became squatters in the West. At the time of the 1870 census, the Clantons were squatting on land in San Buena Ventura township, then part of Santa Barbara County, California.[7]

Squatting has a long and complicated history. Until the 1862 Homestead Act, which offered 160 acres of public lands to settlers who improved the claim and stayed for five years, public land was not free. The government sold it for various prices; the minimum price in the years before the Homestead Act was $1.25 an acre, with buyers allowed to purchase no less than eighty acres.[8] Yet squatting persisted in the West even after the passage of the Homestead Act—particularly because at the same time that the federal government was giving away 160-acre homesteads (often on remote tracts), it was granting millions of acres (in prime locations) to various railroad companies, which they in turn sold to settlers or speculators. By the end of the nineteenth century, the federal government had given away 10 percent of the public lands in the West to the railroads.[9] Sometimes settlers misunderstood the Homestead Act and settled not on as-yet-unclaimed public land but on lands allotted to railroad companies. Or they had settled on railroad land prior to its assignment to the railroad company. In California, the mix of railroads, land grants, and squatters was highly combustible. In May 1880, a dispute between squatters and the Southern Pacific Railroad in the San Joaquin valley erupted into a deadly gunfight. When the battle had run its course, seven people—five squatters and two railroad gunmen—were dead.[10] A similar dispute over the title to valuable lands fueled the conflict in Tombstone that led to the deadly street fight of October 26, 1881.

Most landowners preferred to deal peaceably with squatters. In the early 1880s, James Hancock wrote that he and Tom Whitehead "took up 'Squatters Rights' on two big springs about four miles apart" in the San Simon valley not far from Tombstone. Their tenancy lasted less than a year. "We sold out to the San Simon Cattle Company who had just come in from Texas and was buying out the squatters below us some 20 miles."[11] In buying out squatters, the cattle company was not acquiring title to the land—they already owned it. Rather, they were paying trespassers to leave. Likewise, when Michael Gray came to the region in 1879, he found the spot he had chosen for a cattle ranch in the Animas valley across the territorial border in New Mexico occupied by the cowboy Curly Bill Brocius. Brocius extorted $300 from Gray for his "squatter's rights" to the area. According to Gray's son, John, "we had paid this sum to Curly Bill for the sake of peaceable possession of the land."[12]

Rather than paying the Clantons to leave, the legal owner of the property they had settled on in Santa Barbara signed a sharecrop contract with them in 1872: the Clantons were entitled to 160 acres in return for one-fifth of their harvest of corn, barley, and beans.[13] This arrangement was not unusual. Sharecropping was as common in many parts of the West as in the postbellum South; one-quarter of all farms in the United States were operated by tenants or sharecroppers in 1880. Indeed, not long before the Clantons signed their sharecrop agreement in Santa Barbara, Nicholas Earp had been a tenant farmer in San Bernardino. In other words, as late as 1872, the Clantons were not the hardened criminals that Lake or the ABC television program made them out to be. Rather, as the Earps had been, they were poor western migrant farmers, living, for the most part, hand to mouth.

In 1873, however, the Clantons improved their lot by leaving California and establishing a cattle ranch in the southeastern corner of the Arizona Territory, in the valley of the San Pedro River, a "deep, swift, muddy stream" with "not a shrub" on its banks, according to one description, that flows through the Sonora desert northward from Mexico into Arizona.[14] However unimpressive the San Pedro, the valley was excellent grazing land for cattle: extensive grassland interspersed with stands of oak and mesquite. The dry San Pedro valley was ringed by mountains: the Chiricahuas to the east; the Huachucas, rising to ten thousand feet, to the southwest;

the Dragoons, which like the Huachucas were part of the traditional territory of the Chiricahua Apaches, fifteen miles to the north;
and the Whetstones to the west. In contrast to the grassland of the
San Pedro valley, the mountains contained forests of oak, pine, and
juniper.[15]

The 160-acre plot each of the Clantons was entitled to claim
under the Homestead Act was too small for a cattle ranch, even if
the Clantons' claims were contiguous. But no matter: before the end
of the nineteenth century, anyone could graze cattle on public lands.
Aspiring ranchers squatted or claimed a homestead on land containing a stream or a spring, and if that was the only water to be
found, they effectively controlled an extensive area of surrounding
public land. As for cattle, the Clantons may have driven a few head
from California or purchased a few from ranchers just across the
territorial border in New Mexico. The cheapest way for poor but
aspiring ranchers to build up their herds, however, was by rounding
up mavericks—unbranded calves whose mothers had died—and
putting their own brand on them. In the early 1870s in most western territories, mavericks were considered part of the public domain; like unclaimed public land, they were free for the taking. By
the 1880s, powerful ranchers with close ties to state and territorial
legislatures redefined mavericking as rustling.[16] But until then, mavericking remained one of the best ways for the rural western poor to
rise to respectability. In short, the Clantons were propertyless migrants who employed two of the most common means to exploit the
public domain in the nineteenth-century West: squatting and mavericking. Both were, or became, technically illegal. But in the 1870s
they were common enough, and the western political economy still
democratic enough, for most people to tolerate them.

While ranchers in southern Arizona such as the Clantons controlled extensive ranges, they had only a scant market for beef. In
1870, the population of Pima County—which at the time included
virtually all of Arizona south of the Gila River—was only 5,716. The
Clantons and other ranchers in Pima County sold their cattle to
nearby army posts—Fort Bowie near the New Mexican border,

Fort Grant on the San Pedro River, Fort Lowell near Tucson, and
Fort Huachuca near the Mexican border—and to Indian reserva-
tions, notably, after its establishment in 1871, the San Carlos reservation for the Chiricahua Apache.

The fortunes of southern Arizona ranchers such as the Clantons
improved dramatically in August 1877 when the prospector Edward
Lawrence Schieffelin discovered silver deposits beneath a mesa
about twelve miles northeast of Fort Huachuca. Schieffelin had
prospected in Idaho and California before coming to Arizona. In
early 1877, he signed up to serve as an army scout during a round of
the United States' ongoing conflict with the Chiricahuas. (Dis-
affected Chiricahuas, under the leadership of Geronimo and others,
periodically fled the San Carlos reservation, resumed habitation in
the mountains of southeastern Arizona, and, taking advantage of
the international border, raided into Mexico.[17]) When his term as a
scout ended, Schieffelin began prospecting in the San Pedro valley;
prospectors had known of silver in the area since 1858, when a
small mine had briefly operated there. Chiricahuas had killed those
miners in 1860. Infamously, a Fort Huachuca soldier quipped that
the only rock Schieffelin would find prospecting in the San Pedro
valley would be his own tombstone. Schieffelin thus named his
claim to the massive silver vein he located Tombstone.[18]

Schieffelin's claim sparked one of the most intense silver rushes
in the nineteenth-century West. A booster wrote in 1881, "The
great richness and extent of the new discoveries soon spread far and
wide, and thousands rushed to the Silverado of the southwest. An
army of prospectors swarmed over the hills, many other valuable
discoveries were made, a city sprung up as if by magic, mills and
hoisting-works were erected, bullion began to find its way out of the
camp, and to-day, a little more than three years after its discovery,
Tombstone can show a population of 7,000 souls."[19] Tombstone's
growth was indeed rapid—almost doing justice to the booster's breath-
less description. Between June 1879 and March 1882, miners hauled
over fifty thousand tons of silver ore, containing seventy tons of pure
silver, from Schieffelin's Tombstone claim. In 1881 alone, Schieffelin's

mine combined with others around Tombstone produced $6 million in silver bullion. The town grew too large too quickly for an accurate count of its inhabitants. In 1880, the population of Pima County was nearly twenty thousand—more than three times its population ten years earlier. Tombstone's official population in 1882 was fifty-three hundred, but an undercounting of Spanish-speaking inhabitants and the large number of transient Anglos could well have meant that the true total was closer to the booster's claim of seven thousand.[20] A number of satellite mining towns sprang up within Tombstone's orbit: Charleston, Contention, Bisbee, Benson, and Galeyville.

Tombstone was the epitome of the sort of places where Wyatt had made his living for nearly a decade: a dusty, newly constructed town dominated by transient young men, where liquor, gambling, and prostitution prevailed. Hastily assembled in a semidesert, Tombstone had a makeshift character. Clara Brown, who came to Tombstone from southern California in 1880, described the place as "an embryo city of canvas, frame, and adobe." Builders smeared some of the adobe structures with a pine resin to create a mock stone façade and thus affect a more refined exterior. In the middle of town, awnings jutted over the sidewalks to provide some relief from the blazing summer heat. Yet one could do little to guard against the clouds of particles churned up by the near-constant wagon traffic and the hoisting works surrounding the town. Tombstone, Brown wrote, "is one of the dirtiest places in the world." She complained that the wind "makes the eyes smart like the cinders from an engine; it penetrates into the houses, and covers everything with dust."[21] A local newspaper agreed: "The nature of the soil in Tombstone is such that the great ore wagons grind it into an impalpable powder to the depth of several inches. Every breath of wind sets this dust afloat, and it penetrates everywhere."[22] Incongruously, this collection of dusty tents and shacks received telephone service. Belying the Hollywood image of the technologically primitive West, Arizona began to string telephone lines shortly after Alexander Graham Bell patented the technology in 1876. Tombstone's telephone lines were installed in early March 1881—the first lines connected Tombstone with the mines in Contention.[23]

Like the Kansas cow towns, Tombstone drew to itself a population of young male laborers. Working in ten-hour shifts, miners earning $4 a day clustered in shanties on the south side of town, crowding as many as six bunks into one cabin.[24] As in Kansas, the custom of these young male laborers supported a host of saloons, gambling halls, and brothels. Just as in the cow towns, the plain wooden and adobe exteriors of the saloons opened into ornate interiors. The Oriental Saloon, which opened in July 1880, featured chandeliers, a gilded bar, and furnishings appropriated from the lavish Baldwin Hotel in San Francisco. At the Oriental, Occidental, and Crystal Palace saloons, "the liquors were the finest domestic and foreign that money could buy," according to one contemporary.[25] Clara Brown noted that "the only attractive places visible are the liquor and gambling saloons, which are everywhere present, and are carpeted and comfortably furnished."[26]

Brown refrained from entering the saloons, however, because "as long as so many members of the *demi-monder* patronize them, many honest women will hesitate to attend."[27] George Parsons, a California bank clerk who moved to Tombstone and became a mining broker, deplored the shamelessness of prostitutes in Tombstone: "This place holds some of the most depraved—entirely and apparently totally so that were ever known. I have seen hard cases before in a frontier oil town where but one or two women were thought respectable but have never come across several such cases as are here."[28] The Tombstone city council permitted prostitution and regarded it as a source of municipal funds. In Tombstone, prostitutes were jailed only if they failed to pay the city license fee.[29]

For southern Arizona ranchers, the establishment of Tombstone represented a lucrative opportunity. Only a few ranchers in the region had herds that were large enough to supply beef to the mining town sustainably, however. Henry C. Hooker—the father-in-law of Wyatt's would-be biographer Forrestine—was one of those. He had brought ten thousand longhorns from Texas to the Sulphur Springs valley in 1872. Yet the herds of struggling ranchers such as the Clantons were simply too small to satisfy the new demand for beef in Tombstone. The Clantons and other small ranchers thus looked to northern Mexico, where hundreds of thousands of cattle grazed.[30] The Clantons took to raiding into Mexico, stealing cattle there, and driving them north for sale in Tombstone. The rancher John Gray recalled that when Tombstone was first founded, "cattle ranching had not been started and the butchers got their cattle mostly from across the border with Mexico." Butchers, Gray added, got "the hides off and hid away before the proper owner had time to trail up the 'lost' animals."[31]

Cross-border raiding was new to neither the Arizona-Sonora region nor the U.S.-Mexico borderland generally. Apaches and Comanches had long raided the towns and ranches of northern Mexico.[32] Many cowboys had come to southern Arizona from Texas, where cross-border cattle raids—committed by both Mexicans and Texans—were common in the years after the Civil War.[33] Mexican outlaws had robbed stages in southern Arizona and California since the early 1870s.[34]

Most businesses in Tombstone had few scruples about buying stolen cattle. John Gosper, the acting governor of Arizona, complained in late 1881 that "hotels, saloons, restaurants &c" were "dealing *dishonestly* with one hand *secretly* behind them, handling *stolen* property of the 'Cow-Boys,' while with the other hand openly before them they are disposing of the stolen property (mostly beef cattle) to honest citizens, afterwards dividing with the regular thieves." Such businesses, Gosper lamented, "are both weak and wicked in their sympathy for & protection of this lawless class."[35] Similarly, many southern Arizona ranchers tolerated the rustlers. "Most of the early cattlemen were none too good to do a little business with the Rustlers in the way of buying a bunch of cattle or horses if they thought there was no chance of being found out," according to James Hancock.[36]

Just as ranchers, butchers, and consumers in Tombstone did not inquire too closely into the provenance of the cattle that cowboys such as the Clantons provided, authorities in Mexico and the United States were either unwilling or unable to put a stop to cattle rustling. Local authorities in southern Arizona turned a blind eye to the rustlers' activities so long as they committed their thefts in Mexico. U.S. marshals and Mexican federal police had a mandate to confront cross-border criminals, but the remoteness of the Arizona-Sonora borderland from national authorities in the United States and Mexico, and the outlaws' ability to cross the border to evade pursuit, had long allowed outlawry to persist in the region. The Rurales, the Mexican federal police, were ineffective in countering borderland criminality. Created in 1861, their ranks included numerous former borderlands bandits.[37] Moreover, through most of the 1870s, a climate of mutual distrust and contempt both encouraged cross-border raiding and discouraged Mexican and U.S. authorities from cooperation. Only by the end of the 1870s had authorities made a few hesitant steps toward dealing with cross-border raiding. For instance, in 1880, a deputy U.S. marshal, Joseph Evans, arrested a small group of Mexican revolutionaries hiding in southern Arizona.[38]

In the lightly policed borderland of southern Arizona, the number of active rustlers grew to roughly one hundred by 1881. They could hardly be judged hardened criminals, however. The southern Arizona rustlers were "mostly young men and boys hardly out of their teens who fell into this life in search for adventure," according to John Gray.[39] Like the cowboys in Kansas, their worst form of lawbreaking—apart from rustling cattle—was to hurrah a town. The manager of a smelter in Galeyville complained that "the cowboys frequently visit our town and often salute us with an indiscriminate discharge of firearms, and after indulging in a few drinks at the saloons, practice shooting at the lamps, glasses &c."[40] George Hand of Contention wrote how "some festive young fellows without brains at a late hour of night commenced firing pistols in the Main Street for their own amusement to the discomfort of families and other persons."[41]

Yet rustling was dangerous. John Gray's brother Dick threw in his lot with the rustlers and was killed, by Mexican soldiers patrolling the border, while on a cattle raid in 1881. The Clantons were also active rustlers. John Clum, a former agent for the Chiricahuas at San Carlos who moved to Tombstone in 1879, founded a newspaper, and served as mayor in 1881, wrote that "the Clanton clan had a 'ranch' west from Tombstone in the San Pedro valley which was headquarters for the outlaws in that section, and which served as a sort of clearing-house for the cattle stolen by rustlers in Mexico and smuggled across the line down the valley." The brothers Tom and Frank McLaury—both of whom would be killed in the 1881 gunfight— "had a 'ranch' about 25 miles east from Tombstone in the Sulphur Springs valley where they harbored and fed the cattle thieves and other desperadoes of that locality, and looked after the interests of those rustlers who 'imported' their stolen stock by way of Agua Prieta."[42] Clum was a partisan of the Earps', but his charges were probably accurate: in July 1880 the McLaurys were keeping stolen livestock at their ranch, according to an officer from Camp Rucker; in August 1881 Newman Clanton was killed along with Dick Gray by Mexican soldiers while trying to drive a herd of stolen cattle to the north. Far from being the boss of the rustlers, Gray's brother John described Newman as the outfit's cook.[43]

Newman Clanton died a cattle thief. Yet he was not a lifelong criminal. He rather spent most of his life on the move, scratching out a living as a squatter and a sharecropper—one of the thousands of rural poor wandering on the margins of American settlement in the nineteenth century. He slipped into rustling by degrees: squatting on public land, appropriating unbranded cattle as his own, and then, in the last years of his life, when the opportunity for wealth presented itself, raiding into Mexico. The historian Eric Hobsbawm might have called Clanton a "social bandit" or "peasant outlaw," that is, "a poor man who refuses to accept the normal rules of poverty" and whose banditry, though not intended as a form of social or political protest, expresses the proto-revolutionary aspirations of the rural poor.[44] Rustling certainly enjoyed the tacit support of southern Arizona cowboys, but in southern Arizona in the 1870s rustling was not a rebellion against the political order. The political economy of the nineteenth-century West not only permitted settlers to stake claims to land, underground minerals, lumber, and water, but encouraged it. Rustling was a twisted derivative of that scramble for resources.

If Newman Clanton was not the Robin Hood of southern Arizona, neither was he its Al Capone. Popular culture remembers Clanton as a frontier crime boss for much the same reason that Wyatt Earp is usually remembered as a duty-bound lawman: the action-detective genre demands that a sharp distinction be drawn between the criminal and the crime-solving hero. Forrestine Hooker, John Flood, and Stuart Lake each made that distinction clear. Yet as a poor, rural migrant who ventured into crime, Clanton was not so different from the bootlegger Nicholas Earp or Nicholas's son Wyatt, the onetime horse thief and brothel enforcer.

Newman Clanton slipped into rustling after spending many years helping himself to unclaimed land and cattle in the American West—appropriations that were perfectly legal. Indeed, exploiting the public domain for private gain was commonplace in the nineteenth-century West. The mineral rushes that spurred the economic development of the West—California in 1849, Colorado in 1858, Nevada in 1859, the Black Hills in 1874, and Tombstone in 1879—were made possible by federal laws that permitted prospectors such as Schieffelin to stake claims to the mineral rights beneath public land.[45] Railroad companies that extracted huge grants of public land from the federal government practiced such exploitation on a large scale. Small-timers such as the Clantons or the Earps squatted on public land, rounded up unbranded calves for their own herds, or resorted to booty politics, using municipal offices for private enrichment. The legal traditions that permitted—or, rather, encouraged—the arrogation of public resources blurred the lines between public and private, preemption and extortion, claim and theft.

Much of the violence in Tombstone in the early 1880s stemmed from conflict over the appropriation of public lands and resources.

Such conflicts were notorious in mining regions, as merchants and investors sidestepped the speculative work of prospecting and instead tried for quick wealth by claiming land on which to develop cities to serve as commercial centers for the mines. Such claims were often faulty, and disputes led to violence. For instance, in 1850 in Sacramento, California, the commercial capital of the California gold fields, over a dozen people were killed in a street battle over the legitimacy of townsite property rights.[46]

For over a year after Schieffelin's silver strike, miners, saloon-keepers, and prostitutes simply clustered near the Tombstone mine. By late 1878, however, Schieffelin and his partners had grown weary of having so many tenants on their mining property and began to evict them. Most found their way to a spot north of the Toughnut Mine, where a number of veterans of Gold Rush California, including the rancher Michael Gray, had staked out a 320-acre townsite under the name of the Tombstone Townsite Company.

The U.S. Land Office did not patent the claim, however, because when the townsite company had filed its claim, it had failed to pay the required $1.25 per acre. The partners ignored this oversight as a mere technicality and pressed ahead, selling titles to city lots—though without a patent, the townsite company did not have legitimate titles to sell. In March 1880, a Tucson newspaper reported that the Land Office would not issue a patent. Immediately, Tombstone residents began appropriating empty lots for themselves. To maintain their claim to their property, the townsite company arranged to have the plot resurveyed and to have the Tombstone mayor, Alder Randall, a saloonkeeper and a crony of the townsite partners, re-register the claim with the Land Office. In late May, Randall quietly deeded most of the town—2,168 of 2,394 lots—to the townsite partners, now known as Clark, Gray & Company.[47]

By early August, residents had begun to meet to discuss the townsite problem.[48] The issue proved to be a political boon to John Clum, the editor of the *Tombstone Epitaph*. Over the previous months he had tried—and failed—to build a political base by agitating against the handful of Chinese immigrants in Tombstone.[49]

Clum hammered away at the patent issue in the *Epitaph* throughout the fall of 1880, urging residents not to purchase titles from the townsite company.[50] The campaign culminated in early January 1881 with Clum's election as mayor at the head of the Citizens Protective Party. On the eve of the election, he endorsed himself for mayor in his newspaper, drawing attention to the patent issue: "In Tombstone he has made himself thoroughly the friend of the people by his firmness and activity in protecting the rights of individuals and the community against the unscrupulous demands of Clark & Co."[51]

Clum was not the only Tombstone resident to resist the townsite company. James Reilly was an Irish immigrant, former army sergeant, lawyer, and Tombstone justice of the peace who forced the issue in September 1880. Disputing the legality of the townsite's patent, Reilly appropriated for himself an empty lot—claimed by the townsite company—bordering an office building occupied by Clark himself. Reilly erected a building on the lot overnight and moved his office into it. In December, James Clark, Michael Gray, and a dozen men descended on Reilly's building and began to move the frame structure off the lot and into the street. A crowd of the townsite company opponents also appeared and, under orders from the town marshal, Ben Sippy, partially moved the building back into place.[52]

Before the house was returned to its place, however, for a few tense moments bystanders feared violence might break out between the two groups. "Much artillery was on hand and I expected shooting," George Parsons wrote in his diary. The incident passed without violence, but Clum saw it as a political opportunity. Rather than trying to calm the situation, the mayoral candidate organized a paramilitary force, which he called a Citizens Safety Committee, to combat the townsite company. Years later, he wrote to Lake that the force was composed of between one and two hundred members (in his letter to Lake, Clum had first written "between 200 and 300," before crossing it out). The force "was organized for the purpose of supporting the duly authorized officers of the law in maintaining order

within the city limits and protecting the lives and property of citizens." According to Clum, "I—as mayor of the city—was the official
head of the CITIZENS COMMITTEE. All members of the committee were properly armed and were pledged to assemble on call
in front of my office in the *Epitaph* building on Fremont street. The
Vizina Hoisting Works was located within the city, and a certain
signal from the Vizina whistle was agreed upon as an emergency
call for this committee to report to duty."[53] It was not the first time
Clum had raised a private army: the hallmark of his administration
as Indian agent at San Carlos was the creation of an Indian police
force, which he drilled and paraded on the reservation.

While some threatened violence, both the citizens and the
townsite company pursued their cases in court.[54] The case wended
its way through the courts for several years. Ultimately, the Arizona
Territorial Supreme Court ruled on the townsite question in 1886.
Randall's deed, they decided, was invalid. An officer of the town,
the court ruled, might register a townsite with the Land Office only
for "the use and benefit of the occupants"—not to benefit a handful
of investors.[55] Yet in 1881 and 1882 no one yet knew how the conflict would be decided. The citizens' vigilance committee and the
townsite company (which had the support of most of the cowboys
who had come to southeastern Arizona in the late 1870s before the
silver strike) regarded each other suspiciously, wary that the other
side might try to resolve the issue by force.

In the late summer of 1879, as the cattle-trading season in Kansas
reached its end, Wyatt resigned his position on the Dodge City police force and went to Las Vegas, New Mexico.[56] He had quit Dodge
every fall over the previous three years; his pattern was to follow the
cowboys south to spend the winter dealing faro in places such as
Fort Clark and Fort Worth before returning to Kansas in the spring.
To all appearances, nothing had changed in Wyatt's routine. The
spring might find him back in Dodge—or perhaps he would shift to
Caldwell, Kansas, which was already supplanting Dodge as the cap-

ital of the Kansas cattle trade. The gambler and lawman Mike Meagher—who as marshal in Wichita had appointed Wyatt to the police force—would move to Caldwell in 1880 and be elected mayor. Presumably, if Wyatt joined him there, he could have found work on the city police force. Or he might remain in Las Vegas—Dave Mathers, who had traveled with Wyatt through Texas in 1878, had become the town marshal, and Wyatt might have become his deputy.

In 1879, however, Wyatt made a different choice. A professional gambler in the southern plains could hardly avoid hearing of the silver strike in Tombstone, but Wyatt was also encouraged to go to Tombstone by his brother Virgil, who was living in Prescott, Arizona.[57] His brother's enthusiasm notwithstanding, by waiting until the fall—the time of his usual gambling tour—Wyatt hedged his bets. If the town proved to be a disappointment, he could continue on his gambling circuit and eventually return to Kansas. If the town was as wealthy as rumored, however, his prospects as a faro dealer were bright.

Not only Virgil but James arrived in Tombstone with Wyatt; they were later joined by their younger brothers Morgan and Warren. The confluence of Earps in Tombstone was a continuation of their yeoman strategy of family solidarity born in backcountry Kentucky and adapted to small towns in Illinois and Missouri. Along the way, the Earps had gradually abandoned farming but still adhered to the yeoman tradition of clannish cooperation, notably in their various booty-politics schemes. Kinship, as an organizing scheme for society, was giving way to class and capital, but in Tombstone, Nicholas Earp's sons came together to try, for the last time, to adapt the strategies of the backcountry yeomanry to an increasingly modern world.

Wyatt's brothers like him had made a living on the margins of the western economy in the late 1870s. According to his Civil War pension record, after being banished from Wichita, James and his wife, Bessie, moved to Fort Worth, Texas.[58] Virgil met his third wife, Allie, while driving a stage in Nebraska; they had a modest timber claim in Prescott, Arizona, where they had lived since 1873. Morgan came to Tombstone from Butte, Montana, where he had served briefly on the city police force. Like thousands of others who went to Tombstone, they regarded the town as a once-in-a-lifetime chance at riches. It is unlikely that the Earp brothers—least of all Wyatt, who had been on the move since his late teens, rarely staying for more than one year in one place—thought of settling down permanently in Tombstone. Rather, they probably meant to stay in town only so long as the mines continued to produce silver ore.

Wyatt's accounting of his reasons for going to Tombstone evolved over the years. In 1896, Wyatt told a reporter for the *San Francisco Examiner* that he left Dodge because "I was tired of a peace officer's life and wanted no more of it." In Arizona, he first stopped in Prescott, where the brothers, together with their wives (and in Wyatt's case, his concubine, Mattie Blaylock), had arranged to meet before continuing on to Tombstone. There, Wyatt claimed that he met Crawley Dake, the U.S. marshal for the Arizona Territory, who prevailed upon him to accept a commission as a deputy U.S. marshal.[59]

This account is patently false: before Wyatt, Virgil, and their wives left Prescott for Tombstone, Dake appointed not Wyatt but Virgil to be deputy U.S. marshal.[60] Dake knew Virgil because two years earlier he had assisted admirably as a member of a posse confronting two criminals in Prescott. Virgil had been hastily deputized to aid in the arrest of the two men, one of whom was an accused murderer who had been recognized in a saloon. Virgil joined a posse of five that included the town constable, the county sheriff, and the U.S. marshal for Arizona, William Standefer. Following a short pursuit, a brief gunfight ensued. Most of the combatants were armed with pistols; Virgil carried a Winchester rifle. Both outlaws were killed: one was shot eight times while the other—the accused murderer—was killed by a shot to the head.[61] When Standefer was succeeded by Dake in 1878, he likely recommended Virgil as a potential deputy. Wyatt eventually received a commission as a deputy U.S. marshal, but not until two years later, after Virgil had been shot and incapacitated by cowboys in Tombstone.[62]

Twenty years after his interview with the reporter for the *Examiner*, Wyatt told Forrestine Hooker that he entered Tombstone wearing a badge—not that of a deputy U.S. marshal but as deputy sheriff of Pima County. The story is suspiciously similar to the one Wyatt told the *Examiner* in 1896. Stopping in Tucson on the way to Tombstone, Sheriff Charles Shibell of Pima County "persuaded Wyatt Earp to accept the position of Deputy Sheriff," Hooker wrote. "After much hesitation at returning to the same kind of work he had hoped to leave when he resigned at Dodge, Earp accepted."[63] This account is also false: Wyatt eventually became Shibell's deputy, but not until July 1880.

When he reminisced to Flood in the mid-1920s, Wyatt repeated the story he had told Hooker, but this time told Flood that he had declined Shibell's offer.[64] Not long after, called in 1926 to give a deposition in an inheritance case, Wyatt returned to the version he had told Hooker, saying that he had held an appointment as a deputy county sheriff from the time of his first arrival in Tombstone. Moreover, he stated that he brought between twelve and fifteen horses with him to Tombstone from Kansas, and that "I intended to start a stage line when I first started out from Dodge City."[65] Wyatt must have told Lake the same thing he told the lawyers at the deposition: *Frontier Marshal* has Wyatt entering Tombstone as a deputy sheriff and aspiring stagecoach entrepreneur.[66] All of these are at odds with the 1880 census, which lists Wyatt as living in Tombstone and working as a "farmer."

Wyatt's shifting falsehoods are revealing. In claiming Virgil's appointment as a deputy U.S. marshal as his own, Wyatt showed how as a middle-aged man reminiscing about the past, he still remained, in part, the teenaged boy in thrall to his veteran older brother. In 1896, Wyatt still so wanted to emulate Virgil that, nearly fifty years old, he appropriated some of Virgil's deeds as part of his own past. In claiming to have entered Tombstone as either a deputy federal marshal or a deputy county sheriff, Wyatt intuited the requirements of the action-detective genre: he understood popular culture well enough to realize that he needed to present himself as having been—always—on the side of the law. Moreover, Wyatt presented himself as only reluctantly accepting a badge. In truth, by 1880, having learned how lucrative the sheriff's office could be, he had a powerful desire to hold the office. Indeed, Wyatt's ambitions set in motion the events that led to the gunfight of October 1881.

Yet in 1879, Wyatt arrived in Tombstone not yet as a lawman and probably not to run a stagecoach line, either. More likely, Wyatt came to Tombstone as a faro dealer—the profession at which he had come to excel over the previous three years. In the 1926 deposition, Wyatt grudgingly, and using coded vernacular, admitted how he primarily made his living in Tombstone:

Q: What did you do besides being deputy sheriff and marshal?
A: What did I do?
Q: Yes.
A: Well, I dealt awhile in pasteboard and ivory.
Q: Well, you are talking to people who don't know what those things are.
A: Dealing faro bank.[67]

Not long after his arrival in town, Wyatt settled into work dealing faro, primarily at Danner & Owen's Saloon.[68] He found extra work riding shotgun on Wells Fargo stages. Meanwhile, his brothers slipped into the work with which the Earps were familiar: barroom hustlers and hired muscle. While Virgil served as a deputy U.S. marshal, James found work as a bartender at Vogan & Flynn's Saloon, in which capacity he could direct potential customers to the nearest bordello.[69]

Wyatt dealt faro throughout most of his stay in Tombstone, accumulating thousands of dollars in winnings. Some of his gambling wealth probably came in the form of mining claims. Nineteenth-century western mining towns, despite producing great wealth in bullion, were often short of specie for everyday exchanges and relied on foreign coins and homemade scrip.[70] Moreover, successful

professional gamblers such as Wyatt were used to taking their winnings in goods, property titles, or claims rather than cash.[71] For
Wyatt, taking his winnings in mining claims meant investing the
proceeds from one game of chance, faro, in another—the speculative world of mining claims.

The centrality of faro to Wyatt's life in Tombstone became clear
on June 22, 1881, when a fire that ultimately destroyed four city
blocks broke out in the city. When the alarm was raised, Wyatt was
dealing faro in the back of a saloon. "Seemingly instantaneously
with the explosion and the bursting of the flames," the *Epitaph* reported, "the alarm spread and people rushed to the scene."[72] Wyatt,
however, was not among those who rushed to confront the flames.
With thousands of dollars spread before him on the faro layout,
Wyatt risked his life not to fight the fire but to rescue his money.
According to Flood, "he began gathering up the money while the
smoke poured in at the front door." By the time Wyatt had the bills
and coins stacked in his arms, the front exit was impassable, and the
saloon was rapidly filling with smoke. Taking care not to spill his
armload of cash, Wyatt groped his way out the back exit. The fire
continued to rage, but before joining the town residents who were
fighting the fire—including his brothers, who were trying to get into
the front of the saloon, believing that Wyatt was still trapped
inside—Wyatt first stopped by a bank to deposit his winnings.[73]

As in the Kansas cow towns, merchants, investors, and professionals
flocked to Tombstone as well as laborers. These included Clum, who
had been a divinity student at Rutgers College in New Jersey before
joining the federal civil service and who had urged the acculturation
of the San Carlos Apaches to Protestant norms during his tenure as
an Indian agent; Brown, who attended a normal school—an institution that trained teachers—in Massachusetts before emigrating
west with her husband; and Endicott Peabody, a Cambridge-educated
Episcopalian rector who came to Tombstone to establish a church
and later founded the Groton boarding school in Massachusetts.[74]

These merchants and educated professionals maintained a sem-
blance of polite society in the mining town. By the beginning of
1881, they had founded three churches, a school, and several fraternal societies. In February 1881, Clara Brown wrote that "the ladies
of the Methodist society have instituted semi-monthly sociables, for
the purpose of cultivating acquaintance and sociability among the
moral portion of the community." In July, the "Baptist society"
countered with an ice-cream social. The Masons, Odd Fellows, and
Knights of Pythias all founded orders in Tombstone that competed
for fellowship with the volunteer Rescue Hook and Ladder Company, founded after the fire of 1881. The volunteer company was as
much a fraternal society as the Masons or Odd Fellows; it staged a
grand ball on Thanksgiving eve 1881. Brown wrote that the volunteer company was composed of "estimable citizens" and that their
Thanksgiving ball could not have been attended by "a fairer and
more intelligent assemblage."[75]

In Kansas, Wyatt had learned to cultivate the patronage of the
professional class. In Tombstone, even as he dealt faro to miners and
cowboys in the town's saloons, he stayed in the good graces of the
refined class, who rarely ventured into such places as the Oriental.
Most of Tombstone's gamblers comported themselves as gentlemen.
One Tombstone observer claimed that the "bunko-steerers" were "a
peaceable, quiet class of people who outside of the bad habits of
lying and stealing, would make quite respectable Sunday-School
superintendants."[76] With the memory of his reaction to liquor in his
teens still vivid, Wyatt continued to eschew alcohol in Tombstone—
a position approved of by middle-class moralists. George Parsons,
another member of the churchgoing middle class in Tombstone,
told Lake in 1929 that he had never seen either Wyatt or Virgil
drunk.[77] Wyatt preferred ice cream to alcohol; he was a frequent
customer at Tombstone's ice-cream parlor.[78] After the fire of 1881,
he joined the volunteer fire company.

Wyatt's cultivation of these social ties, together with his sober
and calm demeanor, helped him to win the approval of Tombstone's
well-to-do. Clum maintained that the "leading citizens" held both

Virgil and Wyatt in "high esteem."[79] Peabody called the Earps "guardians of the town" and "trustworthy officers."[80] Wyatt and his brothers needed such endorsements if they wanted to work as law officers. In Kansas, Wyatt had enforced the rule of merchants over transient cowboys. The Earp brothers found similar work in Tombstone—although Wyatt would discover that the hold of the dominant class was less secure in Tombstone than it had been in Kansas.

Virgil held two positions as a lawman in Tombstone. In addition to being a deputy U.S. marshal (the same sort of officer who had arrested Wyatt in Indian Territory in 1871) from the time he arrived in Tombstone in late 1879 until shortly before he left in early 1882, he also served two stints as chief of the city police force, for a few weeks in October and early November 1880, and again between June and October 1881. Wyatt was deputy sheriff of Pima County between July and November 1880; served as Virgil's deputy on the city police force episodically in 1881 (including, of course, at the time of the gunfight in October); and was commissioned as a deputy U.S. marshal in early 1882.

Virgil briefly assumed the position of Tombstone chief of police following the shooting death of the city marshal, Fred White, in October 1880. White died attempting to disarm one of a number of drunken cowboys who were hurrahing the town with gunfire after midnight, "firing at the moon and stars," according to the local newspaper.[81] White's killer was Curly Bill Brocius, a cowboy who, according to James Hancock, "was pleasant enough when sober but dangerous when under the influence of liquor. The boys used to take his six-shooter away from him when he got drunk."[82] According to both Wyatt and John Gray, the shooting was an accident—Brocius readily surrendered his weapon but the pistol accidentally discharged just as White took hold of it. Wyatt arrived on the scene as White fell and subdued Brocius. Brocius was tried in Tucson for the shooting and acquitted of any wrongdoing—the court deemed White's death an accident.[83]

White was buried on October 31; a special election to fill his position for the remainder of his term was set for November 12. The

Epitaph endorsed Virgil, whom the city council had appointed to fill White's place temporarily. On election day, however, Virgil was defeated by his deputy, Ben Sippy, 311–259.[84] White's term was soon to end, however—Sippy was compelled to stand for reelection just a few weeks later, on January 5, 1881. Virgil declined to run again, and Sippy was reelected with only token opposition.[85] Sippy was by all accounts an excellent police officer—it was he who restored order when crowds gathered around Judge Reilly's house—but without explanation he left town in June 1881, after first requesting a two-week leave of absence and recommending that Virgil act as city marshal in his absence. Sippy never returned from his leave, and the city council appointed Virgil as his permanent replacement on June 24—two days after the fire that had destroyed much of the city's business district.[86] Michael Gray, a council member, proposed Virgil, whose candidacy Clum had endorsed in November. Thus in mid-1881, Virgil and his brothers were seen as neutral in the clash between Clum's citizens and Gray's townsite company.

Like the Kansas cow towns, Tombstone was characterized by spasms of violence born of drunkenness, impeded desire, and the honor-culture imperative to protect one's reputation at all costs.[87] A municipal ordinance in Tombstone banned the carrying of firearms without a special permit—though as in Dodge City, enforcement of the firearms ban was lax.[88] The city experienced only a handful of shooting deaths in 1880 and 1881. In only one instance—the killing of Fred White—was the shooter a cowboy. In June 1880, the saloon bartender Frank Leslie shot and killed another bartender, Mike Killeen, after Killeen interrupted a tryst between Leslie and Killeen's wife, Mary.[89] A few weeks later, E. L. Bradshaw shot his erstwhile friend Tom Waters in a tragicomic dispute: Waters, having endured some teasing from saloon denizens about a new shirt he was wearing, vowed to punch the next man who mentioned his new wardrobe. Bradshaw, unaware of Waters's pledge, entered the saloon, inquired innocently about the shirt, and was knocked to the floor by Waters. Bradshaw returned home, retrieved his pistol, and shot Waters dead.[90] In February 1881, the Oriental Saloon faro dealer Luke Short shot and killed a fellow gambler, Charles Storms, who had drunkenly accused Short of crooked dealing. After Storms was killed, according to the Tombstone gadabout Parsons, "faro games went right on as though nothing had happened."[91] The shooting of Storms came only a few months after Holliday, who had followed Wyatt to Tombstone, had drunkenly fired a few shots at the Oriental bartender Milt Joyce, striking him in the hand. In response, Joyce battered Holliday over the head with his pistol. Holliday eventually pleaded guilty to assault and battery; Judge Reilly fined him $20.[92]

In late July 1880, Wyatt ceded his position as a Wells Fargo shotgun messenger to Morgan in order to join Virgil as a law officer, becoming the deputy sheriff of Pima County.[93] The sheriff's office was a plum position for booty politics: the sheriff kept 10 percent of all tax moneys he collected. Because the California-based railroad conglomerate that eventually became known as the Southern Pacific was a major landholder and the single largest taxpayer in the county, "the cost of collection was practically nothing," according to John Gray.[94] With the population of southern Arizona booming, most Arizonans expected that Pima County would eventually be divided, creating a new county with Tombstone as its seat. The sheriff of the new county could expect to earn tens of thousands of dollars annually in collection fees.[95] With an eye toward moving up to the top position in the new county, Wyatt, like the partners in the townsite company, envisioned booty politics on a far larger scale than the debt-collection scheme his grandfather and uncles had practiced in Monmouth.

Beyond the potential for booty politics, the deputy sheriff's badge offered Wyatt the same measure of local respect he had enjoyed in the Kansas cow towns. With the sheriff, Charles Shibell, based in Tucson, Wyatt was effectively the leading county law enforcement agent in Tombstone. He held the position for four months, during which time he was busy: serving warrants in far-flung parts of the county; ferrying prisoners from Tombstone to Tucson (including Curly Bill Brocius, following Brocius's arrest for shooting Fred

White); and bringing county residents charged with certain crimes before the local justices of the peace, Michael Gray and James Reilly.[96]

The accounts of Wyatt's tenure as a law officer in Tombstone by Hooker, Flood, and Lake are in accord about a dramatic turn of events in January 1881, which the authors all present as the most important episode in Wyatt's career as a Tombstone law officer prior to the gunfight. All the authors agree that Wyatt faced down a crowd of men intent on lynching a gambler, Johnny O'Rourke, known as Johnny Behind the Deuce for his predilection for betting on the deuce on the faro layout. According to Hooker, O'Rourke, "a weakling and a cheap gambler," killed a mining engineer in Charleston, Arizona, in self-defense, then fled for nearby Tombstone with a lynch mob in pursuit. Upon reaching Tombstone, he surrendered to Wyatt, who, shutting O'Rourke in a bowling alley, stepped into the street with a shotgun to face down the mob that had grown to four hundred. "Guilty or not guilty," Hooker wrote, "Wyatt Earp knew his duty was to protect the man who was his prisoner." Unwilling to confront the lawman, the crowd dispersed.[97]

Flood's version is remarkably similar—though his account intimates that Wyatt possessed some sort of supernatural ability at crowd control. According to Flood, Wyatt barricaded O'Rourke in a bowling alley, then stepped into the street to find "a scene almost from the French Revolution." Wyatt's "face was white and a light shone from his eyes," Flood wrote. "He was mighty, and he beheld them beneath his hypnotic gaze." Sweeping the muzzle of his shotgun before the crowd, Wyatt dispersed the crowd by promising to kill ten men before they overwhelmed him.[98]

Lake's account adheres to that of Hooker and Flood almost to the letter: while O'Rourke cowered in the bowling alley, Wyatt single-handedly dispersed the lynch mob.[99] The 1927 account by Walter Noble Burns, with whom Wyatt met and corresponded, also has Wyatt facing down the lynch mob alone.[100] So, too, curiously, does the brief account by William Breakenridge, whose 1928 memoir of his experiences in Tombstone is otherwise unfriendly to the

Earps.[101] By the time Breakenridge wrote his memoir, Wyatt's version of events had been in circulation so long that even his detractors credited him with the courageous stand.

O'Rourke did indeed kill a mining engineer in Charleston, flee to Tombstone just ahead of a pursuing mob, and surrender to a lawman in a bowling alley. The lawman was not Wyatt Earp, however, but the newly elected city marshal, Ben Sippy. Indeed, Wyatt was not carrying a badge at the time of the O'Rourke incident; he had resigned his position as deputy sheriff in November 1880. According to the *Epitaph*, O'Rourke reached Tombstone and demanded official protection while a crowd jammed the streets. Sippy deputized a posse of about twenty, including Virgil, whom Sippy had defeated in the election for city marshal just a few weeks earlier. The posse may have included Wyatt as well, but it was Sippy who exercised "sound judgment," according to the *Epitaph*. "[C]ool as an iceberg he held the crowd in check. No one who was a witness of yesterday's proceedings can doubt that but for his presence, blood would have flown [*sic*] freely."[102] One witness did contest that characterization, however. James Hancock wrote, "When Johnny was brought in it naturally attracted a bunch of idly curious who gathered around to see what was going on. Just a bunch of harmless 'rubber-necks'—I was one of them myself—no one armed and there was no demonstration of any kind. They put him in the buggy and drove off towards Benson as quietly as if they were going to a picnic."[103]

Yet Wyatt consistently told his biographers that he, not Sippy, had faced down the mob trying to lynch O'Rourke (if indeed it was a lynch mob, and not simply a crowd of curious onlookers). He probably admired Sippy's courage, and this was not the only time he appropriated the accomplishments of someone else as his own. In this instance, he had a compelling motive: in telling his biographers that he faced down a lynch mob, Wyatt cast himself as the defender of the law and an opponent of vigilantism. A year later, he would become Arizona's deadliest vigilante; in inventing a prominent role for himself in the O'Rourke incident, he depicted himself as a man who took the law into his own hands only reluctantly.

•

The criminality that most concerned Arizona territorial authorities was not the occasional drunken honor-culture killing, but the rustling and, increasingly, highway robbery committed by some of southern Arizona's cowboys. Arizonans' earlier tolerance of the cowboys' rustling in Mexico had allowed lawlessness to fester along the border. The boldest cowboys had grown accustomed to thievery. Indeed, by the time of the street fight, "cowboy" had become a euphemism for "outlaw" among many Arizonans. Clara Brown defined "cowboys" as "a convenient term for villains."[104]

By early 1881, American rustlers who had been stealing cattle in Mexico began, predictably, to steal cattle in Arizona, too. Joseph Bowyer, a mine manager in Galeyville, a mining town south of Tombstone, wrote to the territorial governor's office that the cowboys "are in the habit of making raids along the border. Until recently it has been the custom to steal cattle and horses in Arizona and drive them to Sonora for sale, and on the return trip steal stock in Sonora and drive them into Arizona and New Mexico for sale; consequently, quite a traffic was kept up."[105]

The increasing number of cattle thefts on the American side of the border owed itself both to greater Mexican vigilance and to increasing economic ties between Americans and Mexicans. Sonoran ranchers kept a closer guard on their herds, and the Mexican army assumed a higher profile on the border. The increased presence of the army came at the behest of Mexico's president, Porfirio Díaz, who hoped to suppress lawlessness in Sonora in order to attract capital investment from the north. The United States encouraged Díaz to pacify the border in the interests of American investors and, indeed, in 1876 withheld diplomatic recognition of his regime until he had made progress in doing so. By the end of the decade, cross-border trade and investment was on the rise: Sonoran miners increasingly shipped their ore north to Tombstone to have it milled there, and Richard Gird, one of Ed Schieffelin's original partners, acquired half a million acres of ranchland in Sonora.[106] As the Mexican border became increasingly dangerous for rustlers in 1881—Dick Gray and

Newman Clanton were killed while rustling cattle in Sonora in August—the cowboys shifted their attention to targets in Arizona.

In November 1880, to ensure that the Pima County authorities turned a blind eye to their rustling, the cowboys attempted to rig the election for sheriff in favor of the incumbent, Charles Shibell. The San Simon voting precinct, where Ike Clanton was the precinct vote inspector and another cowboy, John Ringo, was a poll judge, delivered 103 votes for Shibell, and only 1 for his opponent, Bob Paul. As James Hancock recalled it in 1927, the cowboys "took possession of the voting precinct and all of them preceded [sic] to vote, and to make sure that none had been left out or overlooked, they voted several times over again." Taking no chances on the outcome, "then they voted all their horses and a dog or two and a stray cat, and finally to make sure no one had been neglected and not given a chance to cast his ballot, they voted everyone over again."[107]

The county elections in November 1880 put Wyatt in a position similar to the one he had faced in Wichita in April 1876: his status as a lawman depended on the reelection of his superior. Anticipating that Paul would defeat Shibell, Wyatt resigned his deputyship a few days before the polls opened, hoping that his competent performance as deputy under Shibell would recommend his reappointment by Paul. Paul ultimately prevailed—after challenging the votes from the San Simon precinct and having them thrown out—but did not appoint Wyatt to be his deputy.[108] Within a few months, Pima County was divided, Tombstone became the seat of the newly created Cochise County, and John Behan, a former territorial legislator from Mohave County and sheriff of Yavapai County, whom Shibell had appointed to a brief term as deputy to replace Wyatt, was appointed sheriff by the territorial governor, John Frémont. Wyatt later claimed that he and Behan had struck a deal sometime in late 1880 or early 1881, whereby "if I would withdraw and not try to get appointed Sheriff of Cochise county that we would hire a clerk and divide the profits."[109] If Wyatt and Behan had made such an arrangement, Behan reneged. In the end, all of Wyatt's maneuvering— resigning as Shibell's deputy and plotting with Behan—left him empty-handed.

Cowboys applauded the appointment of Behan as Cochise County sheriff. John Gray recalled, "Johnny Behan was a 'good fellow' but it takes more than a good fellow to make a good sheriff."[110] Clum agreed: Behan was "inclined to employ methods of parley and palaver and palliation in dealing with this dangerous nomadic element in the country round about Tombstone, and thus avoid the hazards that would be involved in the fearless pursuit, apprehension, prosecution, and punishment of these defiant criminals—which both duty and justice demanded."[111] With the diffident Behan installed as sheriff and the jurisdiction of Ben Sippy, the Tombstone marshal, limited to the town, the only lawman in early 1881 who might have hindered the cowboys in the countryside surrounding Tombstone was deputy U.S. marshal Virgil Earp. Yet the cowboys did not see the Earps as hostile to them: as late as the summer of 1881, Virgil was on friendly terms with Curly Bill Brocius, one of the most notorious rustlers.

While small-time rustlers had contented themselves with driving off Mexican cattle for sale in Tombstone, the wealth of the mines attracted some hardened criminals to southern Arizona who were less interested in rustling cattle than in robbing stagecoaches and pack trains. On February 25, 1881, highwaymen robbed the Tombstone stage five miles outside town and made off with $135 belonging to the passengers.[112] Late in the evening on March 15, 1881, four highwaymen—James Crane, Harry Head, Billy Leonard, and Luther King—attempted to rob a Tombstone stage carrying Wells Fargo moneys. The stage, driven by Bud Philpott with the Pima County sheriff, Bob Paul, riding shotgun, had left Tombstone in the evening for the six-hour trip to Benson. The stage was full—so much so that one of the passengers, Peter Roerig, was obliged to ride on top of the coach. At ten in the evening, the stage slowed as it reached an incline near Drew's Station, about a mile from Contention. As the stage slowly made its way up the hill, the highwaymen emerged from hiding and ordered the stage to hold. In rapid succession, Paul opened fire with his shotgun and the robbers fired on the stage, fatally wounding Roerig and killing Philpott, who pitched forward as the horses bolted. Paul eventually gained control of the team and continued on to Contention to deliver Roerig to a physician.[113] From Contention, Paul alerted Tombstone authorities of the attempted robbery by telephone.[114]

Immediately, a posse including Behan, Wells Fargo agent Marshall Williams, Bat Masterson (who, like Holliday, had come to Tombstone because of the promise of lucrative faro games), and the Earp brothers Virgil, Morgan, and Wyatt set off in pursuit of the highwaymen. According to Hooker, Wyatt picked up their trail when he noted some torn pages from a dime novel at one of their campsites. One of the robbers, he deduced, was tearing the pages from the book as he traveled and leaving them behind. "Camp after camp, he found leaves of the torn novel," Hooker wrote."[115] Whether torn pages of a novel helped their pursuit or not, the posse tracked the robbers to a ranch belonging to Len Redfield. There they found Luther King, heavily armed. The posse arrested King, but to their consternation, they discovered that the Redfields had provided the other three—whom King identified—with fresh mounts. While Behan and Williams escorted King back to Tombstone, the Earps, Masterson, and Paul drove their weary horses in pursuit of Crane, Head, and Leonard. The fugitives, fleeing eastward on their fresh horses, easily outdistanced the posse. Indeed, the horses Wyatt and Masterson were riding gave out, and the two were forced to return to Tombstone by foot.[116]

Shortly after Wyatt returned to Tombstone, King escaped the custody of the Cochise County sheriff. King's jailbreak was neither as bold nor as inventive as Wyatt's escape in Arkansas in 1871. Rather, King simply walked out of the jail while the deputy sheriff, Harry Woods, was distracted by a visitor. Outside the jailhouse, an accomplice was waiting for King with a horse; he mounted and disappeared.[117]

Around the same time that the four highwaymen attempted to rob the Benson stage, four cowboys, having received a contract to provide cattle to Fort Bowie, rode south into Mexico, where, rather than purchase cattle, they simply appropriated a herd and set off back to the north. They were overtaken near Fronteras, about thirty miles south of the international border, and two of the four cowboys were killed. Some months later, in August, a group of roughly twenty cowboys ambushed a Mexican pack train near Fronteras. The cowboys struck the freighters while they were preparing their breakfast. At least three of the freighters were killed. The remaining freighters fled, leaving their mules and roughly $4,000 in bullion, goods, and livestock behind.[118]

Outraged by the attack on the pack train deep within Mexican territory, the Mexican army stepped up its border patrols. Twelve days after the attack on the Fronteras pack train, they exacted their revenge on a party of seven cowboys trailing a herd of cattle in the Guadalupe Canyon on the Arizona-Sonora border. Among the seven were Newman Clanton, Dick Gray, and Jim Crane, the Benson stagecoach robber. John Gray maintained that his elder brother and the other six men were not driving cattle stolen in Mexico, but were simply bringing a herd of one hundred cattle to market in Tombstone from Lang's ranch in New Mexico. The seven were ambushed in almost exactly the same manner as the freighters in Fronteras had been killed: taken by surprise in the early morning by a hail of rifle fire. Clanton, Gray, Crane, and two others were killed; Clanton had been preparing the men's breakfast and fell face-first into the fire. A sixth man, shot through the abdomen, feigned death and survived. The seventh fled on foot northward to the Gray ranch in New Mexico.[119]

Townspeople in Tombstone believed that the deaths were condign. "While no one upholds the recent massacre, those who think dispassionately about the matter realize that the Mexicans were not the first to inaugurate the present unhappy state of affairs along the border," Clara Brown wrote. "They have suffered greatly from the depredations of the outlaws who, under the guise of 'cowboys,' infest this country."[120] Parsons wrote that "this killing business by the Mexicans, in my mind, was perfectly justifiable as it was retaliation for killing of several of them and their robbery by cowboys recently." Parsons was particularly glad that "the notorious Crane" had been killed.[121]

On September 8, only a few weeks after the killings in Guadalupe Canyon, highwaymen struck a Tombstone stage again, near Bisbee. The robbers, Pete Spence and Frank Stilwell—the former an outlaw from Texas whose real name was Elliott Ferguson, the latter one of John Behan's deputy sheriffs—made off with over $1,000 in cash belonging to the passengers and over $2,000 from the Wells Fargo cashbox.[122] Wyatt was among the posse that set out in pursuit of the robbers. Though the posse did not begin their pursuit until an hour after the robbery, they easily picked up the robbers' trail, following it in the direction of Bisbee. Wyatt, playing the role of the action detective, noted the distinctive imprint of one bandit's boots, which he had left when he had dismounted to walk his horse. Wyatt recalled in 1896 that the trail "led directly into Bisbee, to the livery stable kept by Frank Stilwell and Pete Spence." Stilwell's worn boots matched the tracks the robbers had left.[123] Once they were conveyed to court in Tombstone, however, charges against the two were dismissed—their friends provided alibis for them.

In August and September, in the midst of the violence at Fronteras, Guadalupe Canyon, and Bisbee, tension mounted at the San Carlos reservation. Alarmed by reports of a White Mountain Apache holy man who claimed the ability to resurrect the dead, the San Carlos agent, Joseph Tiffany, ordered the religious leader arrested. The army's attempt to arrest the holy man, however, provoked their Apache scouts to mutiny. Rumors that the scouts had killed the entire detachment reached Orlando Willcox, the commander of the Department of Arizona, who hurriedly ordered several units to the reservation to restore order. Faced with troops intent on avenging a massacre that they had only imagined, hundreds of Apaches fled the reservation and headed south to the Dragoon Mountains.[124]

The Apaches' flight from San Carlos panicked citizens of Tombstone, already in a heightened state of agitation because of the spate of violence and robberies that summer. Clum, Behan, and Virgil organized a company of some twenty men, including Wyatt and Parsons, to ride out into the Sulphur Springs valley in search of Apaches. Acting as if they were a volunteer army unit, the little company, which styled itself the Tombstone Rangers, elected Behan "captain" and Virgil "first lieutenant." The company covered 125 miles in three days, encountering no Apaches other than some scouts, known to Clum, attached to an army unit. The company was indeed fortunate that they met with no hostile Apaches, who would have made short work of the hastily assembled amateur force. By the end of their three-day tour, Clum, having talked to the scouts, concluded that "the Indians were driven off of San Carlos by bayonets, and forced into this thing," according to Parsons.

Rather than camp in the open, the company spent their evenings in comfort at various ranches in the Sulphur Springs valley. On their second night out, they stayed at the McLaury brothers' ranch. Parsons wrote that also present at the ranch when the company arrived "was Arizona's most famous outlaw at the present time, 'Curly Bill,' with two followers. He killed one of our former Marshals, and to show how we do things in Arizona, I will say that our present Marshal and said 'C Bill' shook each other warmly by the hand and hob-nobbed together some time."[125] The friendly meeting between Virgil and Brocius—despite the mounting violence of the rustlers and the depredations of the highwaymen—was grounded in their shared familiarity with saloons, prostitutes, and the faro layout. Though as lawmen the Earps served townsmen such as Clum, they had more in common with the cowboys than with the former divinity student from the East.

When Virgil and Brocius met at the McLaury ranch in early October, there was as yet no feud between the Earps and the cowboys. Since the November 1880 election, Wyatt's primary concern had been Behan, whose position as sheriff he openly coveted. Following the robbery of the Benson stage in March, Wyatt had convinced himself that if he could apprehend Crane, Head, and Leonard—who were believed to be in hiding somewhere in Cochise County or New Mexico—he could win the support of the Tombstone townspeople in his campaign for sheriff. As Wyatt put it, "I had an ambition to be Sheriff of this county at the next election, and I thought it would be of great help to me with the people and business men if I could capture the men who killed Philpot [*sic*]." For help, he turned to two cowboys: Ike Clanton and Frank McLaury. Knowing that the fugitives "were friends and associates of the Clantons and McLowerys, and often stopped at their ranch," Wyatt met with Ike Clanton and Frank McLaury behind the Oriental in late May or early June and offered them the $3,600 reward for the highwaymen "if they would put me on the track of Leonard, Crane, and Head and tell me where those men were hid." Clanton was particularly eager to make the deal; he and Leonard were locked in a dispute over the title to some ranch property, and Clanton warmed to the idea of having Leonard out of the way. Each driven by his own ambitions, Wyatt and the cowboys trusted each other well enough to hatch a plan to lure the robbers to the McLaury ranch, where Wyatt would be waiting to arrest them.[126] Yet the intrigue never unfolded: Head and Leonard were killed in New Mexico in early June, and Crane was among the cowboys killed in Guadalupe Canyon in August.[127]

Though Wyatt's ploy to lure the fugitives into his custody never materialized, it set in motion a series of suspicions and misunderstandings that led to the gunfight of October 26. Not long after having struck the deal to betray the highwaymen, Ike Clanton and Frank McLaury began to have second thoughts about having conspired with Wyatt: they feared that they might be killed if their duplicity became known to the robbers' friends. In June, not long after having met with Wyatt behind the Oriental, Ike confronted Wyatt, convinced that Wyatt had shared the details of the plot with Holliday. Holliday denied it, calling Ike a "damned liar." Still anxious, Ike later convinced himself that Wyatt had told the Wells Fargo agent Marshall Williams of the plot.[128] On October 25, Ike together with Tom McLaury rode to Tombstone, and Ike again confronted Holliday, this time at the Alhambra Saloon. Wyatt, Morgan, and Virgil witnessed the argument—but the confrontation was not a rehearsal for the gunfight. Instead, Virgil intervened to calm the quarrel, threatening to arrest both Ike and Holliday.[129]

Indeed, on October 25, Virgil and Wyatt assuaged the fears of Ike and Tom. Virgil told a *San Francisco Examiner* reporter in 1882 that "Clanton and McLaury came to us, and said they heard we had revealed the contract to catch Leonard, and said they could not live in the country an hour if Leonard's friends learned they had plotted against him."[130] Virgil and Wyatt so thoroughly assured the two cowboys that their secret was safe that both Ike and Tom felt comfortable settling down to an all-night poker game at the Occidental with Virgil and John Behan. The men played until the early-morning hours of October 26.[131] Ike spent the long night further soothing his nerves with drink.

By daybreak, however, Ike's anxieties had returned, and he resumed the belligerence he had shown to Holliday at the Alhambra. When Virgil left the poker game around six or seven in the morning to go home to sleep, Ike—to Virgil's surprise—asked him to issue to Holliday a challenge to fight. Virgil refused, and Ike said, "You may have to fight before you know it." Leaving the saloon, Ike, still drunk from his all-night binge and armed with a pistol and a Winchester rifle, stood sentinel on a Tombstone streetcorner and volunteered to passersby that he intended to fight the Earps and Holliday.[132] Ike was, as Wyatt described it, "playing fight." His swaggering, in a town in which the code of masculine honor prevailed, was a staged demonstration of courage. Still fearful that his secret compact with Wyatt might be revealed, he made a public display of contempt for the Earps, in order, as Flood put it, "to divert suspicion from himself."[133] His bluster did not last long, however: Virgil and Morgan (who, like Wyatt, had been deputized by Virgil) arrested him for violating the city firearm ordinance: Virgil clubbed Ike with his pistol and the two conveyed him to court.[134]

After Ike's arrest, Wyatt, too, began to play fight. M. T. Boyle, an Oriental bartender, stoked Wyatt's anger by reporting to him that Ike had stated that "as soon as Earp and Doc Holliday showed themselves on the streets the ball would open and that they would have to fight."[135] Wyatt confronted Ike after his hearing. "You d--n dirty cow thief, you have been threatening our lives," he claimed to have said to Ike at the courthouse. "If you are anxious to make a fight I will go anywhere to make a fight with you, even over to San

Simon, among your own crowd." Like Ike's streetcorner display of bravado, Wyatt's public remonstrance was a demonstration to the community that he would not be cowed. According to Wyatt, outside the courtroom, Tom McLaury, who had heard Wyatt's exchange with Ike, accepted Wyatt's challenge to combat. Wyatt testified that, in response, he slapped Tom with his left hand, drew his pistol with his right, and issued the masculine honor code's ultimatum: "Jerk your gun and use it."[136] Tom made no move, and Wyatt clubbed him over the head with his pistol. Three bystanders witnessed Wyatt beating Tom and testified at the trial following the gunfight. One witness maintained that Tom was unarmed.[137]

The court had confiscated Ike's weapons following his arrest, so he and his younger brother Billy (who had arrived in town by the time Ike had been released from custody), together with Tom and his brother Frank McLaury, who had also arrived in town, proceeded to a gunsmith to rearm. The presence of the Clanton and McLaury brothers at the gun shop alarmed the Earps, who, according to Wyatt, had spent the morning and early afternoon receiving reports from townspeople about the cowboys' intentions. "Several men came to me," Wyatt testified, "who warned me to be careful and said, 'If you turn your backs on that party you will get killed.'" Rather than brushing off the cowboys' threats, Wyatt sought out the cowboys at the gun shop and further provoked them. On the pretext that one of the cowboys' horses was untethered and had wandered onto the sidewalk, Wyatt took the horse by the bridle and led him back to the street—which caused Billy Clanton and the McLaurys to emerge from the gun shop. Billy put his hand to his pistol.[138]

Despite the mounting tensions, neither the Clanton-McLaury group, nor the Earps and Holliday, necessarily anticipated that shots would be fired—much less that anyone would be killed. Both sides probably imagined that a confrontation, if it occurred, would amount to no more than another round of posturing. Satisfying the demands of masculine honor could stop well short of an exchange of bullets—a display of courage was all that was needed. Likewise, for Ike and the McLaurys, a show of courage, rather than an exchange of gunfire, would insulate them from suspicion that they had conspired with Wyatt. The McLaurys and Clantons were hardly desperadoes; they had dealt in stolen cattle but had never robbed stages or been in a shoot-out.

Moreover, the cowboys had every reason to think that the Earps and Holliday would back down. Holliday was a tubercular gambler whom Milt Joyce had easily overpowered during their brief gunfight. To the cowboys, the Earps were dandified faro dealers who, as Tombstone lawmen, bullied unarmed cowboys. Their failed pursuit of the Benson stage-robbers—which ended for Wyatt with a long walk back to Tombstone—and the feckless search for Apaches earlier in October hardly made them seem intimidating.

If it came to shooting, however, the cowboys were at a distinct disadvantage. Wyatt's experience as a gunfighter was not as extensive as Lake imagined it, but Wyatt had drawn his gun on the thieves who had stolen M. R. Moser's wagon in Wichita in 1874 and had participated in the shootings of Hoy and Kennedy in Dodge City in 1878. Holliday had come out on the losing side of gunfights in Dallas and with Milt Joyce, but—unlike with the cowboys—the October 26 gunfight was not his first. Virgil was a Civil War veteran who had been part of a posse in Prescott in 1877 that had killed two fugitives in a shoot-out.

Wyatt also carried into the fight the persona of steely imperturbability that he had honed as a faro dealer, which masked the impulsiveness that had previously led him into trouble in Missouri, the Indian Territory, Illinois, and Kansas. Though Ike Clanton's anxious, drunken bluster was the proximate cause of the shoot-out, Wyatt, more than anyone else, precipitated the gunfight. He coveted the sheriff's office, an aspiration that grew out of long experience in booty politics. He intrigued with Ike Clanton and Frank McLaury, hoping to draw the stage-robbers into a trap much as a faro dealer drew dupes to the gaming table. He publicly challenged Ike and then Tom McLaury to fight, provocations that reflected his deep immersion in the masculine honor culture. The choices that Wyatt made that brought on the gunfight were born of traits that were over a decade in the making.

•

The cowboys—Ike Clanton, Billy Clanton, Tom McLaury, and Frank McLaury—spent the early afternoon of October 26 issuing loud challenges to the Earps from an empty lot on Fremont Street north of the O.K. Corral and between two buildings—C. S. Fly's house on the east and W. A. Harwood's house on the west. Billy Clanton's friend Billy Claiborne, a buggy driver for one of the mine owners, also stopped by the empty lot. For the Earps, Claiborne's presence was ominous: he had killed a man in Charleston a few weeks earlier. (As it turned out, Claiborne was wise enough to avoid the looming conflict—he slipped away just before the shooting began.)

Virgil continued to attempt conciliation. He asked Behan, the cowboys' friend, to join him in disarming them. With Behan, whom the cowboys trusted, present, they might be convinced to leave town without a fight. Behan offered instead to go alone to the empty lot to persuade the cowboys to give up their arms and avoid bloodshed. The Earps agreed.[139]

Almost immediately, however, the Earps began to have misgivings about having sent Behan as their emissary. Behan and Wyatt were, after all, already jockeying for position in the 1882 county election for sheriff. Behan might succeed in persuading the cowboys to leave town and then portray himself as a peacemaker who had averted a potential gunfight precipitated by the impulsive Wyatt. The Earps thus decided not to wait for Behan to return, but to proceed to the empty lot. When Wyatt told the story of the fight to a *San Francisco Examiner* reporter in 1896, he made no mention of Behan's role as go-between. Instead, he stated simply that the cowboys had "sent us word that if we did not come down there and fight they would waylay and kill us. So we started after them—Doc Holliday, Virgil, Morgan, and I."[140]

The presence of the truculent Holliday, who, following a late breakfast, had joined the Earps at Hafford's saloon on Fourth and Allen Streets, doubtless contributed to the Earps' decision to forgo negotiation and force a resolution of the dispute on the cowboys. Wyatt, according to Flood and Lake, tried to dissuade his friend from participating. "There's no call for you to mix in," Wyatt reportedly told Holliday, who replied, "That's a hell of a thing for you to say to me."[141] The honor culture demanded that Holliday fight. Once Ike had accused Holliday of betraying a confidence and had challenged him to fight, Holliday had no choice but to accept. Holliday, unlike Wyatt and Morgan, had not been formally deputized by Virgil, but there was no strict procedure for deputizing city police—anyone aiding the city marshal was, as far as most observers were concerned, his deputy.

The Clantons, McLaurys, and Earps were all products of a determinedly clannish backcountry culture. Just as Tom McLaury and Billy Clanton rallied to their brothers' sides, Virgil closed ranks with his brothers and Wyatt's close friend Holliday. Wells Spicer, the justice of the peace in whose court the Earps and Holliday stood accused of murder following the gunfight, called Virgil's decision to deputize both Wyatt and Holliday "injudicious," as their presence as deputies was more likely to provoke the cowboys to violence than convince them to disarm. Yet Spicer also understood both the demands of the masculine honor culture and the imperative of the yeoman tradition of fraternal solidarity. "Considering the many threats that had been made against the Earps," Spicer ruled, "he needed the assistance and support of staunch and true friends, upon whose courage, coolness and fidelity he could depend."[142]

Shortly before three o'clock, the Earps and Holliday left Hafford's and walked briskly north on Fourth Street toward Fremont. When they turned left onto Fremont, they spotted Behan, still talking to the cowboys. Behan approached the Earps and Holliday, but they pushed past him, with Virgil declaring his intention to disarm the cowboys. Virgil later said that Behan told him, "I have disarmed them." During the post-gunfight trial, Behan, choosing his words carefully, claimed that he told Virgil, "I have been down there to disarm them." It is unlikely, however, that the Earps and Holliday fully believed that Behan had disarmed the cowboys, particularly as Behan followed them as they proceeded down Fremont Street, warning that if they confronted the cowboys, "you will be murdered."[143] Virgil pressed on, leading his deputies to the empty lot.

Holliday was armed with a shotgun—at Hafford's, he had given Virgil his walking stick in exchange for it. As the four lawmen made their short walk through town, Holliday concealed the shotgun beneath his long coat in order not to draw townspeople's attention to it. His effort to keep the shotgun hidden apparently worked well enough so that neither Claiborne nor Behan noticed it—an oversight that undermined their testimony at the hearing that followed the shoot-out. The Earps held their pistols at their sides—at least until they encountered Behan. According to Virgil, when he understood Behan to say that the cowboys had been disarmed, he put his pistol in his belt on his left hip and approached the empty lot with Holliday's cane still in his right hand.[144] Wyatt testified that after encountering Behan, he put his pistol in his overcoat pocket. If this is true, Wyatt likely kept his hand on the grip, because he was one of the first to fire. Frank McLaury and Billy Clanton were armed with pistols. Ike Clanton was unarmed—Virgil had confiscated his weapons and deposited them with the clerk at a hotel. Tom McLaury was also unarmed, but a rifle was within his reach in a scabbard strapped to the saddle of one of the cowboys' horses.

The McLaurys and Clantons, standing at the northern edge of the lot where it opened into Fremont Street, backpedaled toward the Harwood house as the Earps and Holliday marched a few feet into the lot between the two buildings. Claiborne withdrew; the Earps and Holliday let him slip off—their attention was on the Clantons and McLaurys. The antagonists were standing less than ten feet apart. According to Virgil, when he reached the empty lot, Billy Clanton and Frank McLaury had their hands on their pistols, and Tom McLaury was reaching for the rifle. Behan and Claiborne stated that when Wyatt reached the empty lot, he said, "You sons of bitches, you have been looking for a fight, and now you can have it."[145] Virgil, however, continued to try to avoid shooting. "Throw up your hands, I want your guns," Virgil ordered, followed quickly by "Hold, I don't want that," as the antagonists drew their weapons.[146]

Eyewitnesses to the gunfight could not agree who fired first. According to a prepared statement Wyatt read at a hearing following the shoot-out, he drew his pistol from his overcoat pocket only after he saw both Billy and Frank draw their revolvers. "The first two shots which were fired were fired by Billy Clanton and myself; he shot at me, and I shot at Frank McLowery," Wyatt stated.[147] Behan testified, "The first two shots were fired by the Earp party."[148] Claiborne maintained that Holliday fired first, followed by Morgan, and that the "Earp party" fired the first five shots of the gun battle.[149]

Wyatt's first shot struck Frank in the belly; Frank staggered backward but was not yet finished. Morgan and Billy Clanton, who were standing near each other when the shooting began, exchanged shots. Billy shot Morgan, who was standing sideways in a duelist's stance to present a smaller target, in the shoulder. The bullet passed through Morgan's body, chipping a vertebra and exiting out the other shoulder. Morgan shot Billy, probably fatally, in the chest; both slumped to the ground. Tom McLaury dodged behind one of the cowboys' horses, either to get out of the way of the gunfire or to pull the rifle from the scabbard attached to the saddle. Holliday blasted him in his right side with the shotgun.

Ike, unarmed, rushed forward to Wyatt. According to Ike, he grappled with the lawman, "taking hold of Wyatt and his pistol with my left hand" and grabbing Wyatt's shoulder with his right, trying to prevent him from shooting, before running from the scene.[150] Wyatt's account of the fight in his hearing testimony corroborates Ike's statement. "After about four shots were fired, Ike Clanton ran up and grabbed my left arm," Wyatt testified. Seeing no weapon in Ike's hand, Wyatt pushed him away.[151] (When Wyatt told his story to Hooker almost forty years later, he cast Ike as a coward. In Hooker's version, Ike was armed but did not draw his pistol. Instead he begged Wyatt not to shoot him.[152]) The few moments that Ike distracted Wyatt were significant in a gun battle that lasted only thirty seconds: by the time Wyatt disengaged himself from Ike, the battle was nearly over.

Virgil fired four shots altogether, one at Frank and three at Billy. He may have hit Billy (who was struck by three bullets altogether, in the chest, belly, and wrist) once or even twice. Frank, though shot in the abdomen by Wyatt, kept shooting; one of his shots hit Virgil in the calf, bringing him to the ground. Frank then stumbled out into Fremont Street and leveled his pistol at Holliday, who had discarded the shotgun and drawn his own pistol. Frank shot at Holliday, nicking him in the hip—Holliday, like Morgan, stood sideways, presenting as small a target as possible. Holliday ("as calm as if at target practice," according to the *Epitaph*)[153] and Morgan fired at Frank simultaneously, hitting him in the heart and the head, killing him instantly. Tom and Billy were taken into a nearby house, where they soon died.

Wyatt recalled in 1896 that as soon as the fight had ended, "the citizens were out a hundred strong to back us up."[154] Indeed, in 1881, Clum's Citizens Safety Committee had evolved from a vigilance committee intended to protect townspeople's property from the dubious claims of the townsite company to resisting "the lawless element in the country about Tombstone." The members of the vigilante group had agreed to assemble with their weapons at Clum's office upon a signal from the whistle at the Vizina Hoisting Works. When the gunfight had ended, the whistle blew, and within ten minutes the vigilantes had assembled.[155] As Clara Brown described it, "Well armed citizens appeared from all quarters, prepared for any emergency. This revealed what was not before *generally* known, the existence of a 'Vigilance Committee,' composed of law abiding citizens."[156]

When Wyatt related his story to Hooker, he portrayed the vigilance committee as celebrating the defeat of the cowboys in the gunfight by bearing the wounded Virgil and Morgan from the empty lot in an impromptu triumphal procession. Hooker wrote, "The town owned one hack, or closed carriage. This was appropriated by the crowd, but they refused to allow any horses to be hitched to it, and after placing the wounded brothers in it, the best, wealthiest and most prominent men, officials and private citizens, millionaire mine-owners, attorneys, store-keepers and hotel owners, caught the pole of the carriage with their hands or with ropes, and hauled it—a modern triumphal chariot—through the streets of Tombstone for a distance of almost half a mile, accompanied by the yelling, cheering crowd, until the home of the Earp boys was reached."[157] The parade may not have happened as Wyatt remembered it—no other source relates the bearing of the wounded Earp brothers from the scene of the shooting as a triumphal procession—but Wyatt, who had boiled with resentment against wealth and privilege in Kansas and who had sought to win the support of the wealthy class in Tombstone, preferred to remember it that way.

The Earps had considerable support from the townspeople in the immediate aftermath of the fight. "So long as our peace officers make an effort to preserve the peace and put down highway robbery—which the Earp brothers have done," Clum editorialized the day after the shoot-out, "they will have the support of all good citizens." He went on to express his hope that the gunfight had impressed upon "the cow boy element that they cannot come into the streets of Tombstone in broad daylight, armed with six-shooters and Henry rifles, to hunt down their victims."[158] Yet the support of Tombstone's merchants and professionals in Wyatt's campaign for sheriff proved to be fleeting. Indeed, the gunfight marked the beginning of the end for Wyatt in Tombstone. Only a few days after the gunfight Clara Brown reported that "opinion is pretty fairly divided as to the justification of the killing. You may meet one man who will support the Earps, and declare that no other course was possible to save their own lives, and the next man is just as likely to assert that there was no occasion whatever for bloodshed."[159] By the time Wyatt left Arizona for good in March 1882, many of his former supporters had come to think of him as recklessly violent.

As soon as the firing had ended, Behan attempted to place Wyatt and Holliday under arrest. Wyatt scorned Behan's authority, and the sheriff retreated.[160] On October 28, however, two days after the shoot-out and a day after a lavish funeral for the three cowboys, the Tombstone coroner, Henry Matthews, opened an inquest into the killings. Behan testified at the inquest that Billy Clanton and Tom McLaury had tried to surrender when the Earps and Holliday arrived at the empty lot, but that Holliday had nonetheless started shooting. The ten jurors at the inquest were not persuaded that the killings were criminal, but neither did they decide that they were "excusable or justifiable by law."[161] The jurors simply declared what everyone already knew: that the cowboys died "from the effects of pistol and gunshot wounds inflicted by Virgil Earp, Wyatt Earp, Morgan Earp, and one Holliday, commonly called Doc Holliday."[162]

The jurors' reluctance to clear the Earps and Holliday of wrong-doing reflected the opinion of Clum's "good citizens." On October 29, the very day that the coroner released his report, Mayor Clum and the city council relieved Virgil of his duties as marshal. Still recovering from the bullet wound to his leg, Virgil was in no condition to act as marshal in any case. Yet the council members were more concerned with the charges that had been leveled against Virgil during the inquest than they were with his injury. Moreover, on the same day that Virgil was suspended as marshal, Ike Clanton, at Behan's urging, charged the Earps and Holliday with first-degree murder in the killing of the three cowboys. The city council suspended Virgil pending further investigation of the charges. He was never reinstated.

Wyatt and Holliday were arrested and immediately brought before Judge Wells Spicer, who set bail at $10,000 each (he did not require bail for Virgil and Morgan, both still recovering from their wounds). Moving swiftly, Judge Spicer began hearing testimony (in the Mining Exchange on Fremont, a few steps east of the empty lot where the shootings had occurred) on Monday, October 31. The proceeding was not a trial, but a preliminary hearing to determine whether sufficient cause existed for one. Yet as the legal historian Steven Lubet explained, both the prosecution and the defense treated the hearing as a trial. The lawyers for the Earps and Holliday mounted an energetic defense, hoping to have the case dismissed; the prosecutors—a team that included Will McLaury, a Fort Worth lawyer and brother of the slain cowboys—were well aware that territorial Arizona courts routinely dismissed cases for insufficient cause at hearing and were determined that this case go to trial.[163]

Will McLaury arrived in Tombstone three days after the hearing started. His first motion—which proved successful—was to revoke bail for Wyatt and Holliday. The two were remanded to the Cochise County jail on Sixth Street. McLaury crowed to a law partner in Fort Worth that the two submitted to their confinement "as quiet as lambs." McLaury thought he had humbled Wyatt and Holliday, but in all likelihood he misinterpreted their stoicism: after all, this was not the first time either of them had been locked up. They remained in the county jail for two weeks; then, with the prosecution's case falling apart, Spicer released them again on bail.[164]

The jailing of Wyatt and Holliday proved to be the high point for the prosecution. Behan, testifying over three days, repeated an assertion he had made at the inquest: the first man to fire in the affray was one of the lawmen, and he fired a "nickel-plated pistol"—a type of pistol Holliday was known to favor. The pistol "was in the hands of the Earp party, I think Doc Holliday," he said. Claiborne was yet more certain: Holliday, armed with the nickel-plated pistol, was the first to fire.[165] Holliday may have fired first, but he had entered the gunfight carrying a shotgun; only after emptying it (into Tom McLaury) did he draw his revolver. This lapse was minor compared to Ike Clanton's fabulations. Holliday, Ike testified, not only fired one of the first two shots of the battle (Morgan, he stated, fired the other), but Holliday was in fact the highwayman who had killed Bud Philpott. Wyatt Earp—who, according to Ike, had fenced the loot Holliday robbed from stages—had schemed with Ike to lure Holliday's fellow stage-robbers Leonard, Crane, and Head to their deaths, to prevent them from implicating Holliday. And the Earps and Holliday had orchestrated the gunfight to eliminate Ike himself because he knew their secret.[166]

In contrast to Ike's outlandish tale, Wyatt and Virgil—the only two defendants to testify—adhered to a straightforward story: the cowboys had threatened their lives; they had gone to disarm the cowboys; Behan had given them the impression that he had already disarmed them; Virgil, surprised to discover that they were still armed, ordered them to throw up their hands; the cowboys opened fire first.

Wyatt, taking no chances in his testimony, was advised by his lawyer, Tom Fitch, to make use of a territorial law that permitted a defendant in a preliminary hearing to read a prepared statement and not submit to cross-examination.[167] While the prosecuting attorneys fumed, Wyatt read a statement—which Fitch had probably drafted—that carefully narrated the Earps' version of the gunfight. Wyatt moreover took advantage of the format to color his prepared testimony with implications about legal doctrine and the trustworthiness of witnesses for the prosecution—all designed to encourage Spicer to dismiss the charges. First, Wyatt implied that he, his brothers, and Holliday were merely acting in self-defense. "You have been threatening our lives," Wyatt testified to have told Ike a few hours before the gunfight. "I think I should be justified in shooting you down any place I should meet you." Secondly, Wyatt narrated the story not only of Behan's alleged broken promise to appoint him as deputy sheriff but of Ike Clanton's and Frank McLaury's willingness to betray the stage-robbers into his hands.[168] The implication of Wyatt's mention of the double-dealing was clear: the prosecution's lead witnesses were not to be trusted.

Wyatt concluded his prepared testimony with a naked appeal to class consciousness. Forgoing subtlety, he introduced two affidavits that praised his work as a police officer in Kansas—one from business leaders, professionals, and elected officials of Dodge City and one from a similar group of citizens of Wichita, which included Jimmy Cairns, Wyatt's old partner and by then Wichita's marshal. The Wichita affidavit further testified to Wyatt's honesty and integrity (it conveniently omitted his dismissal from the police force and his embezzlement of city funds); the Dodge City affidavit asserted that Wyatt "occupied a high social position."[169] The social function of the police, Wyatt's affidavits reminded Spicer, was to protect the lives and property of the dominant class from highwaymen and cattle thieves. On November 30, Spicer brought the hearing to a close by issuing a ruling exonerating the Earps and Holliday.

Spicer's decision did nothing to end the conflict between the Earps and the cowboys. Clara Brown aptly read the divisions in Tombstone over Spicer's ruling. "A smoldering fire exists, which is liable to burst forth at some unexpected moment," she wrote only a week after Spicer announced his decision. "If the Earps were not men of great courage, they would hardly dare remain in Tombstone."[170] Over the next four months, the two factions continued to battle. Men in both factions wore badges. The cowboys, through Behan, controlled the sheriff's office. Virgil had lost his position as Tombstone's town marshal, but he still had his appointment as a deputy U.S. marshal. Both factions tried, without success, to prosecute their enemies in court. Both sides resorted to violence: the dispute did not end until Morgan Earp and three more cowboys—Frank Stilwell, Florentino Cruz, and Curly Bill Brocius—had been killed.

Thus, despite the fact that the Earps defeated the cowboys both in the gunfight and in the courtroom, southern Arizona became more rather than less dangerous for them.[171] The violence resumed only a month after the hearing ended. "On the 29th of December [1881] I stepped out of the Oriental Saloon," Virgil reported. He was headed a few steps down the street to the Cosmopolitan Hotel, where the Earps and their wives had holed up since the gunfight. "Three double-barreled shotguns were turned loose on me from about sixty feet. I was shot in the back and in the left arm."[172] The injury to Virgil's arm was serious; most of the bone between his shoulder and elbow was splintered and was removed by physicians. The would-be assassins fired from an empty building across the street from the Oriental. Investigating the building after the shooting, Wyatt claimed to have found Ike Clanton's hat.[173] The claim was consistent with his other tales of his police work, in which he recalled having found physical evidence such as pages torn from a dime novel or the imprint of a boot.

One of the first things Wyatt did after the attempted assassination was to telegraph Crawley Dake to petition for an appointment for himself as a deputy U.S. marshal. Fearing that Virgil, the only Earp still wearing a badge, was mortally wounded, the Earps realized that without him they would be at the legal mercy of the cowboys. Wyatt received the appointment the next day and immediately organized a posse to pursue the Clantons. The posse, which stayed with Wyatt until he fled Arizona at the end of March, included Holliday; Sherman McMasters and "Turkey Creek" Jack Johnson, two cowboys who had served as Wyatt's informants until the shooting of Virgil, when they openly threw in with the Earps; John "Texas Jack" Vermillion, a gambler and Confederate veteran; Morgan; and Wyatt's youngest brother, Warren.[174]

A federal posse's official mission was to pursue stage-robbers—particularly of stages carrying U.S. mail—and interdict criminals who crossed the border with Mexico. Cowboys rightly suspected that Wyatt intended to employ his posse in search of the Clantons, however.[175] Suspecting that the Clantons were in Charleston, the posse kept a close watch on the town. Joined by a large number of Clum's vigilance committee, the posse patrolled Charleston and halted all traffic in and out of the town. The *Tombstone Nugget* called them a "pestiferous posse" who were terrorizing the town simply to serve the Earps' private grudge against the Clanton brothers. Fearing that if they surrendered to Wyatt's posse they would be killed, Ike and his brother Phin gave themselves up to a Wells Fargo shotgun guard they trusted on January 30.[176]

The Tombstone common council apparently agreed with the *Nugget*: they saw Wyatt's federal posse as a vigilante force perpetuating a feud. The council asked Crawley Dake, who was in Tombstone at the time, to consider other candidates for deputy U.S. marshal in southern Arizona. Stung by the criticism, both Virgil and Wyatt tendered their resignations. "There has arisen so much harsh criticism in relation to our operations, and such a persistent effort having been made to misrepresent and misinterpret our acts," that "it is our duty to place our resignations." Yet the resignations were not entirely what it seemed: the Earp brothers noted that they would stay in their positions "until our successors are appointed."[177] To placate the common council, Dake appointed another deputy for southeastern Arizona, but, at the same time, he did not accept the Earps' resignations.

Having surrendered to authorities, the Clanton brothers made a brief appearance in county court to face charges for the attempted murder of Virgil in December. The charges were dismissed after seven witnesses swore that the Clantons were in Charleston at the time of the shooting.[178] According to the *Nugget*—which was reliably opposed to the Earps and Clum—Wyatt sent word to Ike that he had hopes of "reconciling their differences and obliterating the animosity that now exists between them."[179] Whether Wyatt actually contacted Ike in an effort to put their differences behind them—which seems unlikely, as he had just spent weeks tracking down the Clanton brothers to see them prosecuted for attempted murder—Ike had no such intentions. Less than a week after the charges against him in Tombstone were dismissed, Ike refiled murder charges against the Earps and Holliday in Contention—a town far friendlier to the cowboys than Tombstone. While Virgil remained behind because of the wound to his arm, Wyatt, Morgan, and Holliday were conveyed to Contention—accompanied by a large group of Clum's vigilantes, "armed to the teeth," according to Parsons.[180] The charges were, predictably, dismissed—the presiding judge having no interest in rehearing the testimony that had consumed Spicer's court for a month.[181]

With the dismissal of the charges against the Clantons on one side and against the Earps and Holliday on the other, tensions in Tombstone seemed to abate. Both factions recognized that they could not successfully prosecute the other. What that realization meant, however, was that both factions were prepared to seek vengeance outside the law.

The cowboys took their revenge on Morgan—whom they held responsible for the shooting of Billy Clanton—on March 18, as Morgan and Wyatt were shooting pool late at night in a billiards hall on Allen Street. Firing from behind a glass door at close range, the assassin shot Morgan from behind as he was "leaning across the table to make a difficult shot," according to Hooker.[182] The bullet entered Morgan on the right side of his abdomen, severed his spinal column, exited on his left side, and then lodged in the leg of a bystander. Morgan died within an hour. Another shot, perhaps intended for Wyatt, struck a wall near to where Wyatt was sitting.[183]

Witnesses, notably Marietta Duarte, quickly identified the suspects in the killing as her husband, Pete Spence; Frank Stilwell; Frederick Bode; and two "half-breeds": Hank Swelling and "Indian Charlie."[184] In Hooker's telling, Wyatt was well aware of the killers' identities (like Ike Clanton after the attempt on Virgil's life, one of them, according to Hooker, also dropped his hat at the scene of the shooting). Called to court to identify them, Wyatt refused—having resolved to impose justice on them himself. The jurors "knew that even should he give those names, obtain warrants, arrest and bring them to trial, it would result in the usual way. Alibi and perjury combined with intimidation to block the wheels of Justice in Cochise County." Hooker went further, however, writing that the killing of Morgan marked a change in Wyatt's character. Before Morgan's death, Wyatt "had been merely an officer of the law, carrying out his oath of office conscientiously at the risk of his life, but now he was a man who had sworn a sacred oath of vendetta."[185]

Wyatt, with the posse he had assembled to hunt the Clantons after the attempted assassination of Virgil already in place, swiftly set to work exacting his revenge. On March 20, he and four members of his posse—Holliday, McMasters, Johnson, and Warren Earp—accompanied Virgil and his wife, Allie, to Tucson, the first leg of a journey by rail to bring Morgan's body to southern California for burial. At the Tucson train depot, the posse encountered Stilwell, who, according to Flood, was one of four "bandits" planning to ambush Wyatt at the train station. In Flood's account, Wyatt called out, "Who are you?" and "I don't want to harm an innocent person; hurry and get away from here!" One of the bandits fired at him, however, and Wyatt set off in pursuit. He tracked down the shooter—Stilwell—and in grappling for Stilwell's shotgun, Stilwell was killed.[186] Hooker's version is remarkably similar.[187]

The story—which is found in the accounts by both Flood and Hooker and thus likely originated with Wyatt—is at odds with the available evidence. Stilwell had a reason to be in Tucson other than to ambush Wyatt: he was there to face federal charges for having robbed the Bisbee stage in September. He and Ike Clanton had come to the train station to meet a fellow cowboy who was to testify in the case—no doubt to provide Stilwell with an alibi. When Stilwell's body was found, he had indeed been hit by a shotgun in the chest at close range—powder burns were around the wound. That much is consistent with Wyatt's story—though it was likely not Stilwell who brought the shotgun to the station but Wyatt, who was part of a posse armed to the teeth. But travelers at the train station heard six shots, and Stilwell had five more wounds—he had been shot twice with a shotgun and four times with rifles. Stilwell's pistol had not been fired. But his watch had been stolen.[188]

After Tucson, Wyatt's posse—now including Jack Vermillion—set out for Pete Spence's wood camp in the Dragoon Mountains. There, two days after killing Stilwell, they found Florentino Cruz, described by Hooker as a "wily half-breed Mexican." Cruz might have been the "Indian Charlie" whom Duarte identified, but it is by no means certain. Under questioning, according to Hooker, Cruz confessed to have taken part in the killing of Morgan. Wyatt, in Hooker's account, allowed Cruz to keep his revolver to "give him a chance to fight like a man." Cruz attempted to draw his revolver but Wyatt drew first and killed him with one shot.[189] Flood described Wyatt as calling out to Cruz when the posse first encountered him but before he had been identified, "fearful that an innocent person might be the victim of a doubtful impulse." When Cruz turned and fired, Wyatt killed him.[190]

Both accounts are at odds with the evidence. Like Stilwell, Cruz was shot multiple times: in the leg, shoulder, right temple, and right abdomen. Either of the latter two shots could have been fatal—the bullet to the temple smashed into Cruz's skull; the bullet to his abdomen struck his liver and exited out his back. According to Theodore Judah, one of the men who worked at the wood camp with Cruz, Wyatt's posse came to the camp around noon and questioned him closely about the whereabouts of Spence (who was in town) and a man named Hank Swelling, one of the two "half-breeds" alleged to have taken part in the killing. After the interrogation of Judah, the posse "passed out of sight toward the main road leading to Tombstone." Just a few minutes later, however, Judah heard a round of gunshots and saw two or three of the posse walking back to their horses on the road "very leisurely."[191]

Only two days later, Wyatt and the posse stumbled into a cowboy encampment at Burleigh Springs in the Whetstone Mountains west of Tombstone. Worn out from a long day's ride, the posse entered a canyon to discover a group of cowboys around a campfire—with Curly Bill Brocius preparing the meal. Wyatt told Hooker that the posse approached within fifty feet of the cowboys before the two groups saw each other. While Wyatt dismounted and aimed his shotgun at Brocius, the rest of his posse retreated. Wyatt killed Brocius with a shotgun blast, but, now under fire from the cowboys, was unable either to remount his rearing horse or pull his rifle from the scabbard strapped to the saddle. Nor could he draw his revolver—on the long ride, he had loosened his gunbelt, and once he dismounted, it had slipped down to his knees. Thus hobbled—and still taking fire from the cowboys—he was unable to swing his leg into the saddle. Finally jerking the gunbelt back up to his waist, he remounted and fled with the rest of his posse.[192]

Flood's version is almost entirely the same, with one important difference. In Flood's version, Wyatt lost faith in his posse after they fled. "These were the men he had eaten with and slept with; these were the men he had fought for and fought with, and these were the men he loved and who had run away." In Flood's account, Wyatt was distraught that one of the "men he loved" in particular, Holliday, had retreated. On sensing Wyatt's disappointment, Holliday immediately volunteered to resume the attack on the cowboys' camp with his friend, but for Wyatt, "it was all over now and he couldn't say a word; his heart was full."[193] Wyatt and Holliday remained in close company for another year as fugitives in Colorado, and as late as 1896 Wyatt described Holliday in warm terms. By the time he dictated his memoirs to Flood, however, he sought to distance himself from Holliday. The image that Wyatt sought to create in the 1920s was of a lone lawman—thus in Flood's account, the posse is reduced to bystanders. Moreover, the type of close male relationship that

Wyatt and Holliday had in the West of the 1880s, when homosocial relationships were the norm, was regarded with considerably more skepticism by the 1920s. Wyatt thus deemphasized his relationship with Holliday, portraying Holliday's alleged cowardice at Burleigh Springs as the reason for the cooling of the friendship.

Whether the posse killed anyone in a gunfight at Burleigh Springs, and if they did, whether that person was Brocius, is another matter. Brocius may have left Cochise County long before March 1882. He was last seen in southern Arizona on December 2, 1881, when he was indicted for rustling. Facing such a charge would not on its own have forced Brocius to flee: the cowboys cheerfully went to court to face charges for crimes more serious than cattle theft, confident that their friends would perjure themselves to provide alibis for them. Yet Cochise County ranchers, weary of Brocius's rustling, had put a $1,000 bounty on him—which, incidentally, may have been a motivation for Wyatt's posse to claim to have killed him. No body was ever recovered in the Whetstone Mountains—the *Epitaph* reported, rather dubiously, that "during the night the friends of Curly Bill went out with a wagon and took the body back to Charleston where the whole affair has been kept a profound secret."[194] The evidence that Brocius was killed rests largely on the fact that he was not seen again after the gun battle. But he had not been seen since December, either.[195] In an interview Holliday granted to a Colorado reporter in June 1882, the reporter asked, "You say three cow-boys were killed on the twenty-sixth of October; are there any of that gang still living?" Holliday replied, "Two of them have since been laid out."[196] If the two cowboys Holliday referred to were Stilwell and Cruz, then no one was killed at Burleigh Springs.

Would Wyatt claim to have killed an outlaw when he had not? He did in another instance. In mid-July, almost four months after Wyatt had left Arizona, a teamster discovered the body of John Ringo in a clump of oak trees in the countryside outside of Tombstone. The only mark of violence was a bullet wound to Ringo's right temple. Ringo's revolver was in his right hand, and the coroner ruled the death a suicide.[197] When Wyatt reminisced to Hooker, however, he said that he and his posse killed Ringo shortly after they dispatched Brocius. In Hooker's account, the posse kept up a steady gunfire, pinning Ringo down, while Wyatt circled behind him for the killing shot.[198] In the Flood version, while Ringo was pinned down, Wyatt circled behind him. Then—per the Flood formula—Wyatt called out Ringo's name; Ringo turned and fired, missing; and Wyatt returned fire, killing him.[199]

Two things are certain about the story of Wyatt's killing Ringo. First, the account is false. Ringo did not die at the hands of Wyatt and his posse in March 1882. He died four months later, by which time the posse had partly disbanded and Wyatt was in Colorado. Although Wyatt was actively resisting efforts to extradite him to Arizona to face murder charges, it is technically possible that he might have slipped back into Arizona, killed Ringo, and then returned to Colorado—but this far-fetched hypothesis seems like an effort to squeeze facts to make them fit legend. The second certainty about the story is that Wyatt was the source of it: the story, in nearly identical versions, appears in both the Hooker and Flood manuscripts. Wyatt's claim to have killed Ringo makes little sense as history, but it makes perfect sense according to the formula of the action-detective story, in which the hero always prevails over the villain.

Rather than proceeding from the Whetstones to kill Ringo, shortly after the incident at Burleigh Springs, Wyatt and the posse left Arizona for New Mexico, eventually making their way to Colorado. Perhaps Wyatt had tired of killing or had finished dealing out justice as he saw it to those he held responsible for killing Morgan. Or perhaps his posse had simply run out of money. Wyatt told Flood that he refused the $1,000 reward for killing Brocius when a rancher tried to give it to him. Nonetheless, the posse was supported by both $500 in federal money appropriated by Crawley Dake, and by $3,000 supplied by Wells Fargo.[200]

Support for Wyatt's posse among the merchant and professional class of Tombstone was fast ebbing away. The first reports of the posse's vigilante killings met with approval from the Earps' staunch supporters in Tombstone. Parsons wrote of the killing of Stilwell: "a bad character sent to Hell." And of the killing of Cruz two days later: "More killing by Earp party. Hope they'll keep it up."[201] Endicott Peabody, however, was disturbed by the bounties on the cowboys and the Earp posse's summary justice. "Best they will leave Arizona & then we shall have peace," he wrote in his diary after the killing of Cruz.[202] While the merchants and professionals of Tombstone had been glad of the protection offered by the Earps in the fall of 1881, they were repulsed by the killings in the spring of 1882.

Moreover, Wyatt and the other members of the posse were indicted for murder shortly after the killing of Stilwell. Behan, leading his own posse of some twenty men, ventured into the countryside in pursuit of Wyatt and his men.[203] According to Peabody, Behan could have remained in Tombstone if he were serious about apprehending the Earp posse: after killing Stilwell, Wyatt and his men returned to Tombstone and stayed at the Cosmopolitan Hotel before setting off for Spence's wood camp, where they killed Cruz. Behan watched the heavily armed posse emerge from the hotel but, Peabody wrote, was "afraid to confront them."[204] It would only be a matter of time before even the feckless Behan caught up with Wyatt, however. So Wyatt, as he had departed so many other places having run into trouble with the law, left Tombstone in ignominy.

Wyatt, much like the cowboys against whom he feuded in late 1881 and early 1882, came to southern Arizona to exploit the public domain. The cowboys rounded up unfenced cattle; Wyatt sought lucrative public office. When Wyatt, his brothers, and Holliday walked to the empty lot on Fremont Street to do battle with the Clantons and the McLaurys, and later when Wyatt and his posse hunted down Stilwell, Cruz, and Brocius, they blurred the lines between public office and private feud. Yet the political economy of southern Arizona encouraged exactly that sort of muddying of the distinction between public and private. Wyatt used his authority as a lawman to settle a private grudge, but in the general scramble to exploit the public domain in southern Arizona, he was little different from homesteaders who settled on public lands, speculators who filed townsite claims, prospectors who staked claims to mineral rights beneath that land, or cowboys who put their own brand on motherless calves. In his bid to become the sheriff of Cochise County, Wyatt eagerly joined the scramble for wealth in southern Arizona. The gunfight and Wyatt's vigilante ride were the consequences of his ambitions.

6

ROPING THE MARK

O n December 2, 1896, two prizefighters met in a bout before fifteen thousand spectators in the Mechanics' Pavilion in San Francisco, to determine who would be the professional heavyweight champion. One of the contestants, Bob Fitzsimmons, was a former middleweight who fought carefully and strategically. His opponent—shorter, heavier, and ten years younger—was an ex-sailor, Tom Sharkey, whose preferred strategy, if it could be called that, was to batter his opponents into unconsciousness. In the eighth round, Fitzsimmons straightened up Sharkey with a jab to the face, followed by a quick hook to the midsection and a blow to the jaw. Striking the solar plexus was Fitzsimmons's signature penultimate punch, and one that he liked to employ late in a bout to stun his opponent for the finishing blow. Fitzsimmons had timed his move well: Sharkey crumpled to the canvas, and Fitzsimmons appeared to have won. Yet the referee ruled that Fitzsimmons's body blow had been illegal—that he had fouled Sharkey by striking him below the belt. Fitzsimmons was disqualified, and Sharkey, as he was being carried from the ring, was declared the new heavyweight champion. The referee who called the controversial foul was Wyatt Earp.

Boxing enthusiasts immediately suspected that the bout had been fixed, and suspicion centered on the referee. Before the fight had begun, Fitzsimmons's manager had taken the unprecedented step of announcing to the crowd that he objected to the eleventh-hour selection of Wyatt as referee because reports had surfaced that Wyatt intended to ensure that Sharkey would win the fight.[1] Indeed, Fitzsimmons had been a 3–1 favorite until hours before the fight. When word began to filter through the gambling community that Wyatt was to referee the match, large amounts were bet on Sharkey and the odds dropped to 3–2.[2] Fitzsimmons had nonetheless dominated Sharkey throughout the fight, knocking him down in the first and fifth rounds. Knowledgeable boxing fans knew of Fitzsimmons's tactic of striking his opponent in the solar plexus, and ringside spectators believed that Fitzsimmons's blow to Sharkey's midsection was above the belt.[3] The *San Jose Evening News* reported that the crowd "dispersed amid cries of 'swindle,' 'robbery,' 'jobbery,' and similar evidences of disapproval." As conflicting reports emerged from Sharkey's locker room as to whether or how badly the fighter's groin was swollen and discolored, his $10,000 purse was withheld pending an investigation. Though most observers agreed with Fitzsimmons that there was a "preconceived arrangement" to award the fight to Sharkey, Wyatt's decision was upheld.[4]

For most Americans who followed professional sports, the Sharkey-Fitzsimmons fight exemplified the problem of match-fixing. Indeed, the fight's notoriety was not eclipsed until 1919, when players for baseball's Chicago White Sox conspired with gamblers to throw the World Series to the underdog Cincinnati Reds.[5] The infamous fight may have inspired "Fifty Grand," Ernest Hemingway's short story, first published in *The Atlantic Monthly* in 1927, of a fixed championship boxing match in which a punch below the belt figures as a crucial plot point.[6]

Stuart Lake wrote that Wyatt found himself in the middle of this controversy by pure happenstance. On the morning of the bout, the fight's promoters and the two boxers' handlers had not yet agreed on a referee. Wyatt, Lake explained, was minding his own business in the lobby of the Baldwin Hotel when the promoters approached him and begged him to step in as referee—just as municipal authorities had once begged him to bring law to cow towns and mining camps in Kansas and Arizona. Wyatt, ever susceptible to appeals to his sense of duty and order, reluctantly agreed. Wyatt's unpopular decision to award the fight to Sharkey, Lake implied, was no different from such unwavering (albeit imagined) stances as his arrest of Ben Thompson in Ellsworth or his defense of "Johnny Behind the Deuce" O'Rourke from a lynch mob in Tombstone.[7] Writing of Wyatt's role in the fight for the *Encyclopedia Americana*, Lake turned the popular understanding of the fight on its head, depicting Wyatt not as the center of the conspiracy but as the protector of the bout's integrity. "After countrywide talk of the crookedness of the fight he was selected as referee at the last moment," Lake wrote. "The affair was a national scandal but no one who knew Wyatt ever questioned the honesty of his decision."[8]

Yet Wyatt did not stumble naïvely into the controversy, nor was his honesty unimpeachable. The morning after the fight, the *San Francisco Call* identified Wyatt as an "ex-faro dealing sharp" who "divided his time between dealing faro-bank" and "an interest in running horses on different tracks of this State."[9] Others who knew Wyatt in the late 1870s and early 1880s remembered him as not only a faro dealer but a confidence man.[10] A decade and a half before the infamous 1896 bout, Wyatt's detractors had already begun to call him a grifter.[11]

Some of the allegations made against Wyatt were dubious. The *San Francisco Call*, seeking to keep the controversy surrounding the title fight alive in the interest of the paper's circulation (and because the newspaper's publisher, Charles Shortridge, was reputed to have wagered on Fitzsimmons), dredged up Ike Clanton's old allegations from Tombstone in 1881 that Wyatt and Holliday were no more than stage-robbers hiding behind badges.[12] The newspaper further alleged that Wyatt had doped a Utah prizefighter with belladonna in 1891, causing him to lose his bout.[13] Yet not all of the stories published about Wyatt in the wake of the fight were patently untrue. Some accusations—that Wyatt had been a "lot jumper" in an Idaho mining town in 1884; that he was complicit with men running the gold-brick scam in central California in 1895; that he owed money all around San Francisco—are harder to dismiss.

Wyatt's reputation in 1896 was suspect because from the time he left Tombstone in 1882, he slid steadily back into the louche world of gamblers. He became what nineteenth-century Americans called a rounder: a man who made the rounds of saloons, brothels, and gambling halls.[14] Increasingly in the late 1880s and early 1890s, Wyatt made the rounds of racetracks and boxing rings, too. Before the ascendancy of professional baseball in the last years of the nineteenth century, the most popular spectator sports in the United States were horse racing and prizefighting. By the end of the nineteenth century, both sports had risen, like Wyatt himself, from their origins in the rural backcountry to become popular diversions in urban America.[15] With shared roots in the bachelor subculture of saloons and gambling dens, both horse racing and boxing had long associations with wagering, and gamblers often sought to fix the outcomes of important contests on which heavy bets had been laid. In the years after he left Tombstone, Wyatt had largely disappeared from the public eye as he descended into the world of gamblers. In 1896, the surging tide of spectator sports tossed him to the surface and back into popular consciousness.

In March 1882, Wyatt's posse fled Arizona by heading east, to Silver City, New Mexico. From there, they went north, to Albuquerque, where Miguel Otero, the son of a Las Vegas, New Mexico, merchant, received instructions from his father (who knew both Wyatt and Holliday) to look after the posse. The younger Otero, who later became governor of New Mexico, may unintentionally have accelerated the disbanding of the posse by finding lodgings for its members in different houses in the city. Wyatt, for instance, stayed apart from the rest of the posse with Henry Jaffa, a Jewish grocer who later became Albuquerque's mayor.[16] There were more serious signs of discord. During the disintegrating posse's brief stay in Albuquerque, Wyatt and Holliday quarreled.[17] Otero wrote that while eating at a restaurant, "Holliday said something about Earp being a Jew boy. Earp became angry and left." The restaurant's owner said that after Wyatt left, "Holliday knew he had said it wrong," but the owner "never saw them together again."[18]

Holliday—whose ideas about race and ethnicity had not much progressed since his days in Georgia—may have been alluding to Wyatt's staying with Jaffa, but more likely he was referring to Wyatt's relationship with Josephine "Sadie" Marcus, or, as she called herself in Tombstone, Mrs. John Behan. Josephine, the daughter of German Jewish immigrants, was born in New York and migrated via Panama to San Francisco in 1869. As a girl, she became enamored of the theater and attended Saturday matinees with her elder sister most weekends. Her parents paid for dancing lessons, and she befriended Dora Hirsh, the daughter of her voice teacher. In the late 1870s, when Josephine was in her late teens, she and Dora ran away to join a traveling company of actors on their way to Santa Barbara. The troupe, which specialized in performing Gilbert and Sullivan's *H.M.S. Pinafore*, went on to Arizona, and there Josephine met John Behan.[19]

According to Lake, Josephine was not a performer but a dance-hall girl. She "went to Tombstone from San Francisco with the first rush, to work the dance halls of that camp. Bat Masterson, and a score of old timers, have told me that she was the belle of the honky-tonks, the prettiest dame in three hundred or so of her kind. Johnny Behan was a notorious 'chaser' and a free spender making lots of money. He persuaded the beautiful Sadie to leave the honkytonk and set her up as his 'girl.'"[20] As Behan's concubine, Josephine did not have a sterling reputation in Tombstone. During a quarrel with Behan over a faro game in 1882, Holliday reported that he told Behan "in the presence of a crowd that he was gambling with money which I had given his woman."[21]

As Lake explained it, Josephine and Wyatt were attracted to each other, and "the first thing Johnny Behan knew, Wyatt had his girl," even though Wyatt was still living with Mattie Blaylock at the time. Lake believed that the relationship between Wyatt and Josephine was "the key to the whole yarn of Tombstone." Behan's jealousy over the loss of Josephine, Lake argued, was at the root of the antagonism between Behan and Wyatt. Yet out of respect for Josephine's reputation, Lake resigned himself to leaving her out of his tale. In any case, Lake's contention that Wyatt and Josephine were openly a couple in Tombstone might well have been one of his exaggerations; in the same letter in which he sketched out their romance, he also asserted that Behan, distraught over the loss of Josephine, not only fired off a few shots at Wyatt during the October 26, 1881, gunfight but masterminded the assassination of Morgan and the attempted assassination of Virgil.[22]

Josephine had no desire to see her past—as an actress, dance-hall girl, or concubine—in print. She asked William Breakenridge to omit her from his Tombstone memoir, *Helldorado*, and he complied.[23] Both Flood and Lake referred to Josephine only obliquely. According to Flood, when fire consumed several Tombstone city blocks on June 22, 1881, Wyatt—after rescuing his faro bank from a burning saloon—rescued two women from the second floor of a burning building. When he emerged from the conflagration, Flood wrote, "someone threw her arms around his neck and kissed him. Beyond that, the thread of the story seems to have been lost. If that were the beginning of a romance, Earp has been careful to guard the secret all these years."[24] This anecdote was one of Josephine's favorites; in 1930, she complained to Ira Rich Kent, Lake's editor at Houghton Mifflin, that Lake's manuscript made no mention of it.[25] Instead, Lake took Kent's advice and wrote cryptically of an unnamed "object of Johnny Behan's most ardent affections" showing "a decided preference" for Wyatt.[26]

Lake's imaginings notwithstanding, there is no evidence that the relationship between Wyatt and Josephine contributed to the antagonisms in Tombstone leading to the gunfight in the fall of 1881. Wyatt's animus against Behan centered on Wyatt's thwarted ambition to become the Cochise County sheriff. Yet Holliday's slur suggests that the relationship contributed to a cooling of Wyatt's friendship with him. Holliday had cause to feel jilted. His relationship with Kate Harony had deteriorated when he joined Wyatt in Tombstone. Kate was so jealous of Holliday's friendship with Wyatt that in July 1881 before she abruptly left town, she joined Ike Clanton in accusing Holliday of being a stage-robber.[27] Holliday related the story of having paid Behan's "woman"—presumably for sex—to a Denver reporter in May 1882, only a few weeks after his falling-out with Wyatt in Albuquerque. It was a jab not only at Behan but also at Wyatt for having shifted his affections to another. Holliday could not have felt more deceived than Mattie Blaylock. After the death of Morgan, she made her way to Colton, California, with Bessie, Virgil, and Allie Earp, to await Wyatt. Eventually, she gave up and returned to Arizona and a life of prostitution. She committed suicide at age thirty-eight in 1888.[28]

In 1882, Wyatt had no intention of going to Colton to reunite with Mattie. According to Forrestine Hooker, while Wyatt was in Albuquerque, he received a letter from a friend in Gunnison, Colorado, encouraging him to come there.[29] By early May, the posse had made its way to Trinidad, Colorado, and from there north to Pueblo. While Wyatt, Warren, and Texas Jack went west to Gunnison, Holliday traveled north to Denver, where he ran into legal trouble. In May, a man variously representing himself as a Utah county sheriff and a deputy U.S. marshal (but who was, in fact, merely a bounty hunter and an inept liar) arrested Holliday for the murder of Frank Stilwell. Conveyed to the Arapahoe County jail to await extradition to Arizona, Holliday was rescued by Bat Masterson, who hired a pair of lawyers, filed a writ of habeas corpus, had a friendly marshal from Pueblo seek custody of Holliday on a trumped-up charge in order to pry him from the jail in Denver, and eventually petitioned the governor of Colorado to quash the extradition request. The governor complied, and in July, Holliday joined Wyatt in Gunnison—apparently, the two had forgotten their spat in Albuquerque.[30]

In 1882, Gunnison was the West's latest silver boomtown. Prospectors from Leadville, a hundred miles to the northeast, moved into Gunnison in 1880 and established a number of silver mines in the vicinity. Within a year, the Denver & Rio Grande Railroad reached the town.[31] By 1882 the town looked much like Tombstone, with nearly eight thousand residents and scores of saloons. Gunnison's ascendancy was brief, however. While some precious metals were in the ground around Gunnison, the silver ore there proved to be far less valuable than the deposits near Leadville. By mid-1883, Gunnison's population had fallen by half.

Wyatt, together with Warren, Texas Jack, and another man whom Judd Riley, a Gunnison police officer, identified only as "Big Tip"—probably Dan Tipton, a friend from Tombstone who was with the posse in Albuquerque—arrived in Gunnison in May 1882, when the town was at its height. According to Riley, Wyatt's "gang" was "dodging the state officials who were hot on their trail." Initially, the heavily armed men made their camp alongside a river just outside town and ventured into town only to buy supplies. The Gunnison marshal, Sid Byers, briefly considered taking a posse to Wyatt's camp to arrest the fugitives. Faced with the prospect of confronting men with a reputation for deadly violence, however, Byers, according to Riley, "decided to accept the offer of a truce—that stretched into a year's residence in Gunnison," as Wyatt resolved "to stay in Gunnison and keep quiet until the storm blew over about the trouble in Arizona."[32]

To Riley, Wyatt and his band were "professional gamblers and bad men." Yet the group avoided violence in Gunnison, hoping to escape the attention of authorities seeking to extradite them to Arizona. Nor did they want to fall out of the good graces of the authorities in Gunnison. To deter any honor-culture shootings, whenever Holliday had too much to drink, Riley reported, one of the other men in the party "promptly took him in charge and he just disappeared."[33]

While Wyatt's group avoided violence, they had to make a living, and according to a local sheriff, they resorted to a familiar saloon hustle. Sometime during his stay in Gunnison, Wyatt and his confederates pulled the venerable gold-brick scam on a German visitor to Gunnison named Ritchie. This was exactly the same confidence game that Jim McIntire recalled Wyatt running in Mobeetie, Texas, in 1878. According to Doc Shores, the sheriff of Gunnison County, Wyatt and his friends led Ernest Biebel, a German-born saloon owner, "to believe they had stolen a gold brick, and Biebel replied, 'That is all right, I am a thief myself.' Ritchie, a German, got $2,000 together and paid Earp for the fake gold brick."[34]

Biebel was probably a party to the scam rather than a dupe—he was actually Wyatt's business associate. Sometime after arriving in Gunnison, Wyatt took over the faro table in Biebel's saloon. While Wyatt turned the cards himself some of the time, he employed other men to deal for him as well while he, at a discreet distance, backed up the dealer, ready to shoo away cheats, punters, or disgruntled losers—and most important, to dissuade other faro dealers from disrupting the game. During his year in Gunnison, Wyatt had to run off a competing faro dealer from another saloon, Ike Morris, who had accused Wyatt's dealer of cheating. According to Bat Masterson, Wyatt conceded that his dealer was a cheat and challenged Morris to do something about it. Morris instead left town.[35]

For a professional gambler, protecting territory from the inroads of competitors was as important as one's skill in turning cards. Much of the violence in Tombstone at the Oriental Saloon, when Holliday had shot the Oriental bartender Milt Joyce, and later when Luke Short had shot and killed Charlie Storms, had not simply been drunken shooting affrays but part of a territorial war between two aggregations of gamblers, the Slopers and the Easterners. The Slopers were primarily from California and Nevada, especially the mining towns of Bodie and Virginia City. The Easterners were largely from the Kansas cow towns.

Storms, who accused Short of cheating him before being shot, was not an ordinary cardplayer, but a well-known enforcer for the Slopers who had come to Tombstone to drive Short, Masterson, Holliday, Wyatt, and the other Easterners out of the Oriental. Holliday's shooting of Joyce had started as an altercation between Holliday and Johnny Tyler, another Sloper. Their argument had begun outside the Oriental. Disarmed by the town police to prevent violence, the men continued their argument inside the saloon. Holliday asked Joyce to return his pistol, which the police, as was their custom, had given to the bartender for safekeeping. Joyce, who was inclined to favor the Slopers, refused and forcibly removed the slender Holliday from the saloon; Holliday stormed off to find another pistol, returned to the Oriental, and opened fire at Joyce. Wyatt took part in this territorial battle as well; after Storms was killed, he got into an altercation at the Oriental with Storms's partner. The result of the violence was that the Easterners defended their control of the lucrative gaming tables of the Oriental from the inroads of the Slopers.[36]

By early summer 1883, Wyatt left the declining Gunnison and returned briefly to Dodge City, at the request of the fellow Easterners Short and Masterson. Short had returned to Dodge City to become part owner of the Long Branch Saloon. By the beginning of 1883, the Long Branch had become the most popular saloon in Dodge, taking customers from its various competitors, including Al Webster's Alamo Saloon. Webster enjoined Larry Deger, whom he had helped to elect mayor of Dodge City, to use the power of his office to undermine the Long Branch. In particular, Webster had the police selectively enforce the city's prostitution laws in his competitor's saloon. Short, in response to the police harassment, fired a shot at a deputy marshal and was arrested for assault. Deger ordered Short to leave town.[37]

Short was no more willing to be driven from his gambling tables in Dodge City than he had been to cede the faro tables of the Oriental to the Slopers. He called on Masterson, who rallied the Easterners, among them Neal Brown, Frank McLain, Charlie Bassett, and Wyatt. The Easterners, heavily armed, filtered into Dodge in mid-May.[38] Wyatt was one of the first of the gambling fraternity to arrive. Rather than initiating violence, however, he took a lead role in negotiating an end to the conflict with Deger, who had been the city marshal when Wyatt had served as a deputy marshal in Dodge City. By early June, the dispute had been settled, and Short returned to dealing faro at the Long Branch.[39]

From Dodge City, Wyatt made a brief foray to Eagle City, Idaho, near Coeur d'Alene, where prospectors had discovered gold in late 1882. Wyatt arrived with his brother James in late 1883 or early 1884. An account by a traveler to Eagle City in February 1884 noted that Wyatt had by then already acquired a saloon called the White Elephant. (To the traveler, Wyatt represented himself as having been, with his brothers, "cattle kings" in Arizona, but had suffered from "reverses of fortune and the crowding in of sheep men.")[40] In April, Wyatt and James purchased a large tent and established a dance hall (which meant, presumably, a brothel as well).

Wyatt also began speculating in mining claims and town lots. In Eagle City as in Tombstone, titles to town lots were rarely clear. In March, early in his tenure in Eagle City, a gun battle, with some fifty shots fired over ten minutes, erupted between opposing claimants to the same lot. Wyatt helped the Shoshone County deputy sheriff negotiate an end to the brief gunfight. According to a local report, both Wyatt and James, who also helped to restore order, showed "coolness" and "used their best endeavors to stop the shooting."[41]

Yet according to one of the participants in the gunfight, William Buzzard, Wyatt was not a neutral peacemaker but, in fact, the instigator of the violence. Buzzard maintained that Wyatt ran a lot-jumping scheme in Eagle City. Wyatt and his associates "would take a lot away from some one by force and sell it to an innocent purchaser. Then some others of the gang would come around, drive the man off, and re-sell it." The men on one side of the gunfight in Eagle City—Danny Ferguson, Jack Enright, and Albert Holman— were Wyatt's partners in his land-speculation syndicate. Holman was furthermore a partner with James and Wyatt in their dance-hall business. Buzzard charged that Wyatt had directed Ferguson, Enright, and Holman to drive him off his property. Enright, Buzzard alleged, "was a nervy man who did the gun-play act, while Earp, in his saloon, dance hall and gambling-house, arranged the plans and set the gang to work."[42]

Buzzard made his allegations in 1896, after Wyatt had suddenly reappeared in the national media as a result of his disputed decision in the Sharkey-Fitzsimmons fight. His charges might be dismissed as one of the many unsubstantiated allegations made against Wyatt during this period, yet Buzzard had nothing to gain by traducing Wyatt twelve years after the Eagle City gunfight. Unlike some of the more dubious allegations made in 1896, none of Buzzard's recollections contradict known facts. Moreover, in the three years leading up to the Eagle City gunfight, Wyatt had established a pattern of using violence or the threat of violence to drive competitors out of territory he or his allies coveted: he had done so at the Oriental in Tombstone, at Biebel's saloon in Gunnison, and at the Long Branch Saloon in Dodge City.

While Wyatt and his brothers were in Tombstone, their parents had relocated to Colton, California, just south of San Bernardino. By 1880, Wyatt's father, the old bootlegger, ran a saloon there.[43] After leaving Tombstone in March 1882, Virgil went first to Colton and from there to San Francisco to seek medical treatment for his shattered left arm.[44] During his brief stay in San Francisco, he was arrested by the police for dealing faro.[45] By 1887, Virgil had reunited with his father in Colton, and together they reconstructed the Earp family's accustomed version of booty politics: Nicholas was Colton's justice of the peace, and Virgil was constable. In February 1887, Virgil arrested eight "tramps" who had been asleep in a railroad boxcar and brought them before his father. The local newspaper complained that bringing the inoffensive vagrants to justice cost the town "some ten to fifteen dollars each for them in Justice fees, constable fees, board and attention."[46]

When the *National Police Gazette* picked up the story of the gamblers' battle in Dodge City in 1883, the tabloid identified Wyatt as "Wyatt Earp, of California."[47] Wyatt had not resided in California since he had lived on his father's rented farm in San Bernardino in the late 1860s. Indeed, he had avoided Colton—and his erstwhile wife, Mattie—in 1882 when he had headed for Gunnison. At some point after leaving Arizona, however, Wyatt made at least one trip to California—to San Francisco, specifically—to reunite with Josephine. By November 1884, Josephine had joined Wyatt in Albuquerque, where a local newspaper described her as Wyatt's "very handsome" wife.[48] No marriage certificate has survived, and the pair were probably never legally married, but in the 1910 census, Wyatt and Josephine claimed to have been married for twenty-five years, which would date their union to 1885. Josephine's unreliable memoirs record Gunnison as being one of the first places they were together after their marriage. It is unlikely that she was with Wyatt in Gunnison during his stay there in 1882, however; rather, their visit to Gunnison probably took place in 1885, while Wyatt and Josephine were based in Aspen, Colorado.

Aspen was another mining town that, like Gunnison, had spun off from Leadville. By May 1885, Wyatt opened a saloon, called the Fashion. Wyatt and Josephine remained in Aspen until late November, when a local newspaper reported that they had left town.[49] On a visit to Denver during their spell in Aspen, Wyatt and his new wife encountered his old friend Holliday, visibly weakened from tuberculosis. It would be their last meeting. Holliday died in a tuberculosis sanatorium in Colorado two years later.[50]

By the time Holliday died, Wyatt and Josephine had made their way to San Diego: the city directory for 1887 lists them as living at 946 Third Avenue. Just a few years before their arrival, San Diego had been a sleepy border town little distinguished from similarly undeveloped places along the American side of the border such as Yuma or El Paso. The population of San Diego in 1870 was a mere twenty-five hundred—less than half of that of Tombstone at its height. As the extension of railroads to western Kansas had been instrumental in creating the cow towns, San Diego's rise followed the completion of a rail connection to the east. In 1885, the Atchison, Topeka, and Santa Fe reached San Bernardino and connected to a subsidiary line, the California Southern, that ran to San Diego. The rail connection touched off a boom in population: the city's population rose from about five thousand in 1885 to thirty-five thousand by 1888. To accommodate the influx of new residents, enterprising property owners erected large canvas tents and rented cots for $1.50 a night.[51]

Along with the migrants to San Diego came a frenzied speculation in real estate. "From every direction in the city," wrote Theodore Van Dyke, a booster who took part in the boom, "came the
sound of the saw and the hammer; and at National City, the terminus of the Santa Fe Railroad, four miles up the bay, new houses not
yet ready for the paint were glimmering in all the freshness of lumber."[52] The scale of the real estate frenzy was enormous. On one day
in April 1887, a promoter sold twenty-five hundred San Diego lots.
By the end of the year, it was common for $200,000 in property to
change hands in a day.[53] The speculation in property in San Diego
dwarfed earlier real estate speculation Wyatt had known in Tombstone or Eagle City.

According to Van Dyke, who eventually became disillusioned by
the boom, San Diego beckoned to "the rich merchant" and "the
wealthy broker" as well as "schemers and promoters of all kinds,
with a little money which they were anxious to increase at the ex-
pense of some one else and without risking any of their own." In
what Van Dyke called "the shearing of the lambs," he described
how the schemers fleeced buyers. Among the bidders at property
auctions were dozens of cappers: men dressed as prosperous investors who were in league with the auctioneer. Whenever the bidding
lagged, one of the cappers offered a bid, thus driving up the price
that authentic buyers eventually paid. During breaks in the auction,
the cappers mingled with the authentic buyers, spreading rumors
about the other bidders. During such breaks, Van Dyke wrote, it
would be "noised about that the richest banker in Chicago, and the
richest beer brewer in Milwaukee" were among the crowd bidding
for lots.[54]

Wyatt bought property between Washington and University
Streets in the Hillcrest section of the city to the north of the city
center, and a downtown lot at the intersection of Beech and Union
Streets. He spent most of his time south of downtown, however, in
the Stingaree district near the waterfront, a neighborhood where San
Diego's brothels and gambling halls were clustered. On the northern edge of the Stingaree, where it met San Diego's central plaza,

Wyatt leased a building on Fifth Avenue that housed a saloon and gambling hall on the first floor and prostitutes' rooms on the upper floors. Not far away, on Sixth Avenue and E Street, was the St. James Hotel, where Wyatt ran another gambling hall.[55] Wyatt—and Virgil, who moved from Colton to San Diego in late 1887 or early 1888— were not just members of the San Diego gambling fraternity but its leaders. Between 1887 and 1889, San Diego was home to "more professional gamblers, 'con' and 'sure-thing' men, 'tin-horn gamblers' and all round crooks than in any city of like size in the world," according to Adalaska Pearson, the constable of National City, the Santa Fe terminus just south of San Diego. Virgil and Wyatt "were probably the most prominent among the gambling fraternity." At their gambling hall at the St. James, the "sky was the limit" in their faro games, according to Pearson.[56]

In San Diego, Wyatt was drawn to one of the most popular forms of wagering in late-nineteenth-century America: horse racing. Thoroughbred and harness racing had their origins in the rural backcountry. In the late nineteenth century, horse racing began its evolution toward urban spectator sport as a popular event at state fairs.[57] Thoroughbred racing was the main attraction at the California state fair in Stockton in September 1880, for example.[58] John Morrissey—a gambler, Tammany Hall politician, and former brothel bouncer and prizefighter—founded a racetrack in 1863 in Saratoga Springs, New York, to draw attention to his casino there. The gambling and horse-racing resort became popular with the political, financial, and literary elite. Over the next decades, several racetracks catering to elite patrons were founded, notably Pimlico in Baltimore, Maryland, in 1870 and Churchill Downs in Louisville, Kentucky, in 1875. In New York, harness racing rapidly developed the accoutrements of modern professional sports: organization, schedule, standard rules, record-keeping, and a complex system of betting.[59] By the end of the nineteenth century, tens of thousands of urban spectators attended races at these and other tracks, as professional sports joined vaudeville, cinemas, and amusement parks as sites of commercialized leisure for city dwellers.[60]

While the racetrack was an amusement for the working class, owning a stable of racehorses was an assertion of status for the bourgeois. Particularly in the West, horse racing was a way for men who had only recently made fortunes to assert their newfound gentility. Morrissey was one such man: an illiterate immigrant who worked as an enforcer for Irish gangs in New York as a teen, he had made his wealth as a gambler in Gold Rush California. In 1887, Morrissey offered to race his best horse, Montana Regent, against Volante, the winner of the 1885 American Derby and the prized racehorse of the California hotel and real estate magnate Elias "Lucky" Baldwin.[61] Like Morrissey, Baldwin was an arriviste who had made a fortunate investment in a seemingly worthless mine in Nevada shortly before the discovery of the Comstock Lode in 1859. For the nouveau riche such as Morrissey and Baldwin, a stable of horses signaled their aspirations to the status of landed gentry.[62] For such men, their willingness—indeed, eagerness—to wager large amounts on the outcome of a horse race broadcast their status.[63]

In San Diego, Wyatt met Baldwin and, like him, fashioned himself as a gentleman. Wyatt reputedly won the first of his horses from a player in his gambling hall. He assembled a stable of trotting horses and raced them at the Turf Club in Pacific Beach. He eventually branched out to thoroughbred racing at tracks in Tijuana, Mexico, about fifteen miles south of San Diego, as well as in Escondido, California, about fifteen miles to the north.[64]

For Wyatt, however, gambling was always, primarily, his profession rather than an assertion of status. Like any professional gambler of the nineteenth century, he looked for any way he could to increase his advantage. In 1896, Wyatt was accused of having fixed a race, held in Sempreviva, about ten miles east of Tijuana, on May 5, 1890, a Mexican holiday.[65] A bay horse, owned by an American, Harvey McCarthy, was the favorite to win the race over a roan owned by another American. Wyatt advised a group of American gamblers to bet on the roan because, he said, he had arranged with McCarthy to have the bay's jockey hold him back in the race. Yet McCarthy's bay won, and the men who had placed bets on the roan were indignant.

McCarthy, who was a deputy sheriff of San Diego County, protected Wyatt from the irate group.[66] The scheme shared an important similarity with the gold-brick scam (as it did with numerous confidence games): in the hope of making money dishonestly, dupes were enticed to put their own money forward.

Wyatt could similarly be scammed himself at the racetrack. In San Francisco in April 1893, Wyatt was pleased to see a filly he had trained, Lottie Mills, win the fourth race at the Bay District Race Track. Before the race, however, Wyatt had confided in a bookmaker, Billy Roeder, that Lottie Mills would win. Roeder placed so much money on Wyatt's horse that the horse's odds dropped to 1–2. Wyatt's winnings were thus considerably reduced. After the race, Roeder "snickered" at Wyatt, according to a newspaper account. Though his days as an Arizona vigilante were more than ten years behind him, Wyatt still had a capacity for impulsive violence. He slapped Roeder's face "until it was good and red. Then he turned Roeder around and kicked him until his back was sore."[67] In spite of this setback, Wyatt generally enjoyed success as a horse trainer—so much so that he aroused suspicions. "Mr. Earp seems to be a very shifty sort of trainer," a San Francisco newspaper observed in 1895, "for very few of his 'good things' go astray."[68]

Even more so than horse racing, Wyatt was drawn to prizefighting. Pugilism was part of the saloon world that Wyatt had long inhabited. In addition to offering billiards, gambling, and prostitutes, saloons staged cockfights, dogfights, and bare-knuckle prizefights. Before the adoption, in the late nineteenth century, of Marquess of Queensberry rules, which eliminated grappling and mandated that boxers wear gloves, these contests were brutal. Pugilists went a hundred rounds or more in a single bout, each round lasting a minute or less until one of the fighters was knocked down. The fallen fighter was usually allowed thirty seconds to get back to his feet. Holding, wrestling, and tripping were common. The sport took a toll on its participants: most nineteenth-century bare-knuckle fighters died in their midforties. By the 1850s, despite or perhaps because of its brutality, bare-knuckle prizefighting was the most popular sport in America.[69]

The response of cultural elites and legal authorities to bare-knuckle prizefighting was decidedly mixed. In San Francisco in 1885, the city government responded to the death of a pugilist from a cerebral hemorrhage incurred in a bout by passing a series of ordinances regulating boxing.[70] At the same time, however, well-to-do men who were concerned by what they perceived as the debilitating effects of cosmopolitanism on American masculinity embraced the brutal sport as an antidote to a feminizing Victorian culture.[71] An 1889 editorial in a San Francisco newspaper, while deploring the brutality of prizefighting, nonetheless praised a preacher who dealt with a "bully" who had heckled him during his sermon by knocking the man to the floor, holding him down, and "compelling him to repeat the Lord's Prayer and promise to behave like a good Christian ever afterward."[72] The editorialist's confused and contradictory praise for a pugilist preacher reflected the turn-of-the-century ideal of "muscular Christianity," which conflated physical fitness with moral health. Endicott Peabody, who had been the rector of the Episcopalian church in Tombstone in 1882, emerged as a leading proponent of the creed of Christian manliness as headmaster of the Groton preparatory school.[73] Since his time in Kansas, Wyatt had balanced a reputation for physical violence with an outward appearance of Christian rectitude. In 1888, as the doctrine of muscular Christianity was taking hold, a research assistant for the California popular historian Hubert Howe Bancroft described Wyatt as a man who had "killed over a dozen stage robbers, murderers, and cattle thieves." At the same time, the researcher observed, "socially, he could be taken for a minister."[74]

In the early nineteenth century, bare-knuckle prizefighting had been centered in New York. In the 1860s, however, it shifted westward, drawn to the male-dominated saloon subculture of ranching and mining regions.[75] In California saloons, prizefighting joined yet more violent entertainments; in addition to cockfighting and dog-fighting, saloons promoted both bullfighting and bull-and-bear fighting.[76] Wyatt had been part of that culture in the late 1860s when he had worked with Virgil as a freighter and had learned the rudiments of pugilism. By the time he returned to California in the mid-1880s, Wyatt was not just a practitioner of fisticuffs but a promoter.

Wyatt promoted several bouts in Tijuana and San Diego between midlevel pugilists.[77] For instance, in June 1888, Wyatt organized a prizefight at one of his San Diego gambling halls in order to draw patrons to his tables. A reporter for the *Los Angeles Tribune* described the crowd as a "half-drunken, swearing mob" that "surged in, smashing the seats, tearing the canvas, cursing anything and anybody." Moreover, the "street in front of the saloons was thronged with people, who crowded around the tables of the tin-horn gamblers. This fraternity was there in full force: the 'wheel of fortune,' the 'smiler' or shell-game manipulator, the 'monte' dealer, the 'chuck-a-luck' dice expert and others, were all there." Before the bout could begin, however, the police broke in and dispersed the crowd, declaring that the fight would not take place—most California municipalities barred bare-knuckle prizefighting, while allowing the more gentlemanly "glove contests" under Marquess of Queensberry rules.[78]

At the announcement that the fight would not take place, "there arose a mingled snarl and yell of rage from the crowd, and a rush was made for the officers." Before the crowd rioted, Wyatt appeared and promised the crowd that they would stage the fight just across the border in Tijuana, in a wooden amphitheater used for bullfighting. When the crowd reassembled across the border, however, the bout was once again delayed by the arrival of Mexican soldiers. Wyatt "parlayed" with the sergeant who was in command and determined that a $60 bribe to the local judge would ensure that the bout could go forward. "A collection was taken up, the amount quickly raised, and the fight came off."

As for the prizefight itself, the Los Angeles reporter was appalled. "It was a bloody contest. Both men were reeking from head to toe with gore. Their backs were crimson with it. Their faces were soon smashed and turned into a pulpy, purplish, swollen caricature of the human countenance." The crowd was enthralled, however. When one of the boxers "fell as if dead, a roar of delight was given.

When he was found only to be stunned, there was evident disappointment."[79]

By the end of the century, a wider acceptance of the sport was made possible by fighters' embrace of the Marquess of Queensberry rules. (Ironically, the rules requiring gloves made the sport more rather than less dangerous in one respect: bare-knuckle prizefighters, unlike gloved fighters, rarely struck each other on the head, out of fear of breaking the bones in their hands.) John L. Sullivan, who had risen to preeminence as a bare-knuckle fighter, offered in March 1892 to defend his claim to be heavyweight champion against anyone—but the fight had to be according to Marquess of Queensberry rules. Six months later, a San Francisco boxer, James J. "Gentleman Jim" Corbett, finessed his way to a defeat of Sullivan for the heavyweight title in a bout in New Orleans.[80] Corbett was a handsome and well-spoken champion who boxed like a fencer, darting in to jab before pulling away. He defended his title only once, in 1894, against a journeyman boxer whom he knocked out in the third round. Efforts to schedule a bout in Texas against the main challenger, Bob Fitzsimmons, fell through when state authorities prevented the match from taking place. In November 1895, Corbett, who had already played the lead role in a drama entitled *Gentleman Jack*, gave up the heavyweight championship to play a boxer, Ned Cornell, onstage in *A Naval Cadet*—a touring production that paid him $1,000 a week.[81] Corbett's abdication threw the loosely organized boxing world into disarray. This chaos opened the way for Wyatt, who had refereed only a few low-level bouts, to find himself in the ring between Fitzsimmons and Tom Sharkey in December 1896.

By the time of Corbett's abdication, Wyatt's fortunes were in decline. He had moved to San Francisco in 1891, after the real estate bubble in southern California had burst.[82] He held on to his San Diego property as its value plummeted, but, unable to pay the taxes on the property, he was forced to sell the lots. He continued to race horses, but by 1896 he no longer owned them. Instead, he trained horses on behalf of their owner, a woman in Santa Rosa.

Appearing in court after the 1896 fight, Wyatt testified that he "owned only the clothes on his back." This assertion might have been not far from the truth: he had never repaid over $1,000 he owed to Arizona creditors; had run up a tab of $200 at the restaurant at the Ingleside racetrack; owed a central California attorney about $200; and owed about $140 to other creditors in San Francisco.[83] To make ends meet, he took a job as a bodyguard for Andrew Lawrence, the managing editor of the *San Francisco Examiner*, for $50 a week.[84]

When he resigned his title, Corbett gave the title to Peter Maher, who had recently defeated another heavyweight contender, Steve O'Donnell, in a first-round knockout. Maher, who would have preferred to fight Corbett for a large, guaranteed purse and a shot at the title, was in turn knocked out in the first round in a bout against Fitzsimmons in Mexico, just across the border from tiny Langtry, Texas, in February 1896. Fitzsimmons was declared champion, but Corbett had begun to regret his decision to leave the ring, and boxing enthusiasts believed that Fitzsimmons would have to defeat Corbett to legitimize his title. In September 1896, the two agreed to meet in March 1897. In the meantime, Fitzsimmons was scheduled to fight a tune-up match against Sharkey in San Francisco.

Fitzsimmons was nearly six feet tall, had a relatively long reach, and, most notably, was exceptionally light for a heavyweight boxer. A former middleweight champion at 158 pounds, he weighed in at just over 173 pounds for his fight with Sharkey—considerably less than the average turn-of-the-century heavyweight. Most of his weight was in his upper body: he had worked as a blacksmith in New Zealand as a young man and had a broad back and thickly muscled arms. His legs, however, were so thin that they embarrassed him; to conceal them, he often fought wearing long woolen underwear beneath his boxing trunks. Because of his upper-body strength, he was a fearsome puncher—in November 1894 an opponent whom Fitzsimmons had knocked out in an exhibition died the next day. Fitzsimmons was charged with manslaughter, tried, and acquitted in the summer of 1895.[85]

Sharkey was four inches shorter, ten pounds heavier, and ten years younger than Fitzsimmons. In an era when middle- and upper-class men, wary of the debilitating comforts of cosmopolitan life, embraced the boisterous, working-class physicality of boxing, the combatants wore their working-class identities proudly: Fitzsimmons was the "Fighting Blacksmith"; Sharkey, a veteran of the U.S. Navy, was "Sailor Tom."[86] Hardly a "scientific" boxer like Fitzsimmons, Sharkey was a stocky, uncompromising brute who went straight for his opponents, making little effort to avoid their blows, to slug them into submission. When frustrated, he shoved and grappled with his opponent. Corbett fought him in a four-round bout at the Mechanics' Pavilion in San Francisco in June 1896. Frustrated by Corbett's footwork, Sharkey grabbed Corbett around the neck and threw him to the canvas in the third round. In the fourth, Sharkey threw punches both at Corbett and at the referee when he tried to break the two fighters out of a clinch. When the final bell rang, three policemen had to restrain Sharkey from going after his opponent.[87]

Martin Julian, Fitzsimmons's brother-in-law and manager, and Danny Lynch, Sharkey's manager, had agreed to a fight, according to Marquess of Queensberry rules, for a purse of $10,000. Fitzsimmons, the nominal heavyweight champion going into his fight with Sharkey, did not believe that Sharkey would pose much of a problem for him. The casualness with which Julian and Fitzsimmons approached the fight contributed to the controversy that erupted. Though Fitzsimmons had more standing in the sport, Julian did not insist on having the right to approve the referee for the fight. According to the agreement between the two fighters, each side could propose referees for the bout; and each side could veto a proposed referee. If the two sides could not agree, then the National Athletic Club, the San Francisco boxing club that was staging the fight, would select the referee.[88]

Julian suggested eight men as potential referees, including the well-respected referee Hiram Cook of San Francisco, who had refereed more than a dozen professional fights. Lynch vetoed every suggestion. According to Billy Smith, the San Francisco ironworker Lynch had hired to help train Sharkey, Lynch asked Smith "whether he was sufficiently intimate with Cook to 'talk business' with him." Smith answered that "he knew Cook pretty well, but not well enough for that." Lynch himself then interviewed Cook and reported back to the Sharkey camp that "Cook would not do." Sharkey and Lynch then settled on Wyatt, whom they referred to as a "racehorse man." They would offer Wyatt $2,500 to insure Sharkey's victory. Rather than suggest Wyatt themselves, Sharkey and Lynch "intended to object to every referee proposed by the other side, and if they didn't agree upon a referee by 12 o'clock of the day of the fight the club would choose the referee" they wanted.[89]

If the camps could not agree on a referee, the choice was in the hands of J. J. Gibbs and J. D. Groom, the leaders of the National Athletic Club, neither of whom knew Wyatt. He was suggested to them by Andrew Lawrence, the *Examiner* editor. On December 5, two days after the fight, Groom explained that the day before the fight, Lawrence had asked to see him, ostensibly about some tickets to the fight. At the meeting, Lawrence recommended his body-guard as referee: "Select Wyatt Earp. I know he's as good a man as you can get." Gibbs likewise told reporters on December 5 that "it was at Andy Lawrence's suggestion Wyatt Earp went in as referee."[90] The next day, Gibbs and Groom met Wyatt at the Baldwin Hotel—by happenstance, they insisted. Walking through the hotel lobby, they spotted Wyatt, which Groom called "a strange coincidence." The three retired to a quiet corner. Upon being asked to referee the heavyweight championship bout, Wyatt, according to Groom, "hesitated a moment and said, 'Well, I consider it an honor, and consent to serve.'"[91] Wyatt, conscious of the status that officiating at a championship bout would bring, testified that he said, "It would be a little bit of tone to act as referee where the two best men in the world were about to come together."[92]

At ten o'clock on the morning of the fight, according to Sharkey's trainer, Sharkey's camp "had the referee they wanted." The arrangement was that "Fitzsimmons would lose on a foul in the first round—that it had been agreed that Earp would give him the fight on a foul." Wyatt would call a foul on "the first blow that Fitz would deliver on Sharkey's body."[93] Wyatt's reward would be $2,500—enough to settle his various debts. As soon as word that Wyatt was to referee the bout got out, the odds against Sharkey began to drop.[94] Lawrence himself sent one of his reporters to a "pool room" to place a large bet on Sharkey.[95]

When Julian had first been informed of the choice of Wyatt, he had made no objection. By the time of the fight, however, he had heard the rumors of a fix and confronted Wyatt at the arena, saying "that I knew that he was crooked and that he was fixed for Sharkey, and that the best thing that he could do would be to step out and allow the club to select another referee." Julian threatened to denounce Wyatt to the crowd of fifteen thousand if he refused to step aside: "I told him if he got into that ring I would stand up before the audience and tell what I knew about him. He answered that he had been selected by the club and he was going to stay, and he walked away laughing."[96] Wyatt remembered the end of the conversation differently. He testified that he denied the accusations and that Julian was mollified. "I told him that there was nothing in it as far as I knew; that I would give him a fair, square show, the same as I would to Mr. Sharkey. Julian said, 'I am satisfied.'"[97]

Nonetheless, when Wyatt was announced as the referee, Julian spoke to the crowd. "When we first heard that Mr. Earp had been selected it was satisfactory to us," he said. "But since 6:30 o'clock this evening several sporting men belonging to San Francisco have come and told us that the referee is fixed."[98] Despite these serious misgivings, Fitzsimmons agreed to fight. Had he refused, he would have been accused of having been afraid to meet Sharkey in the ring.

When Wyatt, having grudgingly been approved by Fitzsimmons to referee the fight, removed his coat, another surprise awaited: he had a revolver under his coat. A San Francisco police officer confiscated the weapon. A day after the fight, Wyatt was charged with violating the city ordinance against carrying concealed weapons. In court, Wyatt did not provide the obvious explanation as to why he had the weapon: he was Lawrence's bodyguard. Officially, he was no such thing. On the *Examiner's* books, he was listed as a "library attaché." Rather, he told the court that he carried the weapon to protect himself because "a number of Arizona criminals whom he had been instrumental in sending to prison, had vowed to kill him on sight." He was fined the minimum amount, $50.[99]

When Wyatt appeared in court to face the gun charge, he was presented with a claim for $170.45 from a Stockton, California, lawyer, J. G. Swinnerton. In 1895, three con men had swindled a Lodi, California, farmer out of $2,000 using the gold-brick scheme. The men were arrested and jailed in Stockton. According to the *San Francisco Call*, after their arrest, Wyatt "appeared on the scene and showed his friendship for the men by making efforts to get them released." He hired Swinnerton, who secured light sentences. Wyatt, however, left town without paying Swinnerton's fee. When Wyatt's name appeared in the newspapers after the Sharkey-Fitzsimmons fight, Swinnerton took notice and placed a lien on any moneys Wyatt was due to receive for acting as referee.[100]

Sharkey and Fitzsimmons had entered the ring at ten o'clock in the evening. Julian's denunciation of Wyatt and the confiscation of Wyatt's revolver consumed three-quarters of an hour, however, so it was thus close to eleven when the bout began. Wary that the referee would call a foul at the slightest provocation, Julian advised Fitzsimmons "to fight at long range and to be very careful not to give the least opening to any one to claim a foul."[101] Indeed, according to a ringside reporter, Fitzsimmons opened the fight by "fiddling for an opening." The champion easily dodged Sharkey's swings—indeed, he "jump[ed] aside laughing." Forgoing body blows, which might provide an excuse for Wyatt to call a foul, Fitzsimmons concentrated on Sharkey's head, connecting at least three times—on the last blow, knocking Sharkey to the floor. When the gong sounded, Sharkey went to his corner "very groggy" and Fitzsimmons "very cool." Fitzsimmons was on his feet before the gong sounded to start the second round, while Sharkey was "very shaky." Fitzsimmons continued to batter Sharkey's head and, at the end of the round, "went to his corner laughing."[102] By contrast, according to Sharkey's trainer, Smith, "at the end of the second round Sharkey was considerably dazed from the effects of the punches on the head administered by Fitzsimmons, and he was very anxious to know what round it was."[103]

Still wary of a foul, in the third round, Fitzsimmons continued "feinting and fiddling." When the round ended, the crowd began cheering Sharkey and continued to do so during the entire break between the rounds. They were well aware that in his four-round bout against Corbett, Sharkey had stormed into the fourth round and nearly pummeled Corbett into submission. When the gong rang, Sharkey charged out and pounded Fitzsimmons on the body before pushing him to the canvas. Fitzsimmons remained "cool," however, and continued his "fiddling." He managed to land blows on Sharkey's head and face, yet he continued to avoid striking Sharkey's body.

Becoming desperate in the fifth round, Sharkey, in the clinch, grabbed Fitzsimmons by the legs and tried to upend him. The crowd cried "Foul," but Wyatt ignored them. Toward the end of the round, Fitzsimmons, having trapped Sharkey in his corner, knocked him to the canvas again—indeed, Sharkey slipped through the ropes and fell to the floor of the arena. Fitzsimmons helped his opponent back into the ring just as the gong ended the round. Sharkey "stagger[ed] to his corner very groggy"; Fitzsimmons walked back to his corner "very cool and laughing," then ignored his trainers' efforts to rub him down as he paced in his corner, waiting for the next round to begin.

By the sixth round, the pummeling Fitzsimmons had administered to Sharkey's face was noticeable. Sharkey's cheek was cut badly and his nose was bleeding. In the seventh, Fitzsimmons opened a cut above Sharkey's eye that bled profusely. Sensing that the end of the fight was near, Fitzsimmons attempted his first body blow in the sixth, followed by an uppercut—but Sharkey avoided the second blow. Fitzsimmons tried a few more in the seventh, but was unable to follow his body blows with a knockout blow to the head.[104] In the eighth, however, Sharkey was too addled to withstand Fitzsimmons's combination of a right to the face, a left to the body, and a right uppercut. According to George Allen, one of Sharkey's trainers, the last punch knocked Sharkey "into a sitting position, after which he fell back on the flat of his back." Sharkey "was not knocked out or unconscious but he was as limp as a wet rag and groaned."[105] Smith, Sharkey's other trainer, carried him to his corner, where, he testified, Lynch "came up and whispered, 'Now, Tom, keep your hands down and pretend to be in great pain.'" Sharkey was so addled by Fitzsimmons's blows to his head, however, that "he seemed to be dazed and didn't know what he was doing, and he forgot to put his hands down, but kept them on his head and over his ears, where he said he had pains."[106]

Sharkey's confusion made no difference: he had finally fallen to the canvas from a blow to the body—not, owing to Fitzsimmons's caution, in the first round, but in the eighth. Wyatt called Fitzsimmons for a foul—then quickly retrieved his coat and left the arena before most spectators realized that he had awarded the fight to Sharkey. William Abbott, a ringside spectator who helped carry Sharkey to his dressing room, thought that the fighter was not badly injured—but he had little chance to find out, as Lynch ordered him out of the dressing room.[107] Nor did Lynch permit any physicians to examine Sharkey, other than an unlicensed quack, "Dr. Lee," who applied leeches to Sharkey's ear. When the resident physician of the National Athletic Club was permitted to examine Sharkey the day after the fight, he determined that "Sharkey had not been injured in the manner alleged." George Allen, the trainer, agreed that Sharkey did not seem as if he had been struck below the belt. When cross-examined by Sharkey's lawyer during the court proceedings after the fight, Allen was asked whether he had ever seen a boxer who had suffered such an injury. To the lawyer's surprise, Allen answered that he had, and in that case, the man's groin was so swollen that his boxing trunks had to be cut off him.[108]

Fitzsimmons, who was not only unmarked but "not even breathing hard" after the fight, according to a reporter, enjoined Sharkey from cashing the $10,000 check due the winner. On December 10, the principals in the event appeared in court to give depositions: Sharkey's trainers Smith and Allen; Lynch; Julian; Fitzsimmons; the National Athletic Club physician; and Wyatt. The proceeding proved to be of no avail for Fitzsimmons: after hearing several days of testimony, the judge threw up his hands and announced that the contest had been an illegal prizefight over which the court had no jurisdiction. He did suggest, however, that everyone associated with the bout "had violated the statute prohibiting prize-fighting and were amenable to indictment."[109]

Fitzsimmons was soon vindicated. In March 1897, he knocked out Corbett in the fourteenth round in a bout in Carson City, Nevada, and was declared heavyweight champion. Though he lost the title two years later to James Jeffries, who outweighed him by forty pounds, he continued fighting, dropping down to become champion of the new light-heavyweight division in 1903. Before he left the heavyweight ranks, however, he fought Sharkey again, in 1900, at Coney Island. He knocked out "Sailor Tom" in the second round.

There was no immediate vindication for Wyatt, however, nor would there ever again be obscurity. The 1896 prizefight returned him to the public eye. As Americans read about the man who had rendered this controversial decision, they were reminded—or learned for the first time—of the deadly events in Arizona in the 1880s. Had it not been for the prizefight, Wyatt might have remained as obscure as other nineteenth-century gunfighters such as Walter Crow or Tom Horn—men who had fearsome local reputations in their day but never became national media icons. Trying to escape his celebrity, Wyatt liquidated what possessions he and Josephine had and decamped for remote Yuma, Arizona. In August 1897, he left from there for the Yukon, intending to open another saloon in another mining town even farther from media scrutiny.[110] Thirty years before, Wyatt could have outrun the ignominy in San Francisco and reinvented himself in a new town where he was unknown. In the new media age, however, Wyatt's reputation would precede him wherever he went.

7

THE SHADOWS
OF THE PAST

In the first decades of the twentieth century, Wyatt spent much of his time in the deserts of southern California and southwestern Nevada. Ostensibly, Wyatt was in the desert to manage his mining claims. In early 1929, only a few weeks after Wyatt's death, Stuart Lake wrote an entry for Wyatt in the *Encyclopedia Americana* that put a palmy gloss on this last chapter of Wyatt's life: "From 1905 on Wyatt Earp was active at his mining and oil properties and lived the life of a prosperous business man."[1] Yet the claims yielded little, if any, income. Wyatt and Josephine inhabited a primitive cabin near his claim; the cheap one-room bungalow in Los Angeles they sometimes rented in the summer when the desert heat became unbearable was luxurious by comparison.[2] They lived partly on charity, staying as extended guests in the homes of friends in Los Angeles and living on money that Josephine's well-to-do sister sent her.[3]

The Earps' cabin in the desert was the best they could afford— but just as important, the remoteness of the little homestead kept Wyatt out of the glare of the media. Despite his efforts to escape media attention, however, Wyatt continued to make headlines. Deeply unpopular because of his suspicious decision in the 1896 bout between Sharkey and Fitzsimmons, news reports repeatedly suggested that the aging Wyatt had received his comeuppance. In April 1900, the *Call*—his old nemesis—reported that the fifty-two-year-old

Wyatt, during a visit to San Francisco, started a barroom argument with a racehorse owner, Tom Mulqueen, that ended with Mulqueen's punching Wyatt into unconsciousness.[4] That summer, upon his return to Nome, Alaska, where Wyatt managed a saloon until late 1901, it was erroneously reported in the national press that Wyatt had been shot.[5] The reports of the shooting doubtless confused Wyatt with his younger brother, Warren. After the disintegration of the vigilante posse, Warren had returned to Arizona, where he was shot and killed in a saloon in Willcox, a town in Cochise County, in July 1900.[6]

The shooting of Warren was one of several deaths in the Earp family at the turn of the century. Wyatt's mother, Virginia, died in 1893. His father, Nicholas, who had married Virginia in 1839 within months of the death of his first wife, repeated that pattern in 1893. Nine months after Virginia died, eighty-year-old Nicholas married Annie Elizabeth Cadd, a fifty-one-year-old widow. By 1900, however, Nicholas was living with his daughter Adelia's family in Redlands, California; his third wife, who lived until 1931, was not part of the household. Nicholas, who died in 1907, spent the last years of his life in a soldiers' home outside Los Angeles. Virgil died of pneumonia in 1905, leaving Wyatt as the last surviving participant of the 1881 Tombstone gunfight.[7]

Wyatt spent these years in the deserts of the Lower Colorado River Basin, making the rounds of the last mining boomtowns in North America. In early 1902, Wyatt and Josephine made their way to a silver town, Tonopah, Nevada, where Wyatt once more managed a saloon, the Northern. James, whose wife, Bessie, had died in 1887, joined them in Tonopah in mid-1902. By 1905, Wyatt had moved thirty miles south to Goldfield, Nevada, where a local newspaper reported, somewhat wishfully, that he had "forsworn the green cloth and the automatic revolver."[8] Virgil briefly joined Wyatt in Goldfield: he was sworn in as an Esmeralda County deputy sheriff in January, only ten months before his death.[9] The next year Wyatt and Josephine resumed their wandering; a Prescott, Arizona, newspaper reported them near Needles, California, in late 1906 "completely outfitted for desert traveling."[10] Wyatt moved on to Searchlight, Nevada, in 1907, then returned to southern California; in 1908, he was promoting the mining possibilities of the California desert east of San Diego.[11]

Wyatt had forsworn neither the green cloth nor the revolver, however. To make ends meet, he continued to sign on as hired muscle despite his advancing years. In 1910, when he was sixty-two years old, he was one of two dozen men hired by the American Trona Company to protect some of its borax mining claims near Death Valley from a competing company that claimed the same site. Wyatt's group traveled to the region by automobile, pitched tents on the site, and set to work surveying the claim. When men hired by the competition confronted them, Wyatt fired a round at the feet of their leader, causing the men to scatter. When U.S. marshals arrested Wyatt's group for trespassing, Wyatt, hoping to avoid media attention, gave his name as "W. Stapp."[12]

A year later, Wyatt was arrested again, this time by the Los Angeles police's bunco squad, who charged Wyatt with running a crooked faro game. Claiming that he operated a faro bank as an employee, Wyatt proposed to a faro player, J. Y. Peterson, that Wyatt would use a marked deck, so that Peterson could successfully buck the tiger. Wyatt suggested that Peterson bring $2,500 to the game and that the two of them would then split the winnings. Peterson, correctly surmising that it was his $2,500 that Wyatt was after, informed the police, who arrested Wyatt and two other men involved in the scheme. Once again, Wyatt gave his name as W. Stapp—but to no avail. The arrest of the referee from the disputed fight between Sharkey and Fitzsimmons made national news. Though he was unable to make the $500 bail, Wyatt avoided jail time: the police had raided the game too early, before the scam had taken place. The case was dismissed.[13]

Wyatt evaded a jail term, but this latest arrest improved neither his finances nor his reputation. The negative media attention that had followed him after the 1896 debacle so vexed him that to escape it he had removed himself to some of the most remote places in North America: Nome, Alaska, and the California and Nevada deserts. A similar strategy had worked for him in the 1870s, when he had repeatedly escaped the consequences of his deeds and outrun his reputation by moving to new towns. By the twentieth century, however, American media culture was too well developed and Wyatt's celebrity too secure for him ever again to become anonymous.

Unable to outrun the media, instead Wyatt resolved to remake his reputation once more. Four decades before his arrest in Los Angeles, he had lied to his sister Adelia about his arrests in the Indian Territory and Illinois by telling her that he had been hunting bison in the southern plains. He had been reinventing his past ever since. Ironically, it was during a visit with Adelia, who lived near San Bernardino, that he received the inspiration for rebuilding his shattered reputation in the form of a gift from Adelia's husband, William Edwards: a copy of Owen Wister's 1902 novel, *The Virginian*.[14]

Wyatt Earp was not a bookish man, but his brother-in-law chose the gift well. *The Virginian* was a widely read novel in the first years of the twentieth century: it was a bestseller for a year after it was published and went through fifteen printings in its first eight months. It was quickly adapted as a stage drama starring the actor William S. Hart; in 1914, Cecil B. DeMille made a film version.[15] Beyond its general popularity, the novel could not have failed to have a special appeal to Wyatt, who could see himself—or, rather, an ideal version of himself—in the hero. Wister's main character, the Virginian, is a rough-hewn and uneducated ranch hand, but Wister presents him as innately noble and a born leader. The idea that men of quality should lead society—and that the American West was a proving ground for leadership—was one of the main themes of the novel.[16] For Wister, nobility was measured by manliness—much as Endicott Peabody's notion of "muscular Christianity" conflated morality and rugged physicality. Both notions emerged at the end of the nineteenth century, as a robustly virile ideal of masculinity replaced the midcentury ideal of the entrepreneurial man.[17] In Wister's hero, Wyatt could see himself as he wished to be: a child of the backcountry who had risen to dominance in the cutthroat, male-dominated world of cow towns and mining camps. This made him not a western "bad man," as some newspapers characterized him, but a natural aristocrat.[18]

The two most dramatic episodes in the novel must have had an effect on Wyatt. In the last pages of the novel, the Virginian confronts the villain, a rustler called Trampas, in a gunfight. The gunfight is made necessary by Trampas's public insults. The Virginian explains, "I expect he knows he went too far in the hearing of others to go back on his threat. He will have to go on to the finish now." The Virginian, too, has no other recourse: he must meet Trampas or be thought a coward. The two meet in the street and exchange gunfire; the Virginian kills Trampas; and the townspeople congratulate him for having rid the settlement of the bandit. The scenario—the public insults, the honor-culture requirement to meet challenges, and the gunfight in a street—were all too familiar to Wyatt. Yet in the novel, the Virginian guns down Trampas and is immediately congratulated by the townspeople, who dismiss the notion that there would be any legal consequences for the killing. Unlike Wyatt, who endured a monthlong hearing after the 1881 gunfight, in Wister's tale, the fictional gunman's resort to deadly violence is unquestionably justified.

The most affecting scene in *The Virginian*, and the one that must have had the greatest impact on Wyatt, was a description of vigilante justice. The Virginian is a member of a posse on the trail of cattle rustlers. When the posse apprehends the thieves, one of them is discovered to be the Virginian's old friend. The Virginian has no desire to see his friend hanged, but, as he puts it, "A man goes through with his responsibilities." Vigilante justice, in Wister's telling, is not an angry impulse but a sober imposition of justice in a corrupt Old West that would otherwise know no law. Here, Wyatt found the justification that had long eluded him for his vigilante killing spree. The killings were not acts of vengeance but of justice.

Before long, Wyatt, having put a Wisterian gloss on his past, was regaling Hollywood filmmakers with his recollections. In 1914, when

Paramount Pictures released a film version of *The Virginian*, Wyatt made his first visit to a Los Angeles film studio. He met the director Raoul Walsh as he was finishing work on his epic *The Life of General Villa*. Wyatt charmed both Walsh and Charlie Chaplin with tales of his past.[19] Soon, Wyatt established himself as an informal adviser on Westerns, and the director Allan Dwan gave him a walk-on role in a 1916 Douglas Fairbanks Western, *The Half-Breed*.[20] In 1923, Wyatt's best friend from the studios, the Western film actor and director William S. Hart, created a Wyatt Earp character for his film *Wild Bill Hickok*.[21] Wyatt's familiarity with Hollywood convinced him to try to use the new media to his own advantage, defining himself as he wanted to be remembered. "Many wrong impressions of the early days of Tombstone and myself have been created," he wrote to Hart in 1923. "I am not going to live to the age of Methuselah, and any wrong impression, I want to make right before I go away. The screen could do all this." Wyatt believed that Hart might be "the master mind" of a film of Wyatt's adventures.[22] Perhaps Hart, who was in his late fifties, would produce or direct and a younger cowboy actor such as Tom Mix, whom Wyatt had also befriended, might star.

Hart, a New York–born stage actor who had risen to prominence in dramas such as *Ben-Hur* and *The Man in the Iron Mask*, became a star on the stage playing roles in the Western dramas *The Squaw Man* and *The Virginian*. As he came to be identified with Western roles, he began to inflate his brief childhood stints in small towns in Illinois and Minnesota to present himself as an authentic son of the West. By the time he wrote his autobiography in 1929, he felt confident enough to critique Wister's novel for being "at variance with cowboy life as I knew it."[23] In the early 1910s he moved to Los Angeles and began making Western films; from the mid-1910s until the mid-1920s he was easily the most popular and recognizable Western film star. Wyatt knew him at least as early as 1920; he felt himself on close enough terms with Hart in 1922 to offer him words of encouragement during the actor's divorce proceedings. (Hart, aged fifty-seven, had married a much younger starlet;

the couple separated eight months later while she was pregnant.) Wyatt, no stranger either to spousal abandonment or negative media attention, wrote, "I am your friend and I know you have nothing to regret."[24]

Taken both with Hart and with his films, Wyatt gradually became less distrustful of the new media culture. His receptivity to film was common for early-twentieth-century Americans; short, silent newsreels showing prominent Americans in their homes, for instance, not only struck a chord with American viewers but legitimized the opening of previously private spheres of home and family to public scrutiny.[25] Wyatt regaled Hart with stories of his past, and the actor encouraged Wyatt to put his reminiscences into print—as a prelude to a film of Earp's life. Wyatt hoped Hart would not only produce the film but play the part of the hero.[26] Whether Hart, who made what turned out to be his last film at age sixty-one in 1925, would have followed through and played Earp on-screen seems unlikely. Wyatt's stated desire to see Hart play him (he wrote to Hart in 1925, "If it goes on the screen at all, I would not want anyone but you to play the role") was either naïveté or flattery.[27]

Toward the end of the 1910s Wyatt found a Los Angeles writer with a connection to Cochise County, Forrestine Hooker, who agreed to write his story.[28] The daughter of an army officer, Charles Lawrence Cooper, Forrestine—nicknamed Birdie—grew up at army posts throughout the West. Fort Grant in southern Arizona was one of her father's last postings. He was ordered there in 1885, when Birdie was eighteen. There she met her future husband, Edwin Hooker, the son of the cattle baron and Earp supporter Henry Hooker. By 1904, Birdie was living in Los Angeles and had published the first of over one hundred magazine stories.[29]

Hooker probably intended to publish her tale of Wyatt's experiences, "An Arizona Vendetta," as a three- or four-part serial in a weekly magazine such as the *Saturday Evening Post*. The tightly organized story, which starts in 1879, with Wyatt's arrival in Tombstone, and ends with the alleged killing of Ringo in 1882, made Wyatt's vigilantism central. The pivotal moment in the tale is not the gunfight of October 1881, but Morgan's murder in March 1882. In Hooker's account, Wyatt has a premonition that Morgan—who is described as "little more than a boy" but was, in fact, thirty years old when he died—will be killed and warns him against going to the billiards hall where he is shot. After Morgan's death, Wyatt is transformed. "Wyatt Earp had been merely an officer of the law, carrying out his oath of office conscientiously at the risk of his life, but now he was a man who had sworn a sacred oath of vendetta and until that oath to his dying brother was fulfilled, it would drive him day and night."[30]

Hooker's tale was vivid and smartly paced, in the manner of the Western dime novel. Yet Wyatt had in mind Owen Wister's flowery prose and arch pronouncements of a hero's inner nobility, and Hooker's manuscript fell short in these respects. Worse still, Hooker described Wyatt's vigilantism not as justice but as a "vendetta." Hooker depicted the cowboys Wyatt pursued as guilty of murdering Morgan, made clear that in the corrupt Arizona legal system of 1882 they would not have been brought to justice, and even invented a denouement in which President Chester Arthur offers a pardon to Wyatt because he had "merely done his duty."[31] Wyatt nonetheless emerges from the manuscript as a man who dispensed not dispassionate justice but ruthless vengeance. He refused to allow the manuscript to be published.

Having rejected Hooker's manuscript, Wyatt turned to a young friend, John Flood, to write the biography. Wyatt had met Flood, a former Bucknell University track athlete who was many years younger than he, during his years in southern California; the younger man regarded Earp with unqualified admiration. Wyatt selected Flood not because Flood had any experience as a writer but because his loyalty to Wyatt was unquestioned. Flood, attempting an inept imitation of Wister, had a penchant for grandiloquent exposition. As flawed as the manuscript's style may have been, Wyatt approved of it as the definitive account of his life, and in particular of his experiences in Tombstone.[32] In Flood's manuscript, the cowboys, not Wyatt, are ruled by their passions and bent on revenge.

According to Flood, the justice systems in Kansas and Arizona were venal not because institutions in the Old West were in their infancy, but because of the poisonous influence of wealth and class. In Kansas, a cowboy escapes a murder charge when his father, a "man of wealth," buys off the court; in Arizona, the cowboys use their ill-gotten wealth to hire lawyers and buy political influence to persecute the Earps in court. Whereas in Hooker's account Wyatt enjoys the support of the community against bandits, in Flood's account, Wyatt, aided only by his brothers and the members of his posse, must confront them alone.[33] In Flood's West, as in Wister's, men such as Wyatt are borne to the top of society and ultimately vindicated by their innate nobility.

Flood finished the manuscript by early 1926 and sent it immediately to the *Saturday Evening Post*, which rejected it despite a wheedling letter of recommendation from Hart. "Please—please, in the interest for the furtherance of true American history, publish this work," Hart wrote to the *Post* editor, George Horace Lorimer. Citing the "one hundred western pictures" he had made as evidence of his understanding of the West's history, Hart, without any sense of irony, appealed to Lorimer to publish Flood's tale so that "the rising generation may know the real from the unreal."[34] The *Post*'s rejection was followed by rejections from the publishing houses Thomas Crowell and Houghton Mifflin.[35] In February 1927, after a Bobbs-Merrill editor also rejected the manuscript, calling its style "stilted and florid and diffuse," Hart—still advising the project—wrote to Wyatt that they should consider replacing Flood with a new writer.[36]

Hart suggested they turn to Walter Noble Burns, a Chicago journalist and the author of *The Saga of Billy the Kid*.[37] Burns was widely read (he was, for a time, the literary critic for the *Chicago Inter-Ocean*, reviewing novels by H. G. Wells and Maksim Gorky as well as a collection of poems by Edith Wharton) and had a long-standing interest in the American West (as early as 1912, he wrote about the efforts to preserve the bison from extinction).[38] Burns's *Saga* was a spirited but hardly accurate tale that had transformed

William Bonney into a folk hero—and earned Burns a tidy sum. By early 1927, thousands of copies of the book had been sold, and Burns's publisher had sold the motion-picture rights to the film producer Sam Goldwyn for $10,000.[39]

Yet Burns presented a problem: he had already offered to write Wyatt's memoirs, and Wyatt himself had rejected the idea. In the summer of 1926, Burns had turned up unannounced on Wyatt's doorstep with an offer to write the story of the lawman's life, particularly the events in Tombstone in 1881 and 1882—in effect, to do for Wyatt what he had done for Billy the Kid. Although Wyatt later corresponded with Burns, providing him with some details of his life, he declined Burns's offer to write his biography, saying that Flood had the task well in hand—indeed, at the time, Flood's manuscript was being reviewed by potential publishers.[40] At the time, Hart supported Wyatt's rejection of Burns, writing to Wyatt in September 1926 that Burns's book about Billy the Kid was largely plagiarized from a long article by the Pinkerton detective Charlie Siringo.[41]

Despite Wyatt's refusal to cooperate, Burns persisted in writing a book about Tombstone. He traveled to Arizona and scrutinized the newspapers and public documents surrounding the events in Tombstone in the early 1880s. He also got hold of Frederick Bechdolt's *When the West Was Young*, and—confirming Hart's charge that he was a plagiarist—copied long passages from Bechdolt's book word for word.[42] By early 1927, with his dubious research method speeding the process along, he had completed the first few chapters of what would become *Tombstone: An Iliad of the Southwest.*

At the urging of Wyatt and Hart, the unfailingly loyal Flood approached Burns to ask whether he would edit Earp's authorized biography to make it readable. If Flood and Wyatt, humbled by the publishers' rejections of the manuscript, still harbored any hopes for the memoir, Burns dashed them. With his own Tombstone book well under way, Burns scoffed at Flood's request; he privately called the Flood manuscript a "dud."[43]

A few months later, Wyatt became enraged when Burns's publisher, Doubleday, sought to have some of the *Tombstone* chapters serialized in the *Saturday Evening Post*. Burns's depiction of Wyatt was not a factor in Wyatt's outrage: Burns's account of the events in Tombstone praised Wyatt's courage. Nor was Wyatt primarily concerned that Burns's version might prove more salable than the account that Wyatt had authorized. Had money been the only issue, Wyatt might well have accepted Doubleday editor Harry Maule's $1,000 offer to drop any opposition to publication. Burns, wary of a lawsuit that would delay publication, offered to chip in 25 percent of the film rights—an offer that would be worth even more than $1,000 if the price for the film rights to *Billy the Kid* could be replicated. Wyatt flatly rejected this generous offer and instead insisted on 50 percent of all profits from the book—in effect, he demanded that he become Burns's full partner. The negotiations reached a standstill. Wyatt, too proud to accept Doubleday's offer, preferred to accept nothing. Doubleday went ahead with publication.[44]

If Hooker rendered Wyatt as a dime-novel lawman-turned-vigilante, and Flood depicted him as a natural aristocrat battling the forces of social degeneracy, Burns cast Wyatt as a version of the "muscular Christian." "He was unaffectedly genuine," Burns wrote. "Right or wrong, he believed with absolute faith in the righteousness of the justice he administered at the muzzle of a gun."[45] Burns's description closely resembled one he had written in 1910 of Billy Sunday, a former Chicago White Stockings outfielder turned evangelist: "Billy Sunday is a genuine, fearless, aggressive, wholesome soul . . . Billy Sunday preaches like he used to play ball. He swings hard from the shoulder. He hits sin 'on the nose.'"[46] For Burns, Wyatt was a man ordained to combat Tombstone's lawlessness, an avenging angel who appeared in Tombstone deus ex machina: "no man of his day in the West was more logically fitted to become the man of Tombstone's hour."

Wyatt's feelings about his past were too complex to let him settle merely for money and vindication. To Wyatt, Burns was more than a publishing rival. Wyatt could not accept that anyone, much less someone who had rejected an offer to collaborate on an authorized biography, might write about his life without his permission. Burns, for his part, could not help but be exasperated with Wyatt, who had first rejected Burns's offer to collaborate, then tried to force on him an inferior manuscript, then rejected a generous offer for the rights to his story, and finally demanded that Burns share with him half of the profits from his work. Yet Wyatt pursued a consistent goal: more than reward and even more than reputation, he wanted to control the telling of his story. He wrote to Burns's Doubleday editor Harry Maule that "the story of Wyatt Earp, or any portion of it, if it is to be written, must be written, only, by Wyatt Earp." So overweening was Wyatt's desire for control that, as he had in the case of Hooker's manuscript, he tried to put a stop to publication entirely. "My firm stand," he wrote to Maule in May 1927, is "that no story of myself shall be written or published without my sanction or consent, and that, in this instance, I am unwilling to give."[47]

In his reaction to Burns's book, Wyatt's old resentment against the national media returned. He begrudged the media not because the stories circulating about him were inaccurate (some were and some were not) or even negative, but because they limited his ability to reinvent himself and tell the story of his life as he wanted it told. He bristled when unauthorized reports of his past appeared. In March 1925, he went to the trouble of composing a letter to a *Scribner's Magazine* writer pointing out the errors in a recent article about him.[48] The *Scribner's* contributor—perhaps by virtue of residing in Washington, D.C.—was fortunate that all he received from Wyatt was a letter. That same year, Wyatt tracked down a *Los Angeles Times* journalist who had written a negative portrayal of him. Wyatt, aged seventy-seven, bullied the reporter into affixing his signature to a retraction.[49]

Around the same time that Wyatt was frustrating Burns with his intransigence, he was making an even worse impression on another chronicler of Arizona's past, the historian Frank Lockwood. Lockwood had come to southern Arizona in 1916 as a professor of English at the University of Arizona. In the mid-1920s, he became interested in Arizona's frontier history; he wrote a series of vignettes about the lives of Arizona pioneers, which he later collected into a book, *Arizona Characters*. He had hoped to include Wyatt in that collection and had written to him in 1925 asking to interview him. Like Burns, Lockwood received a polite demurral, in the form of "a courteous, but somewhat evasive letter," in which Wyatt explained that he had already entered into an agreement with a "professional writer" (a mischaracterization of John Flood if ever there was one) to produce his biography.

Lockwood pressed on with the research for *Arizona Characters*. In November 1926, he was at work at the Southwest Museum in Los Angeles when he stumbled across a typed copy of Forrestine Hooker's unpublished Earp manuscript. Lockwood asked the librarian where the "interesting, well-written article" had been published and was surprised to learn from her that "it had been prepared for publication in consultation with Earp and supposedly with his approval, but that when it was finished he refused to give his consent for its release." Lockwood's suspicions were aroused, or, as he put it, "troublesome questions arose in my mind. More than ever, I felt it important for me to interview Earp and get his version of his career in Arizona."

Lockwood wrote to Wyatt again asking whether he might interview him; this time, Wyatt invited him to visit. On Sunday, November 28, 1926, Lockwood and his brother, a Pasadena physician, drove to Wyatt's home. Lockwood described Wyatt as "seventy-eight years old, well-preserved, well-dressed, and well-groomed." However impressed he might have been with Wyatt's appearance, Lockwood left the interview convinced that the old gunfighter "was not only a killer but in general a bad citizen." Lockwood found Wyatt's descriptions of the violence in Arizona "not pleasant to listen to." He was appalled by Wyatt's recollections of his actions as a vigilante in 1882, particularly the killing of Frank Stilwell. "Earp's physical reactions that day as he sat talking to us of the way in which he shot Stilwell, the supple slithery fingering of the trigger of his gun as he visualized and re-enacted the scene, somehow fixed the impression in the minds of both my brother and myself that he had been a cold and cruel killer."[50]

Earp did not appear in *Arizona Characters*, but Lockwood mentioned him in a later book, *Pioneer Days in Arizona*, published in 1932. By that time, Lockwood had tempered his suspicions about Wyatt's violence and untruthfulness with a grudging acknowledgment of his steely resolve: "Wyatt Earp was a cold-blooded killer and a very suave and crafty dissimulator, though he was certainly one of the nerviest and skillful men who ever carried a gun."[51] Yet Lockwood could not comfortably place Wyatt on the side of either the forces of light or the forces of darkness—the only two categories as far as he was concerned. "By what standards of ethics, aesthetics, or religion Wyatt Earp was able to reconcile the propriety of drawing big money as a faro dealer or proprietor of a saloon and gambling hall, and at the same time wearing the badge of a city marshal or peace officer of the Federal Government I do not know. But to my simple mind and in the light of my primitive moral instincts (and I, too, was born in Illinois and grew up in Kansas) this does not seem right. I have a deep conviction that a man—especially an officer of the law—should either run with the hare or hunt with the hounds."[52] Lockwood knew of the gambling and the saloons. One can only imagine what he would have made of Wyatt had he known of the prostitutes and the horse theft.

Lockwood was not the only chronicler of Arizona's past to question Wyatt's integrity. Not long after Wyatt met with Lockwood, Houghton Mifflin published *Helldorado: Bringing Law to the Mesquite*, by William Breakenridge, one of Behan's former deputies. Breakenridge depicted Wyatt not as a heroic lawman but as an unscrupulous murderer who wore a steel vest under his clothes to protect himself from bullets and gunned down innocent and unresisting cowboys in Tombstone. "All a pack of *lies*," Wyatt fulminated about *Helldorado* in November 1928. Obsessed with Breakenridge's book, Wyatt took careful note of which Los Angeles department stores stocked it and which ones did not.[53] If Wyatt learned anything from his interview with Lockwood and the publication of Breakenridge's book, it was that in some quarters the characterization of him as a scoundrel and an unscrupulous murderer remained.

•

By late 1927, Wyatt had bigger problems than the poor impression he had made on Lockwood: his plans to see his biography published were in disarray, in no small part because of his own intransigence. Every publishing house that had considered Flood's manuscript had rejected it. Meanwhile, Burns, who had begun work on *Tombstone* only after Flood's manuscript was complete, had already seen his book published. That Burns lionized Wyatt was beside the point for a man who saw it as an affront for anyone to write about his past without his permission.

As this recognition dawned on him, he received a letter from Stuart Lake, dated Christmas Day 1927. The San Diego press agent, former journalist, and would-be screenwriter offered to write Wyatt's memoirs.[54] Lake was a native of Rome, New York, who had attended Cornell University for one year before leaving to become a reporter for the *New York Herald*. In 1916, he left the newspaper to become a press agent for Theodore Roosevelt's preparedness movement—a campaign for an arms buildup and compulsory military service that anticipated American entry into the First World War.[55] When the United States entered the war in April 1917, Lake left Roosevelt to volunteer. Initially turned away as physically unfit, he persisted until he was able to enlist.[56]

Sent to France with the Allied Expeditionary Force, Lake returned in March 1919, having suffered a serious shrapnel wound to his right leg—his femur was splintered and the upper portion of it destroyed. Lake endured a series of operations, including a six-hour procedure in New York in December 1919, during which two surgeons fastened a metal plate to the shattered bone. After two years spent in body casts in various hospitals, and several more operations, Lake was left with a right leg four inches shorter than his left and unable to bear his weight.[57]

Despairing of working again as a journalist, he began submitting stories to literary magazines, but endured a series of rejections throughout the 1920s.[58] Undeterred, he worked up featherlight stories as script ideas for the film industry—and endured more rejections. In 1927, Cecil B. DeMille's studio rejected "The Red-Blooded Blues" and "Clip the Coupon" while another studio turned down "Spotless Smith."[59] He did not sell a script idea to the studios until 1928, when Universal Studios produced *Buck Privates* based on his story idea.

Thus when Lake wrote to Wyatt on Christmas Day 1927, introducing himself and offering to write Wyatt's biography, he had few literary accomplishments with which to recommend himself. Yet he had certain qualities that Wyatt was looking for: a fluency with words, an air of breezy confidence in dealing with the world of publishers, and not least, like Flood, a whiff of East Coast manners. As Wyatt wrote in November 1928, Lake was among "the better class of men."[60] Moreover, like Wyatt, he was no stranger to violence. Best of all, Lake had been acquainted with Wyatt's friend Bat Masterson when Masterson was a journalist in New York in the early 1910s. Wyatt was taken with Lake when he met him in June 1928. He wrote to Hart of having "a feeling of assurance" in him.[61]

Lake synthesized the approaches of Hooker, Flood, and Burns in his biography: Wyatt emerges as equal parts dime-novel lawman, Wisterian natural aristocrat, and muscular Christian. Each of these characterizations represented a kind of masculine ideal. As Lake incorporated each of them into his depiction of Wyatt, he put a special emphasis on Wyatt's flesh-and-blood physicality. In Lake's description, Wyatt possessed "exceptional strength." He lingered over descriptions of Wyatt's physique and appearance. "Six feet tall, weighing not more than one hundred and fifty-five pounds," Lake wrote, "Wyatt's lean and muscular features were smooth-shaven and tanned brown, his slimness further set off by white shirt, black trousers, wide-brimmed black hat, and high-heeled horseman's boots."[62] To complete Wyatt's costume, Lake armed him with the Buntline Special: the imagined revolver with the twelve-inch barrel, an unsubtle symbol of Wyatt's masculinity. Crippled in the war, Lake projected onto Wyatt the strength and vitality that he had lost.

Ira Rich Kent, Lake's editor at Houghton Mifflin, encouraged

Lake to emphasize Wyatt's masculinity after reading drafts of the first chapters. Indeed, he directed Lake toward a line from Burns's book, "Wyatt Earp was a man," almost goading Lake to try to outdo Burns's emphasis on Wyatt's manliness. Lake responded by opening his biography with an even stronger assertion of Wyatt's masculinity: "Wyatt Earp was a man of action," he wrote in his first line. There were, alas, far too many lines in Lake's first draft. Kent insisted that Lake trim the length of the 643-page, 190,000-word manuscript that Lake submitted in the summer of 1930. (Lake struggled to get the final version down to 150,000 words.) Much of Lake's verbiage dwelt "too insistently on the justification and eulogy of your character," Kent wrote, leading to a tone of the manuscript that was "bilious and jaundiced." Moreover, Kent noted that "in the long quotations from Earp himself we have found a little lack of Western flavor and freedom." Kent asked, "Did he really talk in this rather literary and polysyllabic style?" Kent urged Lake to forgo this "overpolished" prose and opt for "straightforward, simple language." In short, the laconic lawman who emerged in the final draft of *Wyatt Earp: Frontier Marshal* might instead have been argumentative and long-winded had it not been for Kent's editorial intervention.[63]

Wyatt tried to exercise editorial control over Lake, too. On January 10, 1929, only days before he died, Wyatt wrote to Lake insisting that he "would not want the manuscript to be seen nor examined by any person other than yourself until it is absolutely complete—that would not be fair to me—there may be changes or corrections that I would want to make, and nobody should know its contents until I have read it over thoroughly."[64] It is not difficult to imagine that if Wyatt had lived longer, his desire to control the text might have frustrated Lake's efforts to complete the book. Indeed, just as Wyatt had prevented the publication of Hooker's manuscript, perhaps the only reason that Lake's version of Wyatt's life was published was that Wyatt died before he could kill the project.

Wyatt had spent decades rehearsing his version of his life story. He was willing to share these practiced reminiscences, but with the exception of Flood's manuscript, he recoiled from seeing his account on the page. Having spent so many decades telling stories about himself, Wyatt resisted conceding to a collaborator any control over the telling of his life story. His reminiscences, however accurate or not, were part of him. Most of all, even at the end of his life, Wyatt was unwilling to settle on a definitive version of a life he had altered so many times. By the 1920s, Wyatt had been reinventing himself for over half a century. Publishing his story meant giving up the flexibility to change his account when it suited him. The finality of publication meant an end to his life of invention and a consignment of his memories to the past—permanently. It meant, in other words, a kind of death.

Without ever approving Lake's draft, Wyatt died in the early morning on January 13, 1929, at his home in Los Angeles.[65] Hart made the arrangements for the funeral and served as a pallbearer along with fellow Western film idol Tom Mix. The pallbearers also included the playwright and gambler Wilson Mizner, as well as two friends from Tombstone: John Clum and George Parsons, figures from all quarters of Wyatt's complex life. Parsons and Clum were part of the professional class in Tombstone who had supported Wyatt's violent imposition of order; Mizner was a rounder who met Wyatt at his saloon in Nome; Hart and Mix were Hollywood film-makers, representatives of the industry that transformed Wyatt into an icon of the Old West marshal.

Lake attended the funeral, too. Forced by Wyatt's death to re-search the details of Wyatt's life on his own, Lake eventually learned some of the truth of Wyatt's dissolute early life. But none of these details found their way into *Wyatt Earp: Frontier Marshal*. Anointed as Earp's authorized biographer, yet following Wyatt's death free to make editorial and publishing decisions, Lake knew that Earp's legacy could be a gold mine for him—and, with Kent to guide him, he proved to be even more skilled than Wyatt himself at character-ization. Lake crafted a portrayal of Earp as a tight-lipped marshal who was as virtuous as he was violent. So admiring was Lake's por-trayal of Wyatt that when the book appeared, a critic for the *New York Herald Tribune* wrote of his astonishment at seeing Wyatt Earp "emerge from the shadows of the past in a halo and a robe."[66]

Wyatt Earp: Frontier Marshal was an immediate success. By the end of 1931, the entire first printing of five thousand had sold out, and Houghton Mifflin had ordered a second printing of two thousand more copies.[67] Lake sold his biography to the Fox film studio in 1932; by the end of the century Hollywood had made dozens of Earp films, including *Frontier Marshal* (1939; starring Randolph Scott); *My Darling Clementine* (1946; directed by John Ford, starring Henry Fonda); and *Gunfight at the O.K. Corral* (1957; directed by John Sturges, starring Burt Lancaster). *The Life and Legend of Wyatt Earp*, an American Broadcasting Company weekly television program starring Hugh O'Brian, aired between 1955 and 1961. The film and television Earp genre institutionalized the Western lawman as a solitary embodiment of duty, order, and sacrifice; the gunfight as the ultimate Western test of manhood; and vigilantism as the necessary imposition of justice upon a lawless West.

Screened and broadcast repeatedly, the films rooted Wyatt in American collective memory. Decontextualized through time and repetition, Wyatt's adventures, first manipulated only by Wyatt himself, then by Lake, actors, and filmmakers, have become part of collective memory's invented tradition.[68] The media culture that once prevented Wyatt from reinventing himself by foisting on him an unwanted celebrity became, after his death, the engine of his ongoing reinvention. Told and retold, Wyatt's story has lost most of whatever authenticity it once had—a process that is a salient consequence of modernity's mass production of culture.[69] Ironically, in Earp's case, mass consumer culture produced an icon of lone resolve.

The dissonance between the Wyatt Earp of history and the Wyatt Earp of our collective memory, a confused combination of the real and the imagined born partly of Hollywood mythmaking and partly of Wyatt's own efforts to edit his past, is his central story. Although Wyatt was deeply conflicted about it, becoming a popular media icon was the abiding concern of the last years of his life. He had no way of knowing that he would be portrayed scores of times on film and television; it is unlikely that he imagined more than that Bill Hart would make a two-reel silent film about him. Yet Hart fell out of the picture, and instead Burns, Lake, and others—including the film director John Ford and the actors who portrayed him, including Henry Fonda, Burt Lancaster, and Hugh O'Brian—became his media heralds. Through them, we have come to know Wyatt Earp, or think we know him. The man who so often changed his recollections of his own past embedded himself in American collective memory, and that is his enduring legacy.

NOTES

1. LEX TALIONIS

1. "Another Assassination," *Tombstone Epitaph*, March 21, 1882.
2. See Steven Lubet, *Murder in Tombstone: The Forgotten Trial of Wyatt Earp* (New Haven, CT: Yale University Press, 2004).
3. "The Clanton Trial," *Tombstone Epitaph*, February 3, 1882.
4. For Wyatt Earp in films, see Lee Clark Mitchell, *Westerns: Making the Man in Fiction and Film* (Chicago: University of Chicago Press, 1996); Paul Andrew Hutton, "Showdown at the Hollywood Corral: Wyatt Earp and the Movies," *Montana: The Magazine of Western History* 45 (Summer 1995): 2–31; John Mack Faragher, "The Tale of Wyatt Earp," in Mark Carnes, ed., *Past Imperfect: History According to the Movies* (New York: Holt, 1995), 154–61.
5. Stanley Corkin, *Cowboys as Cold Warriors: The Western and U.S. History* (Philadelphia: Temple University Press, 2004).
6. Stan Simpson, "Pakistan a Key Piece of the Puzzle," *Hartford Courant*, September 19, 2001.
7. For the nineteenth-century American belief in upward social mobility, see Edward Pessen, "The Egalitarian Myth and American Social Reality: Wealth, Mobility, and Equality in the 'Era of the Common Man,'" *American Historical Review* 76 (October 1971): 989–1034. For self-invention in the eighteenth and nineteenth centuries, see Daniel Walker Howe, *Making the American Self: Jonathan Edwards to Abraham Lincoln* (New York: Oxford University Press, 2009). For the modern version of self-invention, see Micki McGee, *Self-Help, Inc.: Makeover Culture in American Life* (New York: Oxford University Press, 2005).

2. THE SONS OF ISHMAEL

1. Sixty percent of the residents of Warren County in 1850 had been born outside Illinois. For antebellum western cities, see Richard Wade, *The Urban Frontier: The Rise of Western Cities, 1790–1830* (Cambridge, MA: Harvard University Press, 1959); Don Harrison Doyle, *The Social Order of a Frontier Community: Jacksonville, Illinois, 1825–70* (Urbana: University of Illinois Press, 1978).

2. Nonetheless, the Currier & Ives version of antebellum American farms is so seductive and pervasive that it shapes not only popular but scholarly views; most U.S. history textbooks include at least one Currier & Ives illustration. For a discussion of the intensive agriculture necessary to produce the images represented in Currier & Ives illustrations, see Steven Stoll, *Larding the Lean Earth: Soil and Society in Nineteenth-Century America* (New York: Hill and Wang, 2002); Peter G. Boag, *Environment and Experience: Settlement Culture in Nineteenth-Century Oregon* (Berkeley: University of California Press, 1992).

3. See Stephen Thernstrom, *Poverty and Progress: Social Mobility in a Nineteenth-Century City* (Cambridge, MA: Harvard University Press, 1964); James W. Oberly, "Westward Who? Estimates of Native White Interstate Migration After the War of 1812," *Journal of Economic History* 46 (June 1986): 431–40. Generally, Northeasterners migrated to the Old Northwest of Ohio, Indiana, Michigan, Illinois, and Wisconsin; Southeasterners migrated to the Old Southwest. By midcentury, however, hundreds of thousands of Americans migrated beyond the Mississippi River. When Texas had become independent of Mexico in 1836, it had a population of about forty thousand; by 1860, its population stood at six hundred thousand. See David J. Weber, *The Spanish Frontier in North America* (New Haven, CT: Yale University Press, 1992). Between 1840 and 1860, over three hundred thousand Americans migrated overland to California, Oregon, and Utah. See John D. Unruh, *The Plains Across: The Overland Emigrants and the Trans-Mississippi West, 1840–60* (Urbana: University of Illinois Press, 1979).

4. For the westward migration of farmers before the Civil War, see Paul Wallace Gates, *The Farmer's Age: Agriculture, 1815–1860* (New York: Holt, Rinehart and Winston, 1960); for the California gold rush, see Malcolm Rohrbough, *Days of Gold: The California Gold Rush and the American Nation* (Berkeley: University of California Press, 1997); J. S. Holliday, *Rush for Riches: Gold Fever and the Making of California* (Berkeley: University of California Press, 1999); for Colorado, see Elliott West, *The Contested Plains: Indians, Goldseekers, and the Rush to Colorado* (Lawrence: University Press of Kansas, 1998); for migration during the Civil War, see Dean May, *Three Frontiers: Family, Land, and Society in the American West, 1850–1900* (New York: Cambridge University Press, 1994).

5. Genesis 16:12, 25:18.

6. Clarence H. Danhof, "Economic Validity of the Safety-Valve Doctrine," *The*

Task of Economic History, supplement to *Journal of Economic History* 1 (December 1941): 96–106.

7. John Mack Faragher, *Women and Men on the Overland Trail* (New Haven, CT: Yale University Press, 1979), 49–59; Elizabeth Pleck, "Two Worlds in One: Work and Family," *Journal of Social History* 10 (Winter 1976): 178–95.

8. Elizabeth A. Perkins, "The Consumer Frontier: Household Consumption in Early Kentucky," *Journal of American History* 78 (September 1991): 486–510.

9. See Kathleen Neils Conzen, "A Saga of Families," in Clyde A. Milner II, Carol A. O'Connor, and Martha Sandweiss, eds., *The Oxford History of the American West* (New York: Oxford University Press, 1994), 315–57; Philip J. Greven, *Four Generations: Population, Land, and Family in Colonial Andover, Massachusetts* (Ithaca, NY: Cornell University Press, 1970).

10. "Patrimonial family" is Conzen's term from "A Saga of Families."

11. John F. Murray, "Generation(s) of Human Capital: Literacy in American Families, 1830–1875," *Journal of Interdisciplinary History* 27 (Winter 1997): 413–35.

12. See Nathan O. Hatch, *The Democratization of American Christianity* (New Haven, CT: Yale University Press, 1989); Sydney E. Ahlstrom, *A Religious History of the American People* (New Haven, CT: Yale University Press, 1972), 436–39.

13. See Bertram Wyatt-Brown, *Southern Honor: Ethics and Behavior in the Old South* (New York: Oxford University Press, 1982), 219.

14. See Richard H. Steckel, "The Health and Mortality of Women and Children, 1850–1860," *Journal of Economic History* 48 (June 1988): 333–45; Laurel Thatcher Ulrich, *A Midwife's Tale: The Life of Martha Ballard, Based on Her Diary, 1785–1812* (New York: Vintage, 1990), 170.

15. *The Past and Present of Warren County, Illinois* (Chicago: H. F. Kett, 1877), 208.

16. Fred A. Shannon, "A Post-Mortem on the Labor-Safety-Valve Theory," *Agricultural History* 19 (January 1945): 31–37; William Deverell, "To Loosen the Safety Valve: Eastern Workers and Western Lands," *Western Historical Quarterly* 19 (August 1988): 269–85.

17. Ahlstrom, *Religious History of the American People*, 661–63.

18. Lincoln spoke these words in a speech at Peoria, Illinois, in 1854. See Roy P. Basler, Marion D. Pratt, and Lloyd A. Dunlap, eds., *The Collected Works of Abraham Lincoln*, vol. 2 (New Brunswick, NJ: Rutgers University Press, 1953), 254–76. For competition between planters and nonslaveholding whites in the Upper South, see James Oakes, *Slavery and Freedom: An Interpretation of the Old South* (New York: A. A. Knopf, 1990).

19. William Urban, "Wyatt Earp Was Born Here: Monmouth and the Earps, 1845–1859," *Western Illinois Regional Studies* 3 (Fall 1980): 154–67; William Urban, "Wyatt Earp's Father," *True West*, May 1984, 32.

20. "Address Before the Wisconsin State Agricultural Society," in Basler et al., *Collected Works of Abraham Lincoln*, vol. 3; 477–82. See also Michael F. Holt, *The Rise and Fall of the American Whig Party: Jacksonian Politics and the Onset of*

the Civil War (New York: Oxford University Press, 1999); Eric Foner, *Free Soil, Free Labor, Free Men: The Ideology of the Republican Party Before the Civil War* (New York: Oxford University Press, 1970).

21. Paul W. Gates, "Land Policy and Tenancy in the Prairie States," *Journal of Economic History* 1 (May 1941): 60–82; Gates, "Large-Scale Farming in Illinois, 1850–1870," *Agricultural History* 6 (January 1932): 14–25; Gates, "Tenants of the Log Cabin," *Mississippi Valley Historical Review* 49 (June 1962): 3–31; Jeremy Atack, "Tenants and Yeomen in the Nineteenth Century," *Agricultural History* 62 (Summer 1998): 6–32; John M. Faragher, *Sugar Creek: Life on the Illinois Prairie* (New Haven, CT: Yale University Press, 1986).

22. For the economics of hired labor, see David E. Schob, *Hired Hands and Plowboys: Farm Labor in the Midwest, 1815–1860* (Urbana: University of Illinois Press, 1975), 257. For pork, see Edgar W. Martin, *The Standard of Living in 1860: American Consumption Levels on the Eve of the Civil War* (Chicago: University of Chicago Press, 1942), 67; Margaret Walsh, "Pork Packing as a Leading Edge of Midwestern Industry, 1835–1875," *Agricultural History* 51 (October 1977): 702–17.

23. Urban, "Wyatt Earp's Father," 30–31.

24. See Paul Foos, *A Short, Offhand Killing Affair: Soldiers and Social Conflict During the Mexican-American War* (Chapel Hill: University of North Carolina Press, 2002), 49–51.

25. See Nicholas Earp's pension application in Esther Irvine, Data on the Earp Family, Abraham Lincoln Presidential Library, Springfield, IL. See also Urban, "Wyatt Earp's Father," 31–32.

26. The settlement was named after the Jordan valley city where tradition maintains that both Jews and Christians found refuge during the First Jewish Revolt in A.D. 66–70.

27. See Schob, *Hired Hands and Plowboys*, 7. Set-up men or "hoe-boys" eventually became, in American slang, *hoboes*. See Mark Wyman, *Hoboes: Bindlestiffs, Fruit Tramps, and the Harvesting of the West* (New York: Hill and Wang, 2010), 38–39.

28. For economic opportunity in rural midcentury Iowa, see David W. Galenson and Clayne L. Pope, "Economic and Geographical Mobility on the Farming Frontier: Evidence from Appanoose County, Iowa, 1850–1870," *Journal of Economic History* 49 (September 1989): 635–55.

29. William Urban, "Nicholas Earp's Iowa Lands." Unpublished manuscript. See http://department.monm.edu/history/urban/wyatt_earp/nicholas-earp-iowa-lands.htm, accessed August 25, 2012.

30. See Paul W. Gates, *Landlords and Tenants on the Prairie Frontier* (Ithaca, NY: Cornell University Press, 1973); Daniel Feller, *The Public Lands in Jacksonian Politics* (Madison: University of Wisconsin Press, 1984).

31. Stuart N. Lake, *Wyatt Earp: Frontier Marshal* (Boston: Houghton Mifflin, 1931), 7.

32. Urban, "Nicholas Earp's Iowa Lands."

33. The Panic was brought on by the combined effects of the failure of a New York insurance company, inflation resulting from the California gold rush, and the collapse of grain prices at the end of the Crimean War. See Kenneth Stampp, *America in 1857: A Nation on the Brink* (New York: Oxford University Press, 1990).

34. Lake, *Wyatt Earp*, 4–5.

35. Max Weber, "Politics as a Vocation," in H. H. Gerth and C. Wright Mills, eds., *From Max Weber: Essays in Sociology* (New York: Oxford University Press, 1958), 110.

36. William Urban, "The People Versus Nicholas Earp," *Illinois Historical Journal* 90 (Autumn 1997): 178–80.

37. *Monmouth Atlas*, February 4, 1853, 3.

38. W. J. Rorabaugh, *The Alcoholic Republic: An American Tradition* (New York: Oxford University Press, 1979), 10–11.

39. See Charles Sellers, *The Market Revolution: Jacksonian America, 1815–1846* (New York: Oxford University Press, 1991).

40. Rorabaugh, *Alcoholic Republic*, 78–79; Ian R. Tyrrell, *Sobering Up: From Temperance to Prohibition in Antebellum America, 1800–1860* (Westport, CT: Greenwood Press, 1979), 19–20.

41. On the interrelationship of Protestant revivalism, the market revolution, and moral reform, see Paul E. Johnson, *A Shopkeeper's Millennium: Society and Revivals in Rochester, New York, 1815–1837* (New York: Hill and Wang, 1978). See also Ronald G. Walters, *American Reformers, 1815–1860* (New York: Hill and Wang, 1978), 123–43.

42. Mark Edward Lender and James Kirby Martin, *Drinking in America: A History* (New York: Free Press, 1982), 41–85.

43. Johnson, *Shopkeeper's Millennium*, 55–61.

44. Tyrrell, *Sobering Up*, 56.

45. Adelia Earp Edwards, "Wild West Remembrances," 3. Earl Chafin Papers, Autry National Center/Southwest Museum, Los Angeles, CA.

46. Urban, "People Versus Nicholas Earp," 174, 183.

47. Ibid., 184–85.

48. James M. McPherson, *Ordeal by Fire: The Civil War and Reconstruction*, 2nd ed. (New York: McGraw-Hill, 1992), 84, 171–72; Bell Irvin Wiley, *The Life of Billy Yank: The Common Soldier of the Union* (Indianapolis: Bobbs-Merrill, 1951), 37–38.

49. For instance, the Chicago Democratic politician James A. Mulligan organized the Twenty-Third Illinois Infantry—the "Irish Brigade"—almost entirely of Irish immigrants. See James L. Burton, "'Title Deed to America': Union Ethnic Regiments in the Civil War," *Proceedings of the American Philosophical Society* 124 (December 1980): 455–63.

50. Wiley, *Life of Billy Yank*, 45–65.

51. See the *Monmouth Atlas*, November 8; November 15, 1861.

52. Francis was the son of Josiah Earp, a younger brother of Nicholas. Several of the Earps served in the Civil War. Charles Earp served in the Fifty-Seventh Illinois Infantry, Company F; William Earp, a son of Lorenzo Dow Earp, was a private in the Eighty-Fifth Illinois Infantry, Company F—he died of wounds November 30, 1864; Ephraim Earp was a private in the 129th Illinois Infantry; Delos D. Earp was a private in the 138th Illinois Infantry, Company A, which was organized in Monmouth; and Jonathan D. Earp was a private in the Twelfth Illinois Cavalry. See Irvine, Data on the Earp Family, Lincoln Presidential Library.

53. "A Fresh Outrage" and "Guerilla Chase," *83rd Illinoisan*, April 7, 1865; "Guerilla Outrage," *83rd Illinoisan*, May 5, 1865.

54. Lake, *Wyatt Earp*, 9–10.

55. Welch Nossaman Recollections, 1933, Nossaman Family Papers, Central College Archives, Pella, IA.

56. See Peter Levine, "Draft Evasion in the North During the Civil War, 1863–1865," *Journal of American History* 67 (March 1981): 816–34.

57. John Henry Flood, "Wyatt Earp," c. 1925, 9–18, Ford County Historical Society, Dodge City, KS; Lake, *Wyatt Earp*, 9–10.

58. Wiley, *Life of Billy Yank*, 296–99.

59. Flood, "Wyatt Earp," 18.

60. William Barclay Masterson, "Famous Gun Fighters of the Western Frontier, Second Article: Wyatt Earp," *Human Life*, February 1907.

61. Irvine, Data on the Earp Family, Lincoln Presidential Library.

62. Sarah Nossaman Recollections, 1894, Nossaman Family Papers, Central College Archives.

63. Lake, *Wyatt Earp*, 10.

64. See Flood, "Wyatt Earp," 20.

65. See May, *Three Frontiers*, 89–90.

66. See Nicholas Earp's application for a military pension, 1877, in Irvine, Data on the Earp Family, Lincoln Presidential Library.

67. See Unruh, *Plains Across*, 85; Faragher, *Women and Men on the Overland Trail*, 12–16.

68. For Rousseau's account of the journey, see Earl Chafin, ed., *The Rousseau Diary* (Riverside, CA: Earl Chafin Press, 2002). Chafin's transcription appears accurate, although his annotations can be misleading. For the latter part of the journey, see George W. Beattie, ed., "Rousseau Diary: Across the Desert to California from Salt Lake City to San Bernardino in 1864," *San Bernardino County Museum Association* 6 (Winter 1958): 1–17. Beattie's version lacks crucial entries—particularly entries that are critical of Nicholas Earp. For the average length of an overland journey, see Unruh, *Plains Across*, 341.

69. Chafin, *Rousseau Diary*, 9–11. For the effect of emigrants on the environment of the Platte River valley, see Elliott West, *The Way to the West: Essays on the Central Plains* (Albuquerque: University of New Mexico Press, 1995).

70. Unruh, *Plains Across*, 88, 98–99, 144.

71. Chafin, *Rousseau Diary*, 45. For Indian aid to emigrants, see Unruh, *Plains Across*, 118–20.

72. See Andrew C. Isenberg, *The Destruction of the Bison: An Environmental History, 1750–1920* (New York: Cambridge University Press, 2000), 93–122.

73. Chafin, *Rousseau Diary*, 14.

74. Ibid., 16.

75. See Unruh, *Plains Across*, 91.

76. Chafin, *Rousseau Diary*, 17–18.

77. Ibid., 19–20; Nicholas Earp to James Copla, April 2, 1865, Earp Papers, Central College Archives.

78. Chafin, *Rousseau Diary*, 19–20; Nicholas Earp to Copla, April 2, 1865, Central College Archives. For white bandits, see Unruh, *Plains Across*, 150–52.

79. Flood, "Wyatt Earp," 22–26.

80. Lake, *Wyatt Earp*, 18.

81. For Nicholas Earp's claim to have scouted for Boone, see the Earp Brothers Dictations, Bancroft Library, University of California at Berkeley.

82. Chafin, *Rousseau Diary*, 28.

83. Ibid., 39–41.

84. Ibid., 48, 51, 58, 61; Beattie, "Rousseau Diary," 6.

85. Wyatt-Brown, *Southern Honor*, 149–50.

86. Chafin, *Rousseau Diary*, 61. Copley's name is variously spelled *Copla*, *Coplea*, and *Coply*.

87. Nicholas Earp to James Copla, April 2, 1865, Central College Achives.

88. In this respect, Nicholas Earp was typical. While the ideology of upward social mobility dominated in nineteenth-century America, the reality was very different. Despite striving to move up the social ladder, most Americans did not change status. See Edward Pessen, "The Egalitarian Myth and American Social Reality: Wealth, Mobility, and Equality in the 'Era of the Common Man,'" *American Historical Review* 76 (October 1971): 989–1034.

3. YOUTH HATH FAULTY WAND'RED

1. For prisons in nineteenth-century America, see Orlando Lewis, *The Development of American Prisons and Prison Customs, 1776–1845* (Montclair, NJ: Patterson Smith, 1967); Adam J. Hirsh, *The Rise of the Penitentiary: Prisons and Punishment in Early America* (New Haven, CT: Yale University Press, 1992); David J. Rothman, "Perfecting the Prison: United States, 1789–1865," in David J. Rothman and Norval Morris, eds., *The Oxford History of the Prison: The Practice of Punishment in Western Society* (New York: Oxford University Press, 1995), 100–16.

2. John Wesley, *A Collection of Hymns, for the Use of the People Called Methodists* (1780; repr., London: Wesleyan-Methodist Book-Room, 1889).

3. Roger Jay, "Wyatt Earp's Lost Year," *Wild West*, August 2003.

4. Ira Rich Kent to Stuart Lake, August 30, 1929, Stuart Nathaniel Lake Papers, Box 4, Huntington Library, San Marino, California.

5. Stuart Lake, *Wyatt Earp: Frontier Marshal* (Boston: Houghton Mifflin, 1931), 13.

6. Peter Brown, *Augustine of Hippo* (Berkeley: University of California Press, 1967), 173.

7. Ed Ellsworth Bartholomew, *Wyatt Earp, 1848 to 1880* (Toyahvale, TX: Frontier Book Co., 1963).

8. Lake to Kent, July 5, 1929, Lake Papers, Box 7, Huntington Library. Robert Partin, "Biography as an Instrument of Moral Instruction," *American Quarterly* 8 (Winter 1956): 303–15.

9. B. H. Tickman to Lake, October 13, 1931, quoting from Lewis Gannett's review of *Wyatt Earp: Frontier Marshal* in the *New York Herald Tribune*, Lake Papers, Box 4, Huntington Library.

10. William Barclay Masterson, "Famous Gun Fighters of the Western Frontier, Second Article: Wyatt Earp," *Human Life*, February 1907.

11. For Nicholas Earp's height, see his application for a military pension, April 9, 1877; Newton Earp gave his height as five feet eight and a half inches in his application for a military pension, dated May 17, 1912; James Earp reported himself five feet eight inches tall in his undated pension application, in Esther Irvine, Data on the Earp Family, Abraham Lincoln Presidential Library, Springfield, IL.

12. See Robert A. Margo and Richard H. Steckel, "Heights of Native-Born Whites During the Antebellum Period," *Journal of Economic History* 43 (March 1983): 167–74; Dora L. Costa, "Height, Weight, and Disease Among the Native-Born in the Rural, Antebellum North," *Social Science History* 17 (Autumn 1993): 355–83.

13. E. Anthony Rotundo, "Body and Soul: Changing Ideals of American Middle-Class Manhood, 1770–1920," *Journal of Social History* 16 (Summer 1983): 23–38; Michael T. Smith, "The Beast Unleashed: Benjamin F. Butler and Conceptions of Masculinity in the Civil War North," *New England Quarterly* 79 (June 2006): 248–76.

14. James, quoted in George M. Fredrickson, *The Inner Civil War: Northern Intellectuals and the Crisis of the Union* (Urbana: University of Illinois Press, 1993), 159.

15. See John Henry Flood, "Wyatt Earp," 28–29, Ford County Historical Society, Dodge City, KS.

16. Lake, *Wyatt Earp*, 62.

17. Nossaman Family Papers, Central College Archives, Pella, IA. "Gat," from Gatling gun, was slang for a revolver.

18. Adelia Earp Edwards, "Wild West Remembrances," 4, Earl Chafin Papers, Southwest Museum/Autry National Center, Los Angeles, CA.

19. Elliott J. Gorn, "'Gouge and Bite, Pull Hair and Scratch': The Social Signifi-

cance of Fighting in the Southern Backcountry," *American Historical Review* 90 (February 1985): 18–43; Elliott J. Gorn, *The Manly Art: Bare-Knuckle Prize Fighting in America* (Ithaca, NY: Cornell University Press, 1986), 160–62.

20. Lake, *Wyatt Earp*, 66.

21. Edwards, "Wild West Remembrances," 1, Chafin Papers, Southwest Museum/ Autry National Center.

22. Ibid. Like shooting and fisticuffs, drinking was a virtue both for soldiers and for sons of the southern backcountry. See Bertram Wyatt-Brown, *Southern Honor: Ethics and Behavior in the Old South* (New York: Oxford University Press, 1982), 165–67, 278–80.

23. Alcohol intolerance can also be a symptom of hepatitis C. It seems unlikely that Wyatt suffered from this blood-borne viral infection, however; he showed no other symptoms of chronic hepatitis C, such as fatigue, weight loss, and muscle aches.

24. See R. Douglas Hurt, *Agriculture and Slavery in Missouri's Little Dixie* (Columbia: University of Missouri Press, 1992).

25. For southern yeomen, see Stephen Hahn, *The Roots of Southern Populism: Yeoman Farmers and the Transformation of the Georgia Upcountry, 1850–1890* (New York: Oxford University Press, 1983).

26. According to the 1870 census, Barton County's five thousand inhabitants worked just over seven hundred farms with forty thousand acres of improved land. By comparison, Monmouth's Warren County in Illinois, though smaller, had twice the population, three times as many farms, and six times as many acres of improved land, and its farms were ten times more valuable.

27. "Match Game of Base-Ball," *South-West Missourian*, September 7, 1871, 2. Although baseball remained less popular than boxing or horse racing until the end of the nineteenth century, the sport had grown in popularity during the Civil War, particularly among soldiers who played the game to pass idle hours in camp. In the years after the Civil War, returning veterans brought the game home—with its rules, once reflecting local idiosyncrasies, now standardized through four years of play among men from different regions. For the history of baseball in the period, see Robert F. Burk, *Never Just a Game: Players, Owners, and American Baseball to 1920* (Chapel Hill: University of North Carolina Press, 1994); Robert H. Gudmestad, "Baseball, the Lost Cause, and the New South in Richmond, Virginia, 1883–1890," *Virginia Magazine of History and Biography* 106 (Summer 1998): 267–300.

28. Edwards, "Wild West Remembrances," 2, Chafin Papers, Southwest Museum/ Autry National Center.

29. Marvin Vangilder, *The Story of Barton County: A Complete History, 1855–1972* (Lamar, MO: Reiley, 1972).

30. Irvine, Data on the Earp Family, Lincoln Presidential Library; "Do We Need a Jail?" *South-West Missourian*, March 2, 1871.

31. "A Big R.R. Meeting in Carthage Next Saturday, July 30th" and "Railroad Meeting," *South-West Missourian* (July 28, 1870); "Railroad Election" and "Railroad

Meeting," *South-West Missourian* (August 4, 1870); "Agricultural Society" and "Farmer's Club," *South-West Missourian* (July 13, 1871). For an analysis of the corruption inherent in railroad construction in this period, see Richard White, "Information, Markets, and Corruption: Transcontinental Railroads in the Gilded Age," *Journal of American History* 90 (June 2003): 19–43.

32. Irvine, Data on the Earp Family, Lincoln Presidential Library.

33. See Eric Foner, *Reconstruction: America's Unfinished Revolution, 1863–1877* (New York: Harper and Row, 1988); William E. Parrish, *Missouri Under Radical Rule, 1865–1870* (Columbia: University of Missouri Press, 1965). Barton County, Missouri, was hardly a bastion of support for slavery prior to the war. Like other parts of the South such as northern Georgia and Alabama, western North Carolina, and eastern Tennessee, populated largely by nonslaveholding yeoman farmers, support for the Confederacy declined markedly in the last years of the conflict. Lamar had not only been raided by the Confederate guerrilla Quantrill but had supplied troops for the Union: Company C of the Second Missouri Volunteer Infantry, for instance, was organized in Lamar. Not far from Lamar, in Taney, Christian, and Douglas Counties, tensions between ex-Union Republicans and ex-Confederate Democrats were more pronounced; those tensions eventuated in an outbreak of vigilante violence in the 1880s. See Thomas M. Spencer, "The Bald Knobbers, the Anti–Bald Knobbers, Politics, and the Culture of Violence in the Ozarks, 1860–1890," in *The Other Missouri: Populists, Prostitutes, and Regular Folk* (Columbia: University of Missouri Press, 2004), 31–49.

34. Barton County Records, in Steve Gatto, *The Real Wyatt Earp: A Documentary Biography*, ed. Neil B. Carmony (Silver City, NM: High Lonesome Books, 2000), 9.

35. "Incorporated," *South-West Missourian*, March 3, 1870.

36. "Do We Need a Jail?" *South-West Missourian*, March 2, 1871.

37. "Come to Grief," *South-West Missourian*, June 16, 1870.

38. "Ordinances of the Town of Lamar," *South-West Missourian*, March 17, 1870.

39. "Come to Grief."

40. Barton County Records, in Don Chaput, *The Earp Papers* (Encampment, WY: Affiliated Writers of America, 1994), 18–21.

41. "County Ticket," *South-West Missourian*, October 20, 1870; "County Ticket," *South-West Missourian*, November 17, 1870. Nicholas Earp received 133 votes (25.1 percent); the victor, G. W. Shawen, received 145 (27.4 percent); and the second-place finisher, Samuel Bowman, received 136 (25.6 percent). The fourth-place finisher, Marcellus Pyle, received 116 votes (21.9 percent). Both Bowman and Pyle had been endorsed by the Republican Party.

42. Sutherland advertised his Exchange Hotel as a "new Stone building, one of the cheapest and best in South-West Missouri." "Exchange Hotel," *South-West Missourian*, March 3, 1870.

43. Lake, *Wyatt Earp*, 29.

44. For family size, the rural economy, and migration in the nineteenth-century West, see Daniel Scott Smith, "Family Limitation, Sexual Control, and Domestic Feminism in Victorian America," *Feminist Studies* 1 (Winter–Spring 1973): 40–57; John M. Faragher, *Women and Men on the Overland Trail* (New Haven, CT: Yale University Press, 1979); John M. Faragher, *Sugar Creek: Life on the Illinois Prairie* (New Haven, CT: Yale University Press, 1986); Dean May, *Three Frontiers: Family, Land, and Society in the American West, 1850–1900* (New York: Cambridge University Press, 1994).

45. See Virgil's obituary in the *Portland Oregonian*, October 24, 1905, 10.

46. Mary Beth Sievens, "'The Wicked Agency of Others': Community, Law, and Marital Conflict in Vermont, 1790–1830," *Journal of the Early Republic* 21 (Spring 2001): 19–39; Nancy F. Cott, *Public Vows: A History of Marriage and the Nation* (Cambridge, MA: Harvard University Press, 2000); Norma Basch, *Framing American Divorce: From the Revolutionary Generation to the Victorians* (Berkeley: University of California Press, 1999).

47. Irvine, Data on the Earp Family, Lincoln Presidential Library.

48. Edwards, "Wild West Remembrances," Chafin Papers, Southwest Museum/Autry National Center.

49. Barton County Records, in Chaput, *Earp Papers*, 19.

50. Roger Jay, "Wyatt Earp's Lost Year," *Wild West*, August 2003.

51. Irvine, Data on the Earp Family, Lincoln Presidential Library.

52. Allen Barra, *Inventing Wyatt Earp: His Life and Many Legends* (Edison, NJ: Avalon, 2005), 29, asserts that Urilla died "almost certainly while in childbirth."

53. Barton County Circuit Court Records, 1870–1873, Missouri State Archives, Jefferson City.

54. "Come One, Come All," *South-West Missourian*, April 18, 1870; "The Mass Meeting Last Saturday," *South-West Missourian*, May 12, 1870; "Query," *South-West Missourian*, January 26, 1871; "Lamar School House," *South-West Missourian*, August 14, 1871; "The School Board Again," *South-West Missourian*, September 7, 1871.

55. Barton County Circuit Court Records, 1870–1873, Missouri State Archives, Jefferson City.

56. "Notice to Taxpayers," *South-West Missourian*, September 15, 1870; "Notice to Taxpayers," *South-West Missourian*, March 16, 1871.

57. "Wants—Who Does?—We Don't!" *South-West Missourian*, January 5, 1871; "James Montgomery vs. Nicholas P. Earp," May 15, 1871; "D. A. January & Co. vs. Nicholas P. Earp," May 22, 1871; "James Montgomery vs. Nicholas P. Earp," June 10, 1872, Barton County, Execution Docket Reel C52734, Missouri State Archives, Jefferson City. "Sheriff's Sale," *South-West Missourian*, September 7, 1871; September 14, 1871; September 21, 1871; September 28, 1871; October 5, 1871. Financial failure and outmigration were strongly correlated. In Missouri

in the decades after the Civil War, mobility rates were high in general, but successful farmers and merchants had the highest rates of persistence. Debtors such as Nicholas Earp often pulled up stakes and moved on. See Mary Eschelbach Gregson, "Population Dynamics in Rural Missouri, 1860–1880," *Social Science History* 21 (Spring 1997): 85–110.

58. Larry D. Ball, "Before the Hanging Judge: The Origins of the United States District Court for the Western District of Arkansas," *Arkansas Historical Quarterly* 49 (Autumn 1990): 199–213. See also William G. McLoughlin, *After the Trail of Tears: The Cherokees' Struggle for Sovereignty, 1839–1880* (Chapel Hill: University of North Carolina Press, 1993), 298–300.

59. P. P. Pitchlynn, May 14, 1866, in "Recent Affray in the Indian Territory," S.doc. 70, 42nd Cong., 2nd Sess. (1872).

60. "Western District of Arkansas," H.doc. 626, 43rd Cong., 1st Sess., ix–x, 269.

61. "United States District Court," *Van Buren Press*, May 25, 1869.

62. "Horrible Murder in the Choctaw Nation," *Van Buren Press*, September 21, 1869; "U.S. District Court," *Van Buren Press*, November 23, 1869; "The Hanging of McCurtain," *Van Buren Press*, June 18, 1870.

63. "Cold Blooded Murder," *Van Buren Press*, May 18, 1869.

64. "A Fatal Affray," *Van Buren Press*, August 24, 1869.

65. "U.S. District Court," *Van Buren Press*, November 23, 1869; "The Three K's," *Van Buren Press*, August 31, 1869.

66. Larceny Jacket 59, U.S. District Court for the Fort Smith Division of the Western District of Arkansas, Record Group 21, National Archives, Southwest Region, Fort Worth, TX.

67. "Sworn Statement Made by Anna Shown," Larceny Jacket 59, U.S. District Court for the Fort Smith Division of the Western District of Arkansas.

68. For the posse, see the statement of expenses of William Britton, the U.S. marshal for the Western District. For Wyatt's flight, see the "Sworn Statement Made by Anna Shown," both found in Larceny Jacket 59, U.S. District Court for the Fort Smith Division of the Western District of Arkansas.

69. "Our Public Pasture," *Van Buren Press*, July 12, 1869.

70. Larceny Jacket 59, U.S. District Court for the Fort Smith Division of the Western District of Arkansas.

71. "The Circuit Court," *Van Buren Press*, December 21, 1869.

72. See Lisa Miles Bunkowski, "The Butler County Kansas Vigilantes: An Examination of Violence and Community, 1870" (Ph.D. diss., University of Kansas, 2003). For frontier felonies, see David J. Bodenhamer, "Law and Disorder on the Early Frontier: Marion County, Indiana, 1823–1850," *Western Historical Quarterly* 10 (July 1979): 323–36. Felonies were far less common than misdemeanor prosecutions, especially for such offenses as gambling and violating liquor laws. Most felonies were nonviolent property crimes.

73. *Van Buren Press*, May 16, 1871.

74. Anna Dawes, "A United States Prison," *Lend a Hand*, 1886, 5.

75. "Jail Delivery," *Van Buren Press*, May 9, 1871.
76. Bodenhamer, "Law and Disorder," 335.
77. "Western District of Arkansas," vi.
78. "Biography of Wyatt Earp," Earl Chafin Papers, Southwest Museum/Autry National Center.
79. "Western District of Arkansas," 270–71.
80. Ibid., 282–85.
81. *Cherokee Advocate*, April 20, 1872, quoted in "Difficulties in Cherokee Country," H.doc. 287, 42nd Cong., 2nd Sess. (1872), Ser. 1520. On April 25, 1872, Owen and another deputy U.S. marshal, Joseph Peavy, approached the Going Snake Courthouse as the murder trial of a Cherokee man, Ezekiel Proctor, took place inside the building. The two deputy marshals had come to Going Snake accompanied by a large posse—estimated to be as large as eighteen men—composed of both whites and Cherokees. They aimed to arrest Proctor, who had mistakenly killed his Cherokee sister-in-law in a botched attempt to shoot and kill her white husband. According to an 1866 treaty with the Cherokees, Cherokee courts had jurisdiction over Indian-on-Indian crimes committed in Cherokee Territory. Proctor therefore surrendered himself to Cherokee authorities to be tried before a Cherokee judge. Proctor's intended victim suspected that the Cherokees would acquit him, so he traveled to Fort Smith to petition the authorities to arrest Proctor for the attempted murder of a white man—a crime over which the Western District court had jurisdiction. Owen's intention was to await the outcome of the trial, then arrest Proctor on the new charge when, as expected, the Cherokee court acquitted him. Yet the posse included several Cherokee men, relatives of the woman Proctor had killed, who sought simple vengeance. When the posse arrived at the courthouse, a Cherokee member of the posse who was also a relative of the slain woman pushed his way through the courthouse door and immediately leveled his weapon at Proctor. The defendant pushed the weapon aside but was struck in the leg as the attacker fired. Another member of the posse entered the courthouse and fired, killing Proctor's attorney. In the next few minutes, as the court bailiffs and the posse exchanged fire, ten more men were killed and eight wounded, including a juror and the judge. Owen was shot through the abdomen. He lingered for two days before dying. For criminal jurisdiction in Indian territory, see Sidney Harring, *Crow Dog's Case: American Indian Sovereignty, Tribal Law, and United States Law in the Nineteenth Century* (New York: Cambridge University Press, 1994).
82. For an authentic account of bison hunting that stands in contrast to Earp's memories, see Richard Bussell, "Buffalo Hunting," Panhandle-Plains Historical Society, Canyon, TX. For an analysis of the hide hunters of the southern plains in the 1870s, see Andrew C. Isenberg, *The Destruction of the Bison: An Environmental History, 1750–1920* (New York: Cambridge University Press, 2000), 123–63.

83. Edwards, "Wild West Remembrances," Earl Chafin Papers, Southwest Museum/Autry National Center.

84. Wyatt-Brown, *Southern Honor*, 292–93.

85. John D'Emilio and Estelle Freedman, *Intimate Matters: A History of Sexuality in America* (New York: Harper and Row, 1988), 134; Bell Irvin Wiley, *The Life of Billy Yank: The Common Soldier of the Union* (Indianapolis: Bobbs-Merrill, 1951), 257–58, 261.

86. For prostitution in Nashville, see Wiley, *Life of Billy Yank*, 259–60; D'Emilio and Freedman, *Intimate Matters*, 148. Norfolk was notorious for prostitution even before the war; it had one prostitute for every twenty-six men in the city, a far higher ratio than New York's 1:52. See Wyatt-Brown, *Southern Honor*, 293.

87. *Ellsworth Reporter*, October 3, 1872.

88. See Albert L. Hurtado, *Intimate Frontiers: Sex and Gender in Old California* (Albuquerque: University of New Mexico Press, 1999), 76. For California, see also Susan Johnson, *Roaring Camp: The Social World of the California Gold Rush* (New York: Norton, 2000). For Nevada, see Marion S. Goldman, *Gold Diggers and Silver Miners: Prostitution and Social Life on the Comstock Lode* (Ann Arbor: University of Michigan Press, 1981). For prostitution in the nineteenth-century West in general, see Anne M. Butler, *Daughters of Joy, Sisters of Misery: Prostitutes in the American West, 1865–1890* (Urbana: University of Illinois Press, 1985).

89. For the politics of nonreproductive sexuality, see Estelle Freedman, "Sexuality in Nineteenth-Century America: Behavior, Ideology, and Politics," *Reviews in American History* 10 (December 1982): 196–215. See also Janet Farrell Brodie, *Contraception and Abortion in Nineteenth-Century America* (Ithaca: Cornell University Press, 1994); Stephen Nissenbaum, *Sex, Diet, and Debility in Jacksonian America: Sylvester Graham and Health Reform* (Westport, CT: Greenwood Press, 1980).

90. *Farmer's Cabinet*, January 11, 1866, 3. Brian Page and Richard Walker, "From Settlement to Fordism: The Agro-Industrial Revolution in the American Midwest," *Economic Geography* 67 (October 1991): 281–315; Margaret Walsh, "From Pork Merchant to Meat Packer: The Midwestern Meat Industry in the Mid-Nineteenth Century," *Agricultural History* 56 (January 1982): 127–37; Timothy R. Mahoney, "Urban History in a Regional Context: River Towns on the Upper Mississippi, 1840–1860," *Journal of American History* 72 (September 1985): 318–39.

91. Edwards, "Wild West Remembrances," Earl Chafin Papers, Southwest Museum/Autry National Center.

92. Jay, "Wyatt Earp's Lost Year." The amount of the fine and that Walton and Wyatt were fined the same amount indicate that Wyatt was a confederate of the prostitutes and not a customer.

93. Ibid., 46; John E. Semonche, "Common-Law Marriage in North Carolina: A Study in Legal History," *American Journal of Legal History* 9 (October 1965): 320–22. Recognition of common-law marriage status for cohabitants did not

extend to interracial couples. See Mary Frances Berry, "Judging Morality: Sexual Behavior and Legal Consequences in the Late Nineteenth-Century South," *Journal of American History* 78 (December 1991): 835–56.

94. Robert Wiebe, *The Search for Order, 1877–1920* (New York: Hill and Wang, 1967).

95. History as well as literature abounds with examples, from Siddhartha Gautama (Buddha) to St. Augustine to Malcolm X, of wayward youths who matured to become adults who led lives of moral purpose. Such a biography makes for a compelling allegory of religious conversion—one that transcends any one religion. Buddha, Augustine, and Malcolm X each recounted his life in a way that equated maturation from hedonistic youth to responsible adulthood with religious conversion. See David Edward Shaner, "Biographies of the Buddha," *Philosophy East and West* 37 (July 1987): 306–22; Brown, *Augustine of Hippo*; *The Autobiography of Malcolm X* (New York: Grove Press, 1965). For an analysis of St. Augustine and the problem of memory, see James Olney, "Memory and the Narrative Imperative: St. Augustine and Samuel Beckett," *New Literary History* 24 (Autumn 1993): 857–80.

4. JERK YOUR GUN

1. Stuart Lake, *Wyatt Earp: Frontier Marshal* (Boston: Houghton Mifflin, 1931), 115, 145–46.

2. William B. Shillingberg, "Wyatt Earp and the 'Buntline Special' Myth," *Kansas Historical Quarterly* 42 (Summer 1976): 113–52. For Ned Buntline, see Louis S. Warren, *Buffalo Bill's America: William Cody and the Wild West Show* (New York: A. A. Knopf, 2005), 155–56. In addition to being featured on the *Wyatt Earp* television program, the pistol also featured in 1959 in one of the first episodes of "Peabody's Improbable History," an interstitial segment of *Rocky and His Friends*, the animated series starring Rocky the Flying Squirrel and Bullwinkle Moose—also aired on ABC. In the fourth episode of the series, Mr. Peabody, a genius dog who invents a time machine, travels back in time to aid Wyatt Earp, who has rendered himself helpless by carving so many notches in the handle of his six-shooter that there's nothing of it left. The Earp segment ran in the first season of *Rocky and His Friends*; Earp was the third historical figure Peabody visited, following Napoléon Bonaparte and Horatio Nelson.

3. Harrison Leussler to Lake, March 6, 1929, Stuart Nathaniel Lake Papers, Box 4, Huntington Library, San Marino, CA.

4. Lake, *Wyatt Earp*, 147–49, 295.

5. Ibid., 78–94. For a contemporary account of the shooting of Whitney, which makes no reference to Wyatt Earp whatsoever, see the *Ellsworth Reporter*, August 21, 1873. The transcript of Thompson's trial can be found in the Records of the Ellsworth County District Court, 1868–98, Kansas State Historical Society, Topeka.

6. For the terms of this masculine code, see Bertram Wyatt-Brown, *Southern Honor: Ethics and Behavior in the Old South* (New York: Oxford University Press, 1982).

7. For "green cloth" and "white hood," see *Wichita Eagle*, April 30, 1874.

8. Wilson Purdy Journal, July 23, 1874, Kansas State Historical Society. For the grasshopper plagues of the 1870s, see Jeffrey A. Lockwood, *Locust: The Devastating Rise and Mysterious Disappearance of the Insect That Shaped the American Frontier* (New York: Basic Books, 2004); Annette Atkins, *Harvest of Grief: Grasshopper Plagues and Public Assistance in Minnesota, 1873–1878* (St. Paul: Minnesota Historical Society Press, 1984).

9. David D. Leahy to John Madden, November 11, 1928, Lake Papers, Box 9, Huntington Library.

10. Wilson Purdy Journal, February 6, 1874, June 4, 1874, Kansas State Historical Society. For a comparison of the cowboy and the gaucho, see Richard W. Slatta, *Cowboys of the Americas* (New Haven, CT: Yale University Press, 1990).

11. C. Robert Haywood, *Victorian West: Class and Culture in Kansas Cattle Towns* (Lawrence: University Press of Kansas, 1991). For middle-class culture, see Mary P. Ryan, *Cradle of the Middle Class: The Family in Oneida County, New York, 1790–1865* (New York: Cambridge University Press, 1981); Jacquelyn C. Miller, "An 'Uncommon Tranquility of Mind': Emotional Self-Control and the Construction of a Middle-Class Identity in Eighteenth-Century Philadelphia," *Journal of Social History* 30 (Autumn 1996): 129–48; C. Dallet Hemphill, "Middle Class Rising in Revolutionary America: The Evidence from Manners," *Journal of Social History* 30 (Winter 1996): 317–44.

12. Terry G. Jordan, *North American Cattle-Ranching Frontiers: Origins, Diffusion, and Differentiation* (Albuquerque: University of New Mexico Press, 1993). For the cattle market in nineteenth-century California, see Andrew C. Isenberg, *Mining California: An Ecological History* (New York: Hill and Wang, 2005): 103–30; David Igler, *Industrial Cowboys: Miller & Lux and the Transformation of the Far West, 1850–1920* (Berkeley: University of California Press, 2001).

13. For the Kansas railroads, see Lloyd J. Mercer, *Railroads and Land Grant Policy: A Study in Government Intervention* (New York: Academic Press, 1982), 44–54; and Oscar Osburn Winther, *The Transportation Frontier: Trans-Mississippi West, 1865–1890* (New York: Holt, Rinehart and Winston, 1964). For the industrial consumption of western natural resources in the nineteenth century, see Isenberg, *Mining California*; Andrew C. Isenberg, *The Destruction of the Bison: An Environmental History, 1750–1920* (New York: Cambridge University Press, 2000), 123–63.

14. For the development of the cow towns, see Robert Dykstra, *The Cattle Towns* (New York: A. A. Knopf, 1968); for the incorporation of Texas cattle into a larger system of resource consumption centered in Chicago, see William Cronon, *Nature's Metropolis: Chicago and the Great West* (New York: Norton, 1991). For

contemporary accounts, see "Beef from Texas," *New York Daily Tribune,* November 6, 1867.

15. See William Frank Zornow, *Kansas: A History of the Jayhawk State* (Norman: University of Oklahoma Press, 1957), 162–63; Everett Dick, *The Sod-House Frontier, 1854–1890: A Social History of the Northern Plains from the Creation of Kansas and Nebraska to the Admission of the Dakotas* (New York: D. Appleton-Century, 1937; Lincoln, NE: Johnsen, 1954), 144–45. Citation refers to Johnsen edition.

16. David Lopez, "Cowboy Strikes and Unions," *Labor History* 18 (Summer 1977): 325–40; George N. Green, "The Texas Labor Movement, 1870–1920," *Southwestern Historical Quarterly* 108 (July 2004): 1–26; Andrew R. Graybill, *Policing the Great Plains: Rangers, Mounties, and the North American Frontier, 1875–1910* (Lincoln: University of Nebraska Press, 2007); Mark Wyman, *Hoboes: Bindlestiffs, Fruit Tramps, and the Harvesting of the West* (New York: Hill and Wang, 2010).

17. See Carol Leonard and Isidor Wallimann, "Prostitution and Changing Morality in the Frontier Cattle Towns of Kansas," *Kansas History* 2 (Spring 1979): 34–53.

18. Elliott West, *The Saloon on the Rocky Mountain Mining Frontier* (Lincoln: University of Nebraska Press, 1979), 48–49.

19. City marshal's monthly reports for 1874, Wichita City Records, 1871–81, Kansas State Historical Society.

20. Leahy to Madden, November 11, 1928, Lake Papers, Box 9, Huntington Library.

21. See West, *Saloon on the Rocky Mountain Mining Frontier,* 40.

22. "Important to Texas Drovers. Greetings from citizens of Wichita," April 27, 1875, Wichita City Records, 1871–81, Kansas State Historical Society.

23. City marshal's monthly reports for 1874, Wichita City Records, 1871–81, Kansas State Historical Society.

24. Wyatt Earp to Stuart Lake, October 30, 1928, Lake Papers, Box 3, Huntington Library.

25. For the Earps' residence, see the Kansas State Census, 1875, vol. 55, Sedgwick County, City of Wichita.

26. City marshal's monthly reports for 1874, Wichita City Records, 1871–81, Kansas State Historical Society.

27. John Flood, "Wyatt Earp," 38–46, Ford County Historical Society, Dodge City, KS.

28. Leahy to Madden, November 11, 1928, Lake Papers, Box 9, Huntington Library. Bill Smith was not marshal when Wyatt became a police officer; Smith was the 1876 electoral opponent of Mike Meagher, the marshal who hired Wyatt. Wyatt severely beat Smith on the eve of that election, a violent impulse that cost him his job. Wyatt himself erred in telling Lake that "Bill Smith was the Marshal who put me in." Wyatt Earp to Lake, October 30, 1928, Lake Papers, Box 3, Huntington Library.

29. Lake, *Wyatt Earp,* 95–100.

30. *Wichita Eagle*, October 29, 1874.
31. Gary L. Cunningham, "Gambling in the Kansas Cattle Towns: A Prominent and Somewhat Honorable Profession," *Kansas History* 5 (Spring 1982), 2–22.
32. Wilson Purdy Journal, July 11, 1874, Kansas State Historical Society.
33. Dykstra, *Cattle Towns*; Robert Dykstra, "Body Counts and Murder Rates: The Contested Statistics of Western Violence," *Reviews in American History* 31 (December 2003), 554–63.
34. Roger D. McGrath, *Gunfighters, Highwaymen, and Vigilantes: Violence on the Frontier* (Berkeley: University of California Press, 1984); Clare V. McKanna, Jr., "Alcohol, Handguns, and Homicide in the American West: A Tale of Three Counties, 1880–1920," *Western Historical Quarterly* 26 (Winter 1995): 455–82; Clare V. McKanna, Jr., *Homicide, Race, and Justice in the American West, 1880–1920* (Tucson: University of Arizona Press, 1997); John Boessenecker, *Gold Dust and Gunsmoke: Tales of Gold Rush Outlaws, Lawmen, and Vigilantes* (New York: Wiley, 1999); Randolph Roth, Michael D. Maltz, and Douglas L. Eckberg, "Homicide Rates in the Old West," *Western Historical Quarterly* 42 (Summer 2011): 173–95.
35. A baseball metaphor is perhaps appropriate: if a rookie ballplayer bats for a high average in the first games of his career, no reasonable observer would pronounce him one of the best players of all time, based on that small sample; the player would need to maintain that excellence over a career. For the "fallacy of small numbers," see Robert Dykstra, "Field Notes: Overdosing on Dodge City," *Western Historical Quarterly* 27 (Winter 1996): 505–14; Robert Dykstra, "Violence, Gender, and Methodology in the 'New' Western History," *Reviews in American History* 27 (March 1999): 79–86.
36. Wyatt-Brown, *Southern Honor*, 295, 343, 353, 367–69.
37. Leahy to Madden, November 11, 1928, Lake Papers, Box 9.
38. "An Aristocratic Horse Thief," *Wichita Beacon*, May 12, 1875. See also *Wichita Eagle*, May 6, 1875.
39. *Wichita Beacon*, December 15, 1875.
40. *Wichita Beacon*, January 1, 1876.
41. See Wyatt Earp to Lake, November 30, 1928, Lake Papers, Box 3, Huntington Library. See also Lake to Wyatt Earp, November 24, 1928, Lake Papers, Box 6.
42. Leahy to Madden, November 11, 1928, Lake Papers, Box 9, Huntington Library.
43. B. R. Burg, "Officers, Gentlemen, 'Man-Talk,' and Group Sex in the 'Old Navy,' 1870–1873," *Journal of the History of Sexuality* 11 (July 2002): 439–56.
44. See John D'Emilio and Estelle B. Freedman, *Intimate Matters: A History of Sexuality in America* (New York: Harper and Row, 1988), 124; see also Chris Packard, *Queer Cowboys and Other Erotic Male Friendships in Nineteenth-Century American Literature* (New York: Palgrave Macmillan, 2005); Peter Boag, *Same-Sex Affairs: Constructing and Controlling Homosexuality in the Pacific Northwest* (Berkeley: University of California Press, 2003).

45. Leahy to Madden, November 11, 1928, Lake Papers, Box 9, Huntington Library.

46. John M. Faragher, *Women and Men on the Overland Trail* (New Haven, CT: Yale University Press, 1979); Carroll Smith-Rosenberg, "The Female World of Love and Ritual: Relations Between Women in Nineteenth-Century America," *Signs* 1 (Autumn 1975): 1–29.

47. "Wyatt Earp: Brave, Courageous and Bold, or Murdering Skunk," *Wichita Eagle*, January 21, 1979. For male friends to room together and even to share the same bed was not unusual in nineteenth-century America. In *The Intimate World of Abraham Lincoln*, the author C. A. Tripp tried to use similar evidence—that the young Lincoln shared a bed with a roommate, Joshua Speed—to argue that Lincoln was bisexual. Such an argument takes nineteenth-century men out of their historical context when homosocial relationships were the norm. It imposes modern notions of sexuality upon nineteenth-century Americans, assuming that our understanding of sexual desire and behavior is historically transcendent. C. A. Tripp, *The Intimate World of Abraham Lincoln* (New York: Free Press, 2005).

48. Lake, *Wyatt Earp*, 104.

49. Flood, "Wyatt Earp," 47, Ford County Historical Society.

50. *Wichita Beacon*, April 5, 1876.

51. J. W. Harry, A. W. Allen, "To the Police Comm[ittee]," May 10, 1876; and "Proceedings of the Governing Body," May 22, 1876, Wichita City Records, 1870–81, Kansas State Historical Society; *Wichita Beacon*, April 5, 1876.

52. *Wichita Beacon*, May 24, 1876.

53. Adelia Earp Edwards, "Wild West Remembrances," 2, Earl Chafin Papers, Southwest Museum/Autry National Center, Los Angeles, CA.

54. Robert M. Wright, *Dodge City: The Cowboy Capital* (Wichita, KS, 1913), 8, 74, 137–40.

55. Isenberg, *Destruction of the Bison*, 134.

56. L. C. Fouquet, "Buffalo Days," *Collections of the Kansas Historical Society* 16 (1923–25): 347.

57. Wright, *Dodge City*, 152.

58. O. H. Simpson, Dodge City, Kansas, to the American Bison Society, January 19, 1934, American Bison Society Papers, Box 276, File 7, Conservation Collection, Denver Public Library. See also Joe Killough, interview with D. T. Leachman, December 16, 1945, Panhandle-Plains Historical Society.

59. Wright, *Dodge City*, 255–57.

60. "Dodge City, Kansas, May 28th, 1877," *Kansas City Times*, quoted in Wright, *Dodge City*, 258.

61. Wentin A. Wilson, "Details of a Buffalo Hunt of 1876 in Kansas," November 6, 1876, Kansas State Historical Society.

62. See *Dodge City Times*, February 9, 1878, April 13, 1878, July 13, 1878, July 27, 1878, October 5, 1878; *Ford County Globe*, February 12, 1878, April 16, 1878, August 27, 1878.

63. Wright, *Dodge City*, 138.

64. "Christianity in Dodge City," *Ford County Globe*, January 21, 1879; see also the *Dodge City Times*, June 8, 1878, on the founding of the Presbyterian church.

65. Cyril D. Robinson and Richard Scaglion, "The Origin and Evolution of the Police Function in Society: Notes Toward a Theory," *Law and Society Review* 21 (1987): 109–54. See also Robert Liebman and Michael Polen, "Perspectives on Policing in Nineteenth-Century America," *Social Science History* 2 (Spring 1978): 346–60; Sidney Harring, "The Development of the Police Institution in the United States," *Crime and Social Justice* 5 (Spring–Summer 1976): 54–59; Andrew R. Graybill, "Rural Police and the Defense of the Cattleman's Empire in Texas and Alberta, 1875–1900," *Agricultural History* 79 (Summer 2005): 253–80.

66. Affidavit Re: Wyatt Earp, Lake Papers, Box 3, Huntington Library.

67. Mabel Earp Cason Papers, Arizona Historical Society, Tucson.

68. Flood, "Wyatt Earp," 50, 62, 82–95, Ford County Historical Society.

69. "The Festive Revolver," *Ford County Globe*, March 5, 1878.

70. A. C. Jackson shot up Dodge's Front Street in September 1877. See *Dodge City Times*, September 29, 1877. See also *Ford County Globe*, August 20, 1878; "A Day of Carnival," *Ford County Globe*, September 5, 1879.

71. "Dodge City in Mourning," *Ford County Globe*, April 10, 1878; *Dodge City Times*, April 13, 1878.

72. *Dodge City Times*, July 27, 1878; *Ford County Globe*, August 27, 1878. Both Earp and Masterson recalled that Hoy fired into a theater where the entertainer Eddie Foy was working. Both also claim that Hoy died immediately from his wounds. See Flood, "Wyatt Earp," 96–101, Ford County Historical Society; W. B. Masterson, "Famous Gun Fighters of the Western Frontier, Second Article: Wyatt Earp," *Human Life*, February 1907.

73. Tenth United States Census, 1880, Ford County, Dodge City, Kansas, 19. For Josephine, see Stuart Lake to Ira Kent, February 13, 1930, Lake Papers, Box 7, Huntington Library.

74. For the real and imagined shootings involving James Kennedy, see *Dodge City Times*, October 12, 1878, November 27, 1880.

75. Lake, *Wyatt Earp*, 138.

76. *Dodge City Times*, July 7, 1877; *Ford County Globe*, January 22, 1878, May 8, 1878, June 11, 1878, September 9, 1879.

77. See T. H. Breen, "Horses and Gentlemen: The Cultural Significance of Gambling Among the Gentry of Virginia," *William and Mary Quarterly*, 3rd ser., 34 (April 1977): 239–57.

78. John M. Findlay, *People of Chance: Gambling in American Society from Jamestown to Las Vegas* (New York: Oxford University Press, 1986).

79. In some versions of the game, the dealer draws three cards: a "dead" card, which pays no one, followed by the losing and winning cards.

80. For faro, see James C. Hancock Reminiscences, 1933, James Covington Han-

cock Papers, Arizona Historical Society. See also "The Faro Bank—the Turn,"
Harper's Weekly, February 23, 1867, 120–21; David W. Maurer, "The Argot of
the Faro Bank," *American Speech* 18 (February 1943): 3–11.

81. "Talk with a Tiger: Some Tricks of the Gambler's Trade Explained," *Boston Daily*, October 1, 1882.

82. "Gambling," *Chicago Tribune*, November 6, 1866.

83. "A New Trick at Faro," *Chicago Tribune*, April 2, 1889. See also Ann Fabian, *Card Sharps, Dream Books, and Bucket Shops: Gambling in Nineteenth-Century America* (Ithaca, NY: Cornell University Press, 1990), 21–22.

84. "Talk with a Tiger."

85. "He Isn't a Fool: What an Expert Faro Dealer Must Be to Get On in the World," *National Police Gazette*, December 4, 1886.

86. George Devol, *Forty Years a Gambler on the Mississippi* (1892; repr., New York: Johnson Reprint Company, 1988), 66–67, 156–68.

87. Jim McIntire, *Early Days in Texas: A Trip to Hell and Heaven* (1902; repr., Norman: University of Oklahoma Press, 1992), 70.

88. Lake to Earp, August 5, 1928, Lake Papers, Box 6, Huntington Library.

89. Devol, *Forty Years a Gambler*, 298.

90. Karen Halttunen, *Confidence Men and Painted Women: A Study of Middle-Class Culture in America, 1830–1870* (New Haven, CT: Yale University Press, 1982), 18.

91. See Breen, "Horses and Gentlemen," 241; Gillian Russell, "'Faro's Daughters': Female Gamesters, Politics, and the Discourse of Finance in 1790s Britain," *Eighteenth-Century Studies* 33 (Summer 2000): 481–504.

92. Jackson, quoted in Findlay, *People of Chance*, 38–39.

93. See Gunther Peck, "Manly Gambles: The Politics of Risk on the Comstock Lode, 1860–1880," *Journal of Social History* 26 (Summer 1993): 701–23.

94. Clifford Geertz, "Deep Play: Notes on a Balinese Cockfight," in *The Interpretation of Cultures: Selected Essays* (New York: Basic Books, 1973), 449.

95. Charles G. Sellers, "Who Were the Southern Whigs?" *American Historical Review* 59 (January 1954): 335–46.

96. For Holliday, see Gary L. Roberts, *Doc Holliday: The Life and Legend* (Hoboken, NJ: Wiley, 2006); Karen Holliday Tanner, *Doc Holliday: A Family Portrait* (Norman: University of Oklahoma Press, 1998), 57–65. Tanner maintained that Holliday was born with a cleft palate and lip, and that his uncle, the physician John Stiles Holliday, together with Dr. Crawford Williamson Long, a pioneer in the use of ether as an anesthetic, performed a successful operation to correct the deformity when Holliday was eight weeks old. See Tanner, *Doc Holliday*, 14–16. Roberts has cast doubt on whether such a complicated surgery could successfully have been performed in 1851 without attracting considerable attention. John Henry Holliday was effectively the youngest child in a large Holliday household that included Francisco E'Dalgo (a corruption of *Hidalgo*), a Mexican orphan Henry brought back to Georgia from the war and raised; and, after the

death of Alice's father in 1856, her younger brother and three younger sisters. Just as the extended Earp family stayed close to one another in Monmouth and later in Lamar, the Hollidays—Henry had five younger siblings—lived near Griffin in Fayetteville, Jonesboro, and Atlanta. Roberts, *Doc Holliday*, 14–15, 21.

97. See Jonathan Daniel Wells, *The Origins of the Southern Middle Class, 1800–1861* (Chapel Hill: University of North Carolina Press, 2004).

98. For slavery's domination of the antebellum southern economy, see Gavin Wright, *The Political Economy of the Cotton South: Households, Markets, and Wealth in the Nineteenth Century* (New York: Norton, 1978); James Oakes, *Slavery and Freedom: An Interpretation of the Old South* (New York: A. A. Knopf, 1990).

99. To finance the move, Henry Holliday sold a number of properties in Griffin, raising $34,650 (in Confederate currency), which he used to buy nearly thirty-five hundred acres. Tanner, *Doc Holliday*, 40–46; Roberts, *Doc Holliday*, 29–35.

100. See J. F. DeLacy to Robert N. Mullin, January 9, 1949, Lake Papers, Box 10, Huntington Library.

101. Roberts, *Doc Holliday*, 38–47.

102. Ibid., 53.

103. "A Man of Sand," *Gunnison News-Democrat*, June 18, 1882.

104. Tanner, *Doc Holliday*, 58–59.

105. Roberts, *Doc Holliday*, 70–88; Tanner, *Doc Holliday*, 91–108.

106. Holliday's mother, who had been born a Methodist and had become a Presbyterian when she married Henry Holliday, was "deeply anxious about the faith of her only child" in her last days, according to a local minister. As an encouragement to her son, she rejoined the Methodist church on her deathbed. Following his mother's death, John Henry likewise became a Methodist.

107. Holliday placed an advertisement for his dental services in the *Dodge City Times*, June 8, 1878.

108. Roberts, *Doc Holliday*, 51–52, 77–80.

109. William Barclay Masterson, "Famous Gun Fighters of the Western Frontier, Fourth Article: 'Doc' Holliday," *Human Life*, May 1907. For a somewhat dated but still quite useful analysis of nineteenth-century stereotypes about women, see Carroll Smith-Rosenberg and Charles Rosenberg, "The Female Animal: Medical and Biological Views of Women and Her Role in Nineteenth-Century America," *Journal of American History* 60 (September 1973), 332–56.

110. Wyatt Earp, "How I Routed a Gang of Arizona Outlaws," *San Francisco Examiner*, August 2, 1896.

111. Masterson, "Famous Gun Fighters: 'Doc' Holliday."

112. For the Roman version, see Valerius Maximus, *Memorable Deeds and Sayings: One Thousand Tales from Ancient Rome*, trans. Henry John Walker (Indianapolis, 2004), 152.

113. Touring companies might have as many as fifty plays in their repertory; *Damon and Pythias* was performed both by highbrow companies, who interspersed it with performances of Shakespeare, and by companies that specialized in stage

adaptations of popular novels. Though formal and old-fashioned even by the standards of its day, *Damon and Pythias* was popular with provincial American audiences. J. Alan Hammack, "An American Actor's Diary: 1858," *Educational Theatre Journal* 7 (December 1955): 324–37; Alan Woods, "Fredrick B. Warde: America's Greatest Forgotten Tragedian," *Educational Theatre Journal* 29 (October 1977): 336; Russell Merritt, "Rescued from a Perilous Nest: D. W. Griffith's Escape from Theatre into Film," *Cinema Journal* 21 (Autumn 1981): 19. Griffith, a stage actor before becoming a film director, played Dionysius in *Damon and Pythias* in a touring company in the 1890s.

114. John Banim, *Damon and Pythias: A Play in Five Acts* (New York, c. 1846).

115. H. K. Shackleford, *The Knight's Armor: A History of the Early Origins of the Order of the Knights of Pythias* (New Haven, 1869), 13.

116. *Tucson and Tombstone General and Business Directory for 1883 and 1884, Containing a Complete List of All the Inhabitants, with Their Occupations and Places of Residence; the Public Officers, Secret Societies and Churches, Together with Other Useful Information Concerning Both Cities* (Tucson, AZ: Cobler & Co., 1883), 107, 118–22.

117. See Ros King, *The Works of Richard Edwards: Politics, Poetry, and Performance in Sixteenth-Century England* (Manchester, UK, and New York: Manchester University Press, 2001), 157, 160–61; Louis B. Wright, "The Male-Friendship Cult in Thomas Heywood's Plays," *Modern Language Notes* 42 (December 1927): 510–14. References to homosexual desire were common in early modern English dramas, particularly those that had as their subject friendship, duty, and honor. One scholar has suggested that discourse on chivalry in such dramas was a sublimation for homoerotic attraction. Alan Stewart, *Close Readers: Humanism and Sodomy in Early Modern England* (Princeton, NJ: Princeton University Press, 1997); Alan Bray, "Homosexuality and the Signs of Male Friendship in Elizabethan England," in *Queering the Renaissance,* ed. Jonathan Goldberg (Durham, NC: Duke University Press, 1994), 40–61; Richard E. Zeikowitz, *Homoeroticism and Chivalry: Discourses of Male Same-Sex Desire in the Fourteenth Century* (New York: Palgrave Macmillan, 2003).

118. Marylynne Diggs, "Romantic Friends or a 'Different Race of Creatures'? The Representations of Lesbian Pathology in Nineteenth-Century America," *Feminist Studies* 21 (Summer 1995): 321.

5. WILD JUSTICE

1. The Ten-Percent Ring was an epithet coined by the editors of the *Tombstone Epitaph* in 1881 to characterize corrupt Cochise County officials who allegedly skimmed 10 percent of tax moneys for themselves. See *Tombstone Epitaph*, December 25, 1881. The depiction of the Ten-Percent Ring in the ABC television program may have been based on the Santa Fe Ring, the oligarchs who controlled the governorship and land sales in territorial New Mexico in the

1870s and 1880s. For the Santa Fe Ring, see Howard Lamar, *The Far Southwest, 1846–1912: A Territorial History* (New York: Norton, 1970), 147. NBC countered ABC's *Wyatt Earp* program with *Bat Masterson*, which ran from 1958 to 1961.

2. Stuart Lake, *Wyatt Earp: Frontier Marshal* (Boston: Houghton Mifflin, 1931), 234–35. For the icon of the gangster in the first decades of the twentieth century, see David Ruth, *Inventing the Public Enemy: The Gangster in American Culture, 1918–1934* (Chicago: University of Chicago Press, 1996).

3. Stuart Lake, "Notes on people, places, and situations in Arizona Territory from 1879 to 1883," Stuart N. Lake Papers, Box 16, Huntington Library, San Marino, CA. Lake's characterization of the cowboys resembled that of the writer W. R. Burnett, who followed his 1929 gangland novel, *Little Caesar*, with *Saint Johnson* in 1930—a story based on Tombstone.

4. Richard Gid Powers, "J. Edgar Hoover and the Detective Hero," *Journal of Popular Culture* 9 (Fall 1975): 257–78; Robert Clurman, introduction to *Nick Carter, Detective* (New York: Dell, 1963), 7–13. See also Claire Bond Potter, *War on Crime: Bandits, G-Men, and the Politics of Mass Culture* (New Brunswick, NJ: Rutgers University Press, 1998). Patrick Culhane, *Black Hats: A Novel of Wyatt Earp and Al Capone* (New York: William Morrow, 2007), has the seventy-year-old Earp battling Capone himself.

5. In Earp's defense of justice, Flood compared Earp both to Jesus and the soldiers of the First World War, writing, "Always there has been its defense, sacred from the foundation, from the Man of Calvary to the crimson stream that flowed along the banks of the bitter Marne." John Henry Flood, "Wyatt Earp," c. 1925, 1, Ford County Historical Society, Dodge City, KS.

6. Forrestine C. Hooker, "An Arizona Vendetta: The Truth About Wyatt Earp and Some Others," c. 1918, 1, 4, 9, Southwest Museum/Autry National Center, Los Angeles, CA.

7. W. H. Hutchinson, *Oil, Land, and Politics: The California Career of Thomas Robert Bard* (Norman: University of Oklahoma Press, 1965), 5.

8. John Opie, *The Law of the Land: Two Hundred Years of American Farmland Policy* (Lincoln: University of Nebraska Press, 1994).

9. Richard White, *Railroaded: The Transcontinentals and the Making of Modern America* (New York: Norton, 2011).

10. See Robert J. Orsi, *Sunset Limited: The Southern Pacific Railroad and the Development of the American West, 1850–1930* (Berkeley: University of California Press, 2005), 100–102; Richard Maxwell Brown, *No Duty to Retreat: Violence and Values in American History and Society* (Norman: University of Oklahoma Press, 1994), 87–128.

11. James Covington Hancock Papers, Arizona Historical Society, Tucson.

12. John Pleasant Gray, "When All Roads Led to Tombstone," c. 1940, 50–52, Arizona Historical Society, Tucson.

13. Hutchinson, *Oil, Land, and Politics*, 178–79.

14. Richard J. Hinton, *The Hand-Book to Arizona: Its Resources, History, Towns, Mines, Ruins and Scenery* (San Francisco: Payot, Upham & Co., 1878), 237.

15. *Tucson and Tombstone General and Business Directory for 1883 and 1884, Containing a Complete List of All the Inhabitants, with Their Occupations and Places of Residence; the Public Officers, Secret Societies and Churches, Together with Other Useful Information Concerning Both Cities* (Tucson: Cobler & Co., 1883), 106, Huntington Library, San Marino, CA; J. W. Tourney, "Notes on the Trees and Flora of the Chiricahua Mountains," *Garden and Forest Magazine* 8 (January 9, 1895).

16. For ranching in the nineteenth-century West, see Terry G. Jordan, *North American Cattle-Ranching Frontiers: Origins, Diffusion, and Differentiation* (Albuquerque: University of New Mexico Press, 1993); David Lopez, "Cowboy Strikes and Unions," *Labor History* 18 (Summer 1977): 325–40.

17. For the wars between the Apaches and the United States, see Karl Jacoby, *Shadows at Dawn: An Apache Massacre and the Violence of History* (New York: Penguin, 2008); Chip Colwell-Chanthaphonh, *Massacre at Camp Grant: Forgetting and Remembering Apache History* (Tucson: University of Arizona Press, 2007).

18. For Schieffelin's discovery, see Julius Streidinger, *Report upon the Property Belonging to the Tombstone Mill and Mining Co., Pima County, Arizona*, October 26, 1879, 1, Huntington Library, San Marino, CA.

19. Patrick Hamilton, *The Resources of Arizona* (Prescott, AZ, 1881), 35.

20. "In collating data for a frontier city like Tucson, difficulties of a peculiar or unusual nature present themselves. In the present case a considerable proportion of the population is composed of Mexicans and Spanish speaking people, many of whom are ignorant of the objects or utility of such a publication, and in many instances show great unwillingness to furnish their names, or other requisite information, appearing to fear that the unfortunate compiler is either a Deputy Sheriff, a City marshal or some other limb of the law." *Tucson and Tombstone General and Business Directory*, 3, 103–107; John A. Church, *Annual Report of the Mines and Mills of the Tombstone Mill and Mining Company for the Year Ending March 31, 1882* (Philadelphia: McCalla & Stavely, 1882), 3–6; T. E. Sumner et al., *Report of the Vizina Consolidated Mining Company of Tombstone, Arizona* (New York: John Hamilton, 1881), 5.

21. *San Diego Daily Union*, July 14, 1880, in Lynn R. Bailey, ed., *Tombstone from a Woman's Point of View: The Correspondence of Clara Spalding Brown* (Tucson: Westernlore Press, 2003), 17; *Tucson and Tombstone General and Business Directory*, 107.

22. "The Dust," *Tombstone Epitaph*, April 28, 1881.

23. "Telephones for Tombstone," *Tombstone Epitaph*, March 15, 1881.

24. Streidinger, *Tombstone Mill and Mining Co.*, 9–10; *Tucson and Tombstone General and Business Directory*, 103.

25. Hancock Papers, Arizona Historical Society. See also "The Oriental," *Tombstone Epitaph*, July 22, 1880. For faro at the Oriental, see "About Town," *Tombstone Epitaph*, July 24, 1880.

26. *San Diego Daily Union*, July 14, 1880, in Bailey, *Tombstone from a Woman's Point of View*, 17.

27. *San Diego Daily Union*, August 10, 1880, in Bailey, *Tombstone from a Woman's Point of View*, 21.

28. George Whitwell Parsons Diary, July 16, 1880, in Lynn R. Bailey, ed., *A Tenderfoot in Tombstone: The Private Journal of George Whitwell Parsons* (Tucson: Westernlore Press, 1996), 63.

29. "Local Splinters," *Tombstone Epitaph*, October 26, 1881.

30. Jordan, *North American Cattle-Ranching Frontiers*, 142–45, 228.

31. Gray, "When All Roads Led to Tombstone," 14–15, Arizona Historical Society.

32. Brian DeLay, *War of a Thousand Deserts: Indian Raids and the U.S.-Mexican War* (New Haven, CT: Yale University Press, 2008).

33. Andrew R. Graybill, *Policing the Great Plains: Rangers, Mounties, and the North American Frontier, 1875–1910* (Lincoln: University of Nebraska Press, 2007), 80.

34. Larry D. Ball, *The United States Marshals of New Mexico and Arizona Territories, 1846–1912* (Albuquerque: University of New Mexico Press, 1978), 107–108.

35. John J. Gosper to Crawley Dake, November 28, 1881, Crawley P. Dake Correspondence, 1881–85, University of Arizona Special Collections, Tucson.

36. Hancock Reminiscences, 73, Arizona Historical Society.

37. Paul J. Vanderwood, *Disorder and Progress: Bandits, Police, and Mexican Development* (Lincoln: University of Nebraska Press, 1981), 53–69. In 1870 the Rurales Second Corps revolted against the government; in 1872 the Seventh Corps rebelled; in 1880 it was the turn of the Eleventh Corps.

38. Ball, *United States Marshals of New Mexico and Arizona*, 114–15. For the borderland, see Katherine Benton-Cohen, *Borderline Americans: Racial Division and Labor War in the Arizona Borderlands* (Cambridge, MA: Harvard University Press, 2011); Samuel Truett, *Fugitive Landscapes: The Forgotten History of the U.S.-Mexico Border* (New Haven, CT: Yale University Press, 2006).

39. Gray, "When All Roads Led to Tombstone," 98, Arizona Historical Society.

40. "A Galeyville Robbery," *Arizona Star*, September 10, 1881.

41. George O. Hand, *One Hundred Days on the San Pedro: The Contention City, A.T. Diary of George O. Hand, March 23–July 1, 1882* (Tombstone: Cochise Classics, 1988), May 29, 1882.

42. John P. Clum to Stuart Lake (January 31, 1929), Lake Papers, Box 2, Huntington Library.

43. "Reward!," *Tombstone Epitaph*, July 30, 1880. John Gray maintained that the cattle had been purchased, and not stolen, in Mexico. Killed alongside Clanton were Gray's brother, Dick, as well as Jim Crane, a cowboy who was suspected of robbing a stagecoach earlier in 1881. Gray, "When All Roads Led to Tombstone," 60–62, Arizona Historical Society.

44. Eric J. Hobsbawm, *Primitive Rebels: Studies in Archaic Forms of Social Movements in the 19th and 20th Centuries* (New York: Norton, 1959); Hobsbawm, *Bandits* (New York: Pelican, 1972), 19, 76. See also Hobsbawm, "Social Bandits: Reply," *Comparative Studies in Society and History* 14 (September 1972): 503–505.

45. For these mineral rushes see Malcolm Rohrbough, *Days of Gold: The California Gold Rush and the American Nation* (Berkeley: University of California Press, 1997); J. S. Holliday, *Rush for Riches: Gold Fever and the Making of California* (Berkeley: University of California Press, 1999); Andrew C. Isenberg, *Mining California: An Ecological History* (New York: Hill and Wang, 2005); Elliott West, *The Contested Plains: Indians, Goldseekers, and the Rush to Colorado* (Lawrence: University Press of Kansas, 1999).

46. Sacramento was founded in 1849 at the juncture of the Sacramento and American Rivers by a handful of partners, including a Peter Burnett, future governor of the state. From the outset, the claim was faulty—the town developers had mistakenly plotted the town on land they did not own. Facing competition from the town of Sutterville a few miles away, the investors in the Sacramento townsite company lured most of Sutterville's merchants with promises of lots in the new town and simply razed the stores of those who refused the offer. By 1850, settlers in the town—having discovered the faultiness of the original survey—challenged the townsite company's claim to ownership. In August 1850, the dispute between settlers and the town's founders erupted into violence in which a dozen townspeople and several city officials were killed. Burnett—now governor—ordered the militia to restore order. See Isenberg, *Mining California*, 53–64; David Vaught, *After the Gold Rush: Tarnished Dreams in the Sacramento Valley* (Baltimore: Johns Hopkins University Press, 2007). The investors in the Tombstone Townsite Company included a number of veterans of Gold Rush California. Joseph Palmer opened a bank in San Francisco in 1849. Palmer's sometime partner James Clark operated a saloon and a livery stable in San Francisco. Anson Safford prospected in California before becoming a member of the state legislature; he then became governor of the Arizona Territory between 1869 and 1877. Michael Gray migrated from Texas to California in 1849 and served as the sheriff of Yuba County, just north of Sacramento, from 1852 to 1855. They all knew of the events in Sacramento in 1850, and they drew the lesson that developing a town could mean riches as well as conflict.

47. William B. Shillingberg, *Tombstone, A.T.: A History of Early Mining, Milling, and Mayhem* (Spokane, WA: Arthur H. Clark, 1999), 61–79; Henry P. Walker, "Arizona Land Fraud Model 1880: The Tombstone Townsite Company," *Arizona and the West* 21 (Spring 1979): 5–36.

48. "Citizens Meeting," *Tombstone Epitaph*, August 7, 1880.

49. "Anti-Chinese Meeting," *Tombstone Epitaph*, July 29, 1880; "Anti-Chinese League," *Tombstone Epitaph*, July 30, 1880; "Why Should the Chinese Rejoice?," *Tombstone Epitaph*, May 10, 1881. For anti-Chinese movements in the

nineteenth-century West, see Carlos Schwantes, "Protest in a Promised Land: Unemployment, Disinheritance, and the Origin of Labor Militancy in the Pacific Northwest, 1885–1886," *Western Historical Quarterly* 13 (October 1982): 373–90.

50. "Demand Your Deeds," *Tombstone Epitaph*, October 26, 1880; "He Will Aid the Fraud," *Tombstone Epitaph*, November 7, 1880; *Tombstone Epitaph*, November 11, 1880; *Tombstone Epitaph*, November 14, 1880.

51. The rest of the endorsement reads, "John P. Clum is, by all odds the popular choice for the next Mayor of Tombstone, and there are many reasons why our voters are to be congratulated upon their selection. Mr. Clum is a young man of unusual activity and firmness. His discretion and integrity have been proven beyond a question of doubt, and, what is of greater moment in the present issue, he is, by his association, experience, and education, a thorough frontiersman." "Our Candidate for Mayor," *Tombstone Epitaph*, January 4, 1881.

52. "Helping Himself," *Tombstone Epitaph*, September 30, 1880; "About Town," *Tombstone Epitaph*, October 1, 1880; "Set Her Back, Boys," *Tombstone Epitaph*, December 6, 1880; Parsons Diary, December 4, 1880, in Bailey, *Tenderfoot in Tombstone*, 107–108.

53. Clum to Lake, January 31, 1929, Lake Papers, Box 2, Huntington Library.

54. *The Opinion of the Able and Experienced Lawyers on the Title of Tombstone Town Lots* (Tombstone: Commercial Job Printing Office, 1881).

55. *Clark v. Titus*, 2 Arizona 147, 11 Pacific 312 (1886).

56. *Ford County Globe*, September 9, 1879.

57. Hooker, "Arizona Vendetta," 2–3. Southwest Museum/Autry National Center.

58. James Earp pension record, Data on the Earp Family, Abraham Lincoln Presidential Library, Springfield, IL.

59. Wyatt Earp, "How I Routed a Gang of Arizona Outlaws," *San Francisco Examiner*, August 2, 1896.

60. For Virgil's appointment, see the Virgil Earp Folder, Earp Family Papers, Arizona Historical Society.

61. *Arizona Weekly Miner*, October 19, 1877.

62. See Ball, *United States Marshals of New Mexico and Arizona*, 117, 123.

63. Hooker, "Arizona Vendetta," 3, Southwest Museum/Autry National Center.

64. Flood, "Wyatt Earp," 107, Ford County Historical Society.

65. Wyatt Earp deposition, Lotta Crabtree Will Case, Harvard Law School Library, Cambridge, MA, http://home.earthlink.net/~knuthco1/HistoricalDocuments/crabtree.htm, accessed June 28, 2011.

66. Lake, *Wyatt Earp*, 231–32.

67. Earp deposition, Lotta Crabtree Will Case, Harvard Law Library.

68. Gary L. Roberts, *Doc Holliday: The Life and Legend* (Hoboken, NJ: Wiley, 2006), 127.

69. Flood, "Wyatt Earp," 145–51, Ford County Historical Society. See also Wil-

liam B. Masterson, "Famous Gun Fighters of the Western Frontier, Second Article: Wyatt Earp," *Human Life*, February 1907.

70. Isenberg, *Mining California*, 28–31.

71. By November 1880, Wyatt had sold one mine he had come to own, the Comstock, for $3,000, and leased another, the Mountain Maid, for $400. "Claim Sold and Another Bonded," *Tombstone Epitaph*, November 6, 1880; "Know all men that we Wyatt S. Earp, James C. Earp . . . ," November 12, 1880, Lake Papers, Box 3, Huntington Library. For gamblers taking their winnings in all sorts of property, see George Devol, *Forty Years a Gambler on the Mississippi* (1892; repr., New York: Johnson Reprint Company, 1988), 151.

72. "Baptism of Fire," *Tombstone Epitaph*, June 24, 1881. Wyatt was not the only resident of Tombstone to think first of rescuing his money when the fire broke out. Milt Joyce, the bartender at the Oriental, tried but failed to open the saloon's safe and remove $1,200 in greenbacks before the fire forced him to flee the burning building.

73. Flood, "Wyatt Earp," 145–51, Ford County Historical Society.

74. See Neil B. Carmony, ed., *Apache Days and Tombstone Nights: John Clum's Autobiography* (Silver City, NM: High Lonesome Books, 1997), 2; Douglas Firth Anderson, "Protestantism, Progress, and Prosperity: John P. Clum and 'Civilizing' the U.S. Southwest, 1871–1886," *Western Historical Quarterly* 33 (Autumn 2002): 315–35; Bailey, *Tombstone from a Woman's Point of View*, 7; Frank Davis Ashburn, *Peabody of Groton: A Portrait* (New York: Coward McCann, 1944). Peabody was headmaster at Groton when Franklin Delano Roosevelt attended the school and later officiated at Roosevelt's wedding.

75. *San Diego Daily Union*, January 18, 1881, March 9, 1881, July 23, 1881, December 13, 1881, in Bailey, ed., *Tombstone from a Woman's Point of View*, 22–31. See also *Tucson and Tombstone General and Business Directory*, 118–22.

76. "Cowboys and Bunko-Steerers," *Rocky Mountain News*, May 21, 1882.

77. Parsons to Lake, November 2, 1929, Lake Papers, Box 10, Huntington Library.

78. For Wyatt's partiality to ice cream, see Earp deposition, Lotta Crabtree Will Case.

79. Clum to Lake, October 20, 1928, Lake Papers, Box 2, Huntington Library.

80. Ashburn, *Peabody of Groton*, 45.

81. "The Murderous Pistol," *Tombstone Epitaph*, October 28, 1880.

82. Hancock Reminiscences, 73, Arizona Historical Society.

83. Gray, "When All Roads Led to Tombstone," 32–33, Arizona Historical Society; Flood, "Wyatt Earp," 111–15, Ford County Historical Society; Hooker, "Arizona Vendetta," 8, Southwest Museum/Autry National Center.

84. *Tombstone Epitaph*, November 6, 1880, November 12, 1880, November 13, 1880.

85. "Our City Marshal," *Tombstone Epitaph*, January 4, 1881. Sippy won reelection against Howard Lee by a vote of 556–125.

86. *Tombstone Epitaph*, June 14, 1881, June 15, 1881; Minute Book, Common Council, Village of Tombstone, November 13, 1880, June 6, 1881, June 18, 1881, University of Arizona Special Collections, Cochise County Collection, Reel 26, Arizona Historical Society.

87. For honor culture, see Bertram Wyatt-Brown, *Southern Honor: Ethics and Behavior in the Old South* (New York: Oxford University Press, 1982).

88. At the time of the gunfight in 1881, Ordinance 9 of the city code read, "It is hereby declared to be unlawful to carry in the hand or upon the person or otherwise any deadly weapon within the limits of said city of Tombstone, without first obtaining a permit in writing." See "Seventeenth Day: Continuation of Testimony for the Defense. Virgil W. Earp," *Tombstone Epitaph*, November 20, 1881.

89. *Tombstone Epitaph*, June 26, 1880.

90. "A Fatal Garment," *Tombstone Epitaph*, July 23, 1880.

91. Parsons Diary, February 25, 1881, in Bailey, *Tenderfoot in Tombstone*, 128–29. For the four shootings see Hooker, "Arizona Vendetta," 21, Southwest Museum/ Autry National Center; Clum to Lake, October 20, 1928, Lake Papers, Box 2, Huntington Library. Some killings took place outside Tombstone. In Charleston, a mining community southwest of the city, a gambler opened fire on a friend who refused to loan him money so that he could continue to wager; the friend returned fire and killed the gambler. "The Killing at Charleston," *Tombstone Epitaph*, October 12, 1880.

92. *Tombstone Epitaph*, October 12, 1880.

93. "Good Appointment," *Tombstone Epitaph*, July 29, 1880.

94. Gray, "When All Roads Led to Tombstone," 31–32, Arizona Historical Society.

95. Frank Lockwood, "They Lived in Tombstone," Francis C. Lockwood Papers, Box 5, Arizona Historical Society, Tucson. See also *San Diego Daily Union*, August 28, 1881, in Bailey, *Tombstone from a Woman's Point of View*, 39.

96. See, for instance, "Assault with Deadly Weapons" and "Discharged," *Tombstone Epitaph*, August 6, 1880; "Taken to Tucson," *Tombstone Epitaph*, August 17, 1880; "A Wife Beater," *Tombstone Epitaph*, October 5, 1880.

97. Hooker, "Arizona Vendetta," 10–13, Southwest Museum/Autry National Museum.

98. Flood, "Wyatt Earp," 164–74, Ford County Historical Society.

99. Lake, *Wyatt Earp*, 246–50.

100. Walter Noble Burns, *Tombstone: An Iliad of the Southwest* (New York: Doubleday, 1927), 62–73.

101. William Breakenridge, *Helldorado: Bringing Law to the Mesquite* (Boston: Houghton Mifflin, 1928), 183–84.

102. "Slaughtered. Brutal Murder of an Upright Citizen by a Desperado. The Assassin a Disreputable Villain Who Had Been Driven from Tiger Mine. He Flies to Tombstone and Is Taken Forthwith to Tucson for Safety," *Tombstone Epitaph*, January 17, 1881.

103. Hancock Reminiscences, 73, Arizona Historical Society.

104. *San Diego Daily Union*, February 4, 1882, in Bailey, *Tombstone from a Woman's Point of View*, 49. The acting territorial governor, John Gosper, reported to the secretary of the interior in October 1881 that "within the limits of this Territory there have existed companies of bands of outlaws, commonly called 'cow-boys,' who, in the past year, have committed many murders, and have stolen thousands of dollars' worth of stock and other property. Many times the stages carrying the United States mails, passengers, and the usual express, have been suddenly stopped by armed, masked men, who have rifled the mails, robbed the express, and deprived the passengers of all their valuables." John J. Gosper, "Report of the Acting Governor of Arizona, Made to the Secretary of the Interior, for the Year 1881" (Washington, D.C.: Government Printing Office, 1881), 5.

105. Joseph Bowyer to Acting Governor John J. Gosper, September 17, 1881. Crawley Dake Correspondence, University of Arizona Special Collections, Tucson.

106. Truett, *Fugitive Landscapes*, 63–65; Vanderwood, *Disorder and Progress*, 67; Miguel Tinker Salas, *In the Shadow of the Eagles: Sonora and the Transformation of the Border During the Porfiriato* (Berkeley: University of California Press, 1997).

107. Hancock to the *Arizona Republic*, April 1, 1927, Hancock Papers, Arizona Historical Society. See also Gray, "When All Roads Led to Tombstone," 30, Arizona Historical Society.

108. "Glimpses of Victory," *Tombstone Epitaph*, September 21, 1880; *Tombstone Epitaph*, November 6, 1880; *Tombstone Epitaph*, November 7, 1880; *Tombstone Epitaph*, November 12, 1880.

109. "Fifteenth Day: Testimony for the Defense. The Statement of Wyatt Earp," *Tombstone Epitaph*, November 17, 1881. Behan confirmed that the two had discussed Wyatt's becoming Behan's deputy if Behan won the appointment. See "The Fourth Day: The Continuation of Sheriff Behan's Testimony," *Tombstone Epitaph*, November 4, 1881. See also "Hopeful Holladay [*sic*]," *Rocky Mountain News*, May 17, 1882.

110. Gray, "When All Roads Led to Tombstone," 32, Arizona Historical Society.

111. John Clum, *It All Happened in Tombstone* (1929; repr., Flagstaff, AZ: Northland Press, 1965), 15.

112. *San Diego Daily Union*, March 9, 1881, in Bailey, *Tombstone from a Woman's Point of View*, 27–28.

113. "Hold! Eight Road Agents Attempt to Stop Kinnear's Stage," *Tombstone Epitaph*, March 16, 1881; "The Stage Robbery," *Tombstone Epitaph*, March 17, 1881.

114. Flood, "Wyatt Earp," 195, Ford County Historical Society.

115. Hooker, "Arizona Vendetta," 23–27, Southwest Museum/Autry National Center.

116. "The Long Chase," *Tombstone Epitaph*, March 19, 1881; "The Road Agent," *Tombstone Epitaph*, March 22, 1881; "Who They Are," *Tombstone Epitaph*, March 24, 1881; Flood, "Wyatt Earp," 195–208, Ford County Historical Society.

117. "Escaped," *Tombstone Nugget*, March 29, 1881; Flood, "Wyatt Earp," 203, Ford County Historical Society.

118. Joseph Bowyer to Acting Governor John J. Gosper, September 17, 1881, Crawley Dake Correspondence, University of Arizona Special Collections. See also "An Interrupted Breakfast," *Tombstone Epitaph*, August 5, 1881.

119. Gray, "When All Roads Led to Tombstone," 60–62, Arizona Historical Society; "Border Warfare," *Arizona Star*, August 25, 1881.

120. *San Diego Daily Union*, August 28, 1881.

121. Parsons Diary, August 17, 1881, in Bailey, *Tenderfoot in Tombstone*, 166–67.

122. "Stage Robbery," *Tombstone Epitaph*, September 10, 1881.

123. "Wyatt Earp Tells Tales of the Shotgun-Messenger-Service," *San Francisco Examiner*, August 9, 1896; Flood, "Wyatt Earp," 175–85, Ford County Historical Society; Hooker, "Arizona Vendetta," 8, Southwest Museum/Autry National Center.

124. John Bret Harte, "Conflict at San Carlos: The Military-Civilian Struggle for Control, 1882–1885," *Journal of the Southwest* 15 (Spring 1973): 27–44.

125. Parsons Diary, October 5–8, 1881, in Bailey, *Tenderfoot in Tombstone*, 180–84.

126. "Fifteenth Day: Statement of Wyatt Earp."

127. *Tombstone Epitaph*, June 22, 1881.

128. Flood, "Wyatt Earp," 209–18, Ford County Historical Society.

129. "Fifteenth Day: Statement of Wyatt Earp."

130. "Arizona Affairs," *San Francisco Examiner*, May 28, 1882.

131. "Tenth Day: The Investigation into the Recent Shooting Affair Continued," *Tombstone Epitaph*, November 11, 1881.

132. "Seventeenth Day: Virgil W. Earp."

133. Flood, "Wyatt Earp," 217, Ford County Historical Society.

134. "Tenth Day: The Investigation Continued"; "Fifteenth Day: Statement of Wyatt Earp"; "Seventeenth Day: Virgil W. Earp."

135. "Sixteenth Day: Testimony for the Defense," *Tombstone Epitaph*, November 24, 1881.

136. "Fifteenth Day: Statement of Wyatt Earp."

137. The witness was Appolinear Bauer, a Tombstone butcher. "Tenth Day: The Investigation Continued."

138. "Fifteenth Day: Statement of Wyatt Earp."

139. "Arizona Affairs."

140. Earp, "How I Routed a Gang of Arizona Outlaws."

141. Lake, *Wyatt Earp*, 288; Flood, "Wyatt Earp," 217–45, Ford County Historical Society.

142. "The Decision," *Tombstone Epitaph*, December 1, 1881.

143. "Arizona Affairs."

144. "Seventeenth Day: Virgil W. Earp."

145. "The Third Day: Examination of the Accused Before Justice Spicer. Sheriff Behan's Evidence in Regard to the Tragedy," *Tombstone Epitaph*, November 3,

1881; "Eighth Day: The Examination Drags Its Weary Way Through the Court," *Tombstone Epitaph*, November 9, 1881.

146. "Seventeenth Day: Virgil W. Earp."

147. "Fifteenth Day: Statement of Wyatt Earp."

148. "The Third Day: Sheriff Behan."

149. "Eighth Day." Claiborne had Holliday armed with a "nickel-plated pistol" rather than a shotgun, however, which rather throws his recollection into doubt.

150. "Ninth Day: Continuation of the Examination into the Facts of the Recent Homicide," *Tombstone Epitaph*, November 10, 1881.

151. "Fifteenth Day: Statement of Wyatt Earp."

152. Hooker, "Arizona Vendetta," 37, Southwest Museum/Autry National Center.

153. "Yesterday's Tragedy. Three Men Hurled into Eternity in the Duration of a Moment," *Tombstone Epitaph*, October 27, 1881.

154. Earp, "How I Routed a Gang of Arizona Outlaws."

155. Clum to Lake, January 1, 1929, Lake Papers, Box 2, Huntington Library.

156. *San Diego Daily Union*, November 3, 1881, in Bailey, *Tombstone from a Woman's Point of View*, 41–45.

157. Hooker, "Arizona Vendetta," 38, Southwest Museum/Autry National Center.

158. "Hurled into Eternity."

159. *San Diego Daily Union*, November 3, 1881, in Bailey, *Tombstone from a Woman's Point of View*, 41–45.

160. "Hurled into Eternity."

161. Lubet, *Murder in Tombstone*, 59–67; "The Funeral," *Tombstone Epitaph*, October 28, 1881.

162. "Coroner's Inquest," *Tombstone Epitaph*, October 30, 1881.

163. Lubet, *Murder in Tombstone*, 71–72.

164. McLaury, quoted in Shillingberg, *Tombstone*, 275. See also Lubet, *Murder in Tombstone*, 111.

165. "Third Day: Sheriff Behan"; "Eighth Day."

166. Lubet, *Murder in Tombstone*, 123–27.

167. Ibid., 136–46.

168. "Fifteenth Day: Statement of Wyatt Earp."

169. Ibid.

170. *San Diego Daily Union*, December 13, 1881.

171. And perhaps for Clum, too. On December 14, highwaymen fired on a stagecoach when it was five miles outside Tombstone. They fired between fifteen and twenty shots, killing one of the horses. One of the passengers in the stage was Clum, who—with a certain sense of self-importance—interpreted the attack not as an effort to rob the stage but to assassinate him. See "Tombstone Stage Assailed by Armed Rustler," *Tucson Star*, December 15, 1881; Clum to Lake, January 31, 1929, Lake Papers, Box 2, Huntington Library.

172. "Arizona Affairs."

173. Flood, "Wyatt Earp," 260–65, Ford County Historical Society. Wyatt also held

Frank Stilwell responsible. He told Flood that Stilwell, a deputy sheriff, had left the Oriental moments after Virgil and crossed Allen Street to the place the cowboys had set for their ambuscade.

174. For the constitution of the posse, see "A Pestiferous Posse," *Tombstone Nugget*, January 27, 1882.

175. "Almost a Tragedy," *Tombstone Nugget*, January 18, 1882. The day before the posse was to depart Tombstone, Holliday and the cowboy John Ringo exchanged words—and nearly bullets. Members of both factions were nearby during the standoff, and Parsons feared that there would be "another battle." Yet both Ringo and Holliday were arrested before they drew their weapons, charged with carrying weapons within the city limits, and fined. Ringo had further legal problems—he was a suspect in a robbery in Galeyville and was remanded to the county jail on that charge. While he was in custody, he learned that Wyatt's posse was preparing to leave town. Behan released Ringo from custody without having him post bail so he could speed from Tombstone to warn the Clantons. See the Parsons Diary, January 17, 1882, in Bailey, *Tenderfoot in Tombstone*, 201–202; "Proclamation," *Tombstone Epitaph*, January 24, 1882.

176. "Pestiferous Posse."

177. "Resignation of Virgil W. and Wyatt S. Earp as Deputy Marshals," *Tombstone Epitaph*, February 2, 1882.

178. "The Clanton Trial," *Tombstone Epitaph*, February 3, 1882.

179. *Tombstone Nugget*, February 3, 1882.

180. Bailey, *Tenderfoot in Tombstone*, 206.

181. "The Earp Examination," *Tombstone Nugget*, February 15, 1882.

182. Hooker, "Arizona Vendetta," 49, Southwest Museum/Autry National Center.

183. "The Deadly Bullet," *Tombstone Epitaph*, March 20, 1882. Morgan's autopsy report can be found in the George E. Goodfellow Papers, Arizona Historical Society.

184. *Tombstone Epitaph*, March 22, 1882.

185. Hooker, "Arizona Vendetta," 52A, Southwest Museum/Autry National Center.

186. Flood, "Wyatt Earp," 281, Ford County Historical Society.

187. Hooker, "Arizona Vendetta," 54–58, Southwest Museum/Autry National Center.

188. "Another Assassination," *Tombstone Epitaph*, March 21, 1882.

189. Hooker, "Arizona Vendetta," 54–58, Southwest Museum/Autry National Center.

190. Flood, "Wyatt Earp," 281, Ford County Historical Society.

191. "Coroner's Inquest upon the Body of Florentino Cruz, the Murdered Half-Breed," *Tombstone Epitaph*, March 25, 1882.

192. Hooker, "Arizona Vendetta," 67–69. Southwest Museum/Autry National Center.

193. Flood, "Wyatt Earp," 297–305, Ford County Historical Society.

194. "Battle of Burleigh: The Earp Party Ambushed by Curly Bill and Eight Cow-Boys. A Hand to Hand Encounter in Which Curly Bill Is Killed," *Tombstone Epitaph*, March 25, 1882.

195. The Earp researcher Steve Gatto has suggested that "the evidence that Curly had left Arizona before March 1882 is stronger than the evidence that he was killed by Wyatt at a spring in the Whetstone Mountains." See Gatto, *The Real Wyatt Earp: A Documentary Biography* (Silver City, NM: High Lonesome Books, 2000), 186.

196. "A Man of Sand," *Gunnison News-Democrat*, June 18, 1882.

197. "Statement of Citizens in Regard to the Death of Jno. Ringo," Lake Papers, Box 5, Huntington Library. James Hancock believed that Ringo committed suicide. "'Bull' Lewis who was in the coroner's jury told me there was absolutely no question but that Ringo committed suicide." Hancock Reminiscences, Arizona Historical Society.

198. Hooker, "Arizona Vendetta," 78, Southwest Museum/Autry National Center.

199. Flood, "Wyatt Earp," 321–25, Ford County Historical Society.

200. Leigh Chalmers to A. H. Garland, September 30, 1885, Dake Correspondence, University of Arizona Special Collections; Flood, "Wyatt Earp," 319–20, Ford County Historical Society.

201. Hoping for more murders on one day, the next day the sanctimonious Parsons recorded in his diary, "Church tonight." Parsons Diary, March 21–22, 1882, in Bailey, *Tenderfoot in Tombstone*, 212–13.

202. Endicott Peabody Diary, March 23, 1882, in S. J. Reidhead, ed., *A Church for Helldorado* (Roswell, NM: Jinglebob Press, 2006), 63.

203. Bailey, *Tenderfoot in Tombstone*, 213–14; George O. Hand, "One Hundred Days on the San Pedro: The Contention City, A.T. Diary of George O. Hand, March 23–July 1, 1882," March 25, 1882, University of Arizona Special Collections.

204. Peabody Diary, March 22, 1882, in Reidhead, *Church for Helldorado*, 62.

6. ROPING THE MARK

1. "How the Battle Was Fought," *San Francisco Call*, December 3, 1896.

2. "'Long Green' Is Squirming," *San Francisco Call*, December 7, 1896; Arne K. Lang, *Prizefighting: An American History* (Jefferson, NC: McFarland, 2008), 236–37.

3. "Sharkey Not Much Hurt," *San Francisco Call*, December 15, 1896.

4. "After the Fight," *San Jose Evening News*, December 3, 1896; "Sharkey the Winner," *Chicago Daily Inter-Ocean*, December 3, 1896; "The Fitzsimmons-Sharkey Dispute," *New York Times*, December 5, 1896.

5. Eliot Asinof, *Eight Men Out: The Black Sox and the 1919 World Series* (New York: Holt, 2000).

6. A 1922 welterweight bout between Jack Britton and Mickey Walker also helped inspire the story. Hemingway's biographer Carlos Baker believed the story was based on a bout between Britton and Benny Leonard earlier in 1922. Yet it was the Sharkey-Fitzsimmons fight that closely resembled Hemingway's story of an

aging fighter, Jack Brennan, facing a younger, brutish challenger, Walcott. When criminals instruct Brennan that he must lose to protect their bet on Walcott, Brennan accepts his fate and bets $50,000 on his opponent. The gamblers, having enticed Brennan to bet the money, instruct Walcott to intentionally foul Brennan—with a blow below the belt—and thus lose. Brennan withstands the blow, disdains the foul, and returns the favor to Walcott, thus losing the bout and winning his bet. Carlos Baker, *Ernest Hemingway: A Life Story* (New York: Charles Scribner's Sons, 1969), 157; Phillips G. Davies and Rosemary R. Davies, "Hemingway's 'Fifty Grand' and the Jack Britton–Mickey Walker Prize Fight," *American Literature* 37 (November 1965), 251–58. Baker, as well as Davies and Davies, base their analyses on the similarities between the names of the real boxers and the characters in Hemingway's story: Britton/Brennan and Walker/Walcott. James J. Martine, "Hemingway's 'Fifty Grand': The Other Fight(s)," *Journal of Modern Literature* 2 (September 1971): 123–27, shows that the story might have been based on a bout in France in 1922 in which the referee awarded the victory on a foul at the end of the bout. Yet in other respects, the French fight to which Martine referred bore little resemblance to Hemingway's story. Robert P. Weeks, "Wise-Guy Narrator and Trickster Out-Tricked in Hemingway's 'Fifty Grand,'" in Jackson J. Benson, ed., *New Critical Approaches to the Short Stories of Ernest Hemingway* (Duke University Press, 1990), 275–82, demonstrated that Hemingway had laid out the basis for the story long before 1922.

7. Stuart N. Lake, *Wyatt Earp: Frontier Marshal* (Boston: Houghton Mifflin, 1931), 366–70.

8. Lake wrote his entry for the *Encyclopedia Americana* on March 15, 1929. See the Stuart N. Lake Papers, Box 11, Huntington Library, San Marino, CA.

9. "Fitzsimmons Was Robbed," *San Francisco Call*, December 3, 1896; "They Chose Earp," *San Francisco Call*, December 3, 1896.

10. Jim McIntire, *Early Days in Texas: A Trip to Hell and Heaven* (1902; repr., Norman: University of Oklahoma Press, 1992), 70. See also C. W. Shores interview, Lake Papers, Box 11, Huntington Library.

11. In 1882, an unnamed accuser had Virgil and one of his brothers involved in a scam in Tombstone. According to the allegation, a miner walked into a Tombstone saloon and announced, owing to his good luck at the mines, he would pay for everyone's drinks. A party of well-dressed men—one of whom was one of the Earp brothers—insisted on paying for their own drinks. They agreed to roll dice to determine who would pay. A lively game of dice ensued, and the miner lost a series of wagers. Frustrated, he produced a $100 bill and wagered it. The well-dressed men, unable to cover the bet, looked to the crowd. A dupe, seeing that the miner had consistently lost, produced $100 to cover the bet. On the next roll, the result was different. At that point, Virgil Earp entered the saloon and, using his authority as a deputy U.S. marshal, put a stop to the game. The dupe's money was never recovered. The well-dressed men and the miner—all confederates in

the confidence game—disappeared. "Cowboys and Bunkos," *Rocky Mountain News*, May 21, 1882.

12. "Earp's Many Colors," *San Francisco Call*, December 14, 1896. This story was a reprint of similar stories that had run in other publications. See "Earp's Frontier Life," *Washington Post*, December 5, 1896, and "Old Time Tombstone," *Washington Post*, May 1, 1894.

13. "Doped, with Earp as the Referee," *San Francisco Call*, December 15, 1896.

14. See Richard Maxwell Brown, *No Duty to Retreat: Violence and Values in American History and Society* (New York: Oxford University Press, 1994), 66.

15. Steven A. Riess, *Sport in Industrial America, 1850–1920* (Wheeling, IL: Harlan Davidson, 1995), 9.

16. For Jaffa's grocery, see the *Albuquerque Morning Journal*, November 18, 1882.

17. The quarrel was reported in the *Albuquerque Evening Review*, May 13, 1882, and *Denver Republican*, May 22, 1882.

18. Otero, quoted in Chuck Hornung and Gary L. Roberts, "The Split," *True West* 48 (November–December 2001), 58–61. See also Gary L. Roberts, *Doc Holliday: The Life and Legend* (Hoboken, NJ: Wiley, 2006), 271.

19. Mabel Earp Cason and Vinnolia Earp Ackerman Manuscript, c. 1937, Ford County Historical Society, Dodge City, KS. This manuscript has been heavily redacted by another hand, and I have therefore drawn from it sparingly—and then only facts that can independently be confirmed elsewhere. Josephine dictated her memoir to Cason and Ackerman, two distant relatives of Wyatt's. The manuscript in the Ford County Historical Society is typed on the back of the stationery of a firm called Spicer and Company, based in Glendale, California. Each sheet of the manuscript has, on the reverse side, the same form letter from Spicer and Company, thanking doctors for meeting with a drug representative about the antibacterial drug Edwenil. Spicer and Company indeed manufactured Edwenil beginning in 1933, although by 1936 the product had apparently proven to be ineffective. See the *Journal of the American Medical Association* 106 (January 11, 1936): 126. The manuscript was never published. Cason wrote in 1959 that Josephine refused to "clear up the Tombstone sequence where it pertained to her and Wyatt." See Mabel Earp Cason to Eleanor Sloan, May 20, 1959, Mabel Earp Cason Papers, Arizona Historical Society, Tucson. The Earp researcher Glenn Boyer got hold of the Cason and Ackerman manuscript and, taking it upon himself to "clear up" the things that Josephine had elided, revised it into the book *I Married Wyatt Earp* (Tucson: University of Arizona Press, 1976). The manuscript in the Ford County Historical Society, which Boyer donated to the collection, bears numerous cross-outs and other editorial marks—some apparently by Cason and Ackerman, and some by Boyer. Several large sections are missing.

20. Stuart N. Lake to Ira Rich Kent, February 13, 1930, Lake Papers, Box 7, Huntington Library.

21. "Awful Arizona," *Denver Republican*, May 22, 1882.

22. Lake to Kent, February 13, 1930, Lake Papers, Box 7, Huntington Library.

23. Kent to Lake, February 19, 1930, Lake Papers, Box 4, Huntington Library. Houghton Mifflin published both Breakenridge's *Helldorado* and Lake's *Wyatt Earp: Frontier Marshal*. Kent wrote to Lake that "as I remember it, [Mrs. Earp] asked Breakenridge not to refer to her. He promised her he would not, and he made no reference to her whatever in his book."

24. John Flood, "Wyatt Earp," 151–54, Ford County Historical Society, Dodge City, KS.

25. Kent to Lake, October 23, 1930, Lake Papers, Box 4, Huntington Library.

26. Lake, *Wyatt Earp*, 275–76.

27. After charging Holliday, Kate was arrested twice in two days by Virgil—the first time for being drunk and disorderly, and then the next day for making threats against a person's life. She left town, and the case against Holliday was dropped. "Justice Court-Spicer," *Tombstone Nugget*, July 10, 1881.

28. She overdosed on laudanum. See her obituary in the *Florence Enterprise*, July 7, 1888.

29. Forrestine Hooker, "An Arizona Vendetta," 79, Southwest Museum/Autry National Center.

30. "Doc. Holladay [*sic*], Leader of the Earps, Cleverly Captured Last Night in This City," *Rocky Mountain News*, May 16, 1882; "Hopeful Holladay [*sic*]," *Rocky Mountain News*, May 17, 1882; "'Doc' Holliday, an Alleged Desperado, Well Known Here, Captured in Denver," *Pueblo Daily Chieftain*, May 17, 1882; "Scene at the Sheriff's Office," *Denver Tribune*, May 19, 1882; "A Lively War Between Peace Officers over the Notorious 'Doc' Holladay [*sic*]," *Rocky Mountain News*, May 19, 1882; "Holliday's Hope," *Rocky Mountain News*, May 22, 1882; "Holliday's Chances," *Mountain News*, May 23, 1882; "Holding Holliday," *Mountain News*, May 24, 1882; "Holliday Must Go," *Mountain News*, May 26, 1882; "Helping Holliday," *Mountain News*, May 30, 1882; "Unscathed of Justice," *Mountain News*, May 31, 1882.

31. Frank Fossett, *Colorado: Its Gold and Silver Mines, Farms and Stock Ranges, and Health and Pleasure Resorts*, 2nd ed. (New York: C. G. Crawford, 1880), 564–76.

32. Judd Riley interview, c. 1929, Lake Papers, Box 11, Huntington Library.

33. Ibid.

34. C. W. Shores interview, 1929, Lake Papers, Box 11, Huntington Library.

35. William Barclay Masterson, "Famous Gun Fighters of the Western Frontier, Second Article: Wyatt Earp," *Human Life*, February 1907.

36. Roger Jay, "The Gamblers' War in Tombstone," *Wild West*, October 2004, 38–45.

37. W. F. Petillon to George Glick, May 10, 1883; C. M. Davison et al. to George Glick, May 15, 1883; George Glick Correspondence, 1883, Kansas State Historical Society, Topeka. See also W. B. Masterson, "Luke Short," *Human Life*, 1907.

38. *Kansas City Journal*, May 15, 1883; *Ford County Globe*, June 12, 1883; "Dodge City's Sensation," *National Police Gazette*, July 21, 1883.

39. Masterson, "Luke Short."

40. Cecile I. Duton, "The Boom of the Coeur d'Alenes," *Overland Monthly* 16 (October 1890); 394–403.

41. *Spokane Falls Review*, April 5, 1884.

42. "Earp's Spokane Record," *San Francisco Call*, December 7, 1896.

43. "Gem Saloon," *Colton Semi-Tropic*, November 27, 1880. See also Nicholas Earp's obituary in the *Los Angeles Times*, February 12, 1907.

44. "Arizona Affairs," *San Francisco Examiner*, May 28, 1882.

45. *Phoenix Gazette*, August 10, 1882.

46. *San Bernardino Times*, February 12, 1887.

47. "Dodge City's Sensation."

48. *Arizona Daily Star*, November 16, 1884, reprinting an article from the *Albuquerque Journal*.

49. *Aspen Daily Times*, May 5, 1885, November 30, 1885.

50. "Doc Holliday Dead," *Aspen Daily Times*, November 9, 1887; "Holliday Death," *Denver Republican*, November 10, 1887. For the last meeting of Wyatt and Holliday, see Roberts, *Doc Holliday*, 365–66.

51. Larry Booth, Roger Olmsted, and Richard F. Pourade, "Portrait of a Boom Town: San Diego in the 1880s," *California Historical Quarterly* 50 (December 1971): 363–94; William Deverell, *Railroad Crossing: Californians and the Railroad, 1850–1910* (Berkeley: University of California Press, 1996).

52. Theodore S. Van Dyke, *Millionaires of a Day: An Inside History of the Great Southern California "Boom"* (New York: Fords, Howard, and Hulbert, 1890), 46.

53. Booth et al., "Portrait of a Boom Town."

54. Van Dyke, *Millionaires of a Day*, 64–76. George Devol, the Mississippi riverboat gambler, also used the term *capper* to describe his confederates: fellow confidence men who would lure dupes to his three-card monte game by appearing, asking how to play the game, and enjoying a winning streak. See George Devol, *Forty Years a Gambler on the Mississippi* (New York: George H. Devol, 1892), 66–67, 164–68.

55. Richard H. Peterson, "In San Diego, Wyatt Earp Was All Business—and Business Was Booming for a While," *Wild West*, October 2004, 66–69.

56. Adalaska Pearson reminiscences, San Diego Historical Society, San Diego, CA, quoted in Kenneth R. Cilch and Kenneth R. Cilch, Jr., *Wyatt Earp, the Missing Years: San Diego in the 1880s* (San Diego: Gaslamp Books, 1998), 33–34.

57. Jim L. Sumner, "The State Fair and the Development of Modern Sports in Late Nineteenth Century North Carolina," *Journal of Sports History* 15 (Summer 1988): 138–50.

58. "President Hayes and the Coming State Fair," *San Francisco Bulletin*, August 28, 1880; "The State Fair," *San Francisco Bulletin*, September 25, 1880.

59. Melvin L. Adelman, "The First Modern Sport in America: Harness Racing in New York City, 1825–1870," *Journal of Sport History* 8 (Spring 1981): 5–32.

60. Riess, *Sport in Industrial America*, 49–50, 145. For the commercialization of

leisure, see Kathy Peiss, *Cheap Amusements: Working Women and Leisure in Turn-of-the-Century New York* (Philadelphia: Temple University Press, 1986). For the development of Saratoga Springs, see Dona Brown, *Inventing New England: Regional Tourism in the Nineteenth Century* (Washington: Smithsonian Institution Press, 1995), 27–30.

61. "The Owner of Montana Regent," *San Francisco Bulletin*, April 14, 1887.

62. This group also included Sam Brannan, a merchant, original partner in the Sacramento townsite company, and one of California's first millionaires. See "Racing at Bay District Park," *San Francisco Bulletin*, June 1, 1880.

63. They were in this sense much like the Virginia gentry of the eighteenth century. See T. H. Breen, "Horses and Gentlemen: The Cultural Significance of Gambling Among the Gentry of Virginia," *William and Mary Quarterly*, 3rd ser., 34 (April 1977): 239–57.

64. Cilch and Cilch, *Wyatt Earp*, 54–55; Peterson, "In San Diego, Wyatt Earp Was All Business," 68.

65. Horse racing became popular with Mexico's elite in the 1880s, around the same time that American elites embraced it. See William H. Beezley, *Judas at the Jockey Club, and Other Episodes of Porfirian Mexico* (Lincoln: University of Nebraska Press, 1987), 26–31.

66. "Earp's Straight Tip," *San Francisco Call*, December 11, 1896.

67. "Sporting News," *Los Angeles Times*, May 1, 1893.

68. "A Jockey's Bad Tumble," *San Francisco Call*, April 9, 1895.

69. Elliott J. Gorn, *The Manly Art: Bare-Knuckle Prize Fighting in America* (Ithaca, NY: Cornell University Press, 1986), 24, 124, 129, 133.

70. "Young Kelly's Death: Cerebral Hemorrhage the Cause," *San Francisco Bulletin*, September 8, 1885; "Pugilists Arrested," *San Francisco Bulletin*, December 30, 1885.

71. See Michael Kimmel, *Manhood in America: A Cultural History* (New York: Free Press, 1996), 117–55; Gail Bederman, *Manliness and Civilization: A Cultural History of Gender and Race in the United States, 1880–1917* (Chicago: University of Chicago Press, 1996); John Higham, "The Reorientation of American Culture in the 1890's," *Writing American History: Essays on Modern Scholarship* (Bloomington: Indiana University Press, 1970), 73–102.

72. "The Culture of the Fists," *San Francisco Bulletin*, June 29, 1889.

73. Clifford Putney, *Muscular Christianity: Manhood and Sports in Protestant America, 1880–1920* (Cambridge, MA: Harvard University Press, 2001).

74. Earp Brothers Dictations, 1888, Bancroft Library, University of California, Berkeley.

75. Riess, *Sport in Industrial America*, 146–47; Gorn, *Manly Art*, 165.

76. Susan Lee Johnson, *Roaring Camp: The Social World of the California Gold Rush* (New York: Norton, 2000), 180–81.

77. Earp refereed a fight at the Silver Gate Athletic Club in San Diego on March 3, 1890, between a fighter from San Francisco, Billy Graham, and a San Diegan,

Jack Sullivan. "Wyatt Earp in San Diego," 84, Earl Chafin Papers, Southwest Museum/Autry National Center.

78. San Francisco enacted a law against bare-knuckle fighting in 1889. "An Ordinance to Regulate the Pugilists," *San Francisco Evening Bulletin*, September 17, 1889.

79. G. Rundy, "Sunday over the Line," *Los Angeles Tribune*, June 2, 1888.

80. Gorn, *Manly Art*, 142, 223, 237–47.

81. Armond Fields, *James J. Corbett: A Biography of the Heavyweight Boxing Champion and Popular Theater Headliner* (Jefferson, NC: McFarland, 2001), 94.

82. "Wyatt Earp Exposes the *Examiner*'s Fake Methods," *San Francisco Call*, December 16, 1896.

83. "Earp Attached: He Guaranteed Attorney's Fees of Bunko-Steerers," *San Francisco Call*, December 8, 1896; "Long Green's Bodyguard Swears He Is a Poor Man," *San Francisco Call*, December 9, 1896; "Wyatt Earp Sued," *San Francisco Call*, December 9, 1896; "He Bet for 'Long Green,'" *San Francisco Call*, December 14, 1896; "Wyatt Earp Sued," *San Francisco Call*, December 24, 1896.

84. John Boessenecker, *Lawman: The Life and Times of Harry Morse, 1835–1912* (Norman: University of Oklahoma Press, 1998), 288; "Fitzsimmons Was Robbed," *San Francisco Call*, December 3, 1896.

85. Gilbert Odd, *The Fighting Blacksmith* (London: Pelham, 1976), 91–96.

86. See Gorn, *Manly Art*, 45.

87. "Lynch Tells Why Sharkey May Win," *San Francisco Call*, June 21, 1896; "Sharkey, Once Ace of Ring, Now Option Seller," *San Mateo Times*, May 18, 1932; Fields, *James J. Corbett*, 97–98.

88. "Sharkey Not Much Hurt," *San Francisco Call*, December 15, 1896.

89. "How the Battle Was Fought," *San Francisco Call*, December 3, 1896; "Julian Speaks His Mind Freely," *San Francisco Call*, December 3, 1896; "The Swindle Is Revealed," *San Francisco Call*, December 10, 1896.

90. "Why Earp Was Appointed," *San Francisco Call*, December 5, 1896.

91. "The Club's Statement," *San Francisco Call*, December 7, 1896.

92. "Wyatt Earp Exposes the *Examiner*'s Fake Methods."

93. "The Swindle Is Revealed."

94. "Long Green Is Squirming."

95. "He Bet for 'Long Green.'"

96. "Sharkey Not Much Hurt."

97. "Wyatt Earp Exposes the *Examiner*'s Fake Methods."

98. "How the Battle Was Fought."

99. "Earp Arrested," *San Francisco Call*, December 4, 1896; "Wyatt Earp Fined," *Los Angeles Times*, December 11, 1896; "He Bet for 'Long Green.'"

100. "Earp Attached."

101. "Sharkey Not Much Hurt."

102. "How the Battle Was Fought."
103. "The Swindle Is Revealed."
104. "How the Battle Was Fought."
105. "Crooked Work Was Done by Long Green's Protector," *San Francisco Call*, December 11, 1896.
106. "The Swindle Is Revealed."
107. "Sharkey Was Uninjured," *San Francisco Call*, December 10, 1896.
108. "Fitzsimmons Was Robbed"; "Sharkey Not Much Hurt"; "Crooked Work Was Done by Long Green's Protector."
109. "The Swag Ready for Long Green," *San Francisco Call*, December 18, 1896.
110. "Wyatt Earp Departs," *San Francisco Call*, August 6, 1897.

7. THE SHADOWS OF THE PAST

1. Stuart N. Lake Papers, Box 16, Huntington Library, San Marino, CA.
2. The couple lived elsewhere as well, including, in 1925, 2703 Telegraph Avenue in Oakland, California. See Wyatt Earp to William S. Hart, April 16, 1925, Earp Family Papers, Arizona Historical Society, Tucson.
3. See Casey Tefertiler, *Wyatt Earp: The Life Behind the Legend* (New York: Wiley, 1997).
4. "Gun Fighter Is Knocked Out by Bold Horseman," *San Francisco Call*, April 30, 1900.
5. "Wyatt Earp Shot at Cape Nome," *Washington Post*, July 15, 1900.
6. "A Killing at Willcox," *Arizona Weekly Journal-Miner*, July 11, 1900; "Warren Earp Shot and Killed in a Duel," *San Francisco Call*, July 8, 1900. The *Journal-Miner*'s report painted Warren as a bully, and his killer, John Boyett, as a long-suffering victim of Warren's abuse. Warren certainly had a record of attempted intimidation: he was arrested in Yuma in 1893 for assault and attempted murder—he threatened to kill his victim unless the man gave him $100. See "A Desperate Man," *San Francisco Call*, November 11, 1893. Boyett was acquitted by a coroner's jury. See "Earp's Slayer Exonerated," *San Francisco Call*, July 11, 1900.
7. "Fearless Ranger Succumbs to Death," *Weekly Arizona Journal-Miner*, November 1, 1905.
8. *Tonopah Sun*, February 5, 1905.
9. See the Virgil Earp Folder, Earp Family Papers, Arizona Historical Society, Tucson.
10. "Wyatt Earp Located," *Prescott Courier*, October 3, 1906.
11. "Nicholas Earp Dead," *Daily Arizona Silver Belt*, February 14, 1907. The report of Nicholas's death identified the son in Searchlight as "Nathan." See also "New Gold Rush On," *New York Times*, March 14, 1908.
12. Randy King and James Peterson, "Was Arthur Moore King Wyatt Earp's Last Deputy?" *Tombstone Times*, March 2007.
13. "Earp's Faro Plan Fails," *New York Times*, July 23, 1911.

14. Adelia Earp Edwards, "Wild West Remembrances," 6, Earl Chafin Papers, Southwest Museum/Autry National Center, Los Angeles, CA.

15. See William S. Hart, *My Life East and West* (Boston: Houghton Mifflin, 1929), 174–76.

16. See Max Westbrook, afterword to Owen Wister, *The Virginian: A Horseman of the Plains* (New York: Penguin, 1979), 318–31; Richard Slotkin, *Gunfighter Nation: The Myth of the Frontier in Twentieth-Century America* (New York: HarperCollins, 1992), 175–83.

17. E. Anthony Rotundo, *American Manhood: Transformations of Masculinity from the Revolution to the Modern Era* (New York: Basic Books, 1994); Gail Bederman, *Manliness and Civilization: A Cultural History of Gender and Race in the United States, 1880–1937* (Chicago: University of Chicago Press, 1995); Michael Kimmel, *Manhood in America: A Cultural History* (New York: Free Press, 1996); Clifford Putney, *Muscular Christianity: Manhood and Sports in Protestant America, 1880–1920* (Cambridge, MA: Harvard University Press, 2001); Thomas Winter, *Making Men, Making Class: The YMCA and the Workingman, 1877–1920* (Chicago: University of Chicago Press, 2002).

18. For Wyatt as a "bad man," see "The Last of the Man Killers," *Chicago Tribune*, January 5, 1896.

19. Raoul Walsh, *Each Man in His Time* (New York: Farrar, Straus and Giroux, 1974), 102–104.

20. Stephen Hanson and Patricia Hanson, "The Last Days of Wyatt Earp," *Retrospect*, March 1985.

21. Josephine Earp to William S. Hart, December 18, 1923, Earp Family Papers, Arizona Historical Society.

22. Wyatt Earp to Hart, July 7, 1923; Earp to Hart, April 11, 1925; Earp Family Papers, Arizona Historical Society.

23. Hart, *My Life East and West*, 175.

24. Wyatt Earp to Hart, October 26, 1922, Earp Family Papers, Arizona Historical Society. For an account of Hart's messy separation, see "Bill Hart, Movie Wild West Hero, to Be Sued Shortly for Divorce," *Baltimore Sun*, August 10, 1922.

25. Jonathan Auerbach, "McKinley at Home: How Early American Cinema Made News," *American Quarterly* 51 (December 1999): 797–832.

26. Wyatt Earp to Hart, July 7, 1923, Earp Family Papers, Arizona Historical Society.

27. Wyatt Earp to Hart, April 11, 1925, Earp Family Papers, Arizona Historical Society.

28. Wyatt probably reminisced to Hooker sometime in 1917 or 1918: the conclusion to her manuscript identifies Wyatt as being seventy years old.

29. Forrestine C. Hooker, *Child of the Fighting Tenth: On the Frontier with the Buffalo Soldiers* (New York: Oxford University Press, 2011), 14.

30. Forrestine C. Hooker, "An Arizona Vendetta," 51, Southwest Museum/Autry National Center.

31. Ibid., 79.

32. Wyatt Earp to Hart, April 11, 1925, Earp Family Papers, Arizona Historical Society.

33. John H. Flood, "Wyatt Earp," 94, 249, Ford County Historical Society, Dodge City, KS.

34. Flood to Hart, February 19, 1926; Hart to George Horace Lorimer, February 22, 1926; Earp Family Papers, Arizona Historical Society.

35. Wyatt Earp to Hart, December 6, 1926; Wyatt Earp to Hart, December 14, 1926; Hart to Wyatt Earp, January 25, 1927; Hart to Wyatt Earp, January 31, 1927; Wyatt Earp to Hart, February 1, 1927; Earp Family Papers, Arizona Historical Society.

36. Anne Johnston to Hart, February 21, 1927; Hart to Wyatt Earp, February 26, 1927; Earp Family Papers, Arizona Historical Society.

37. Hart to Wyatt Earp, February 26, 1927, Earp Family Papers, Arizona Historical Society.

38. Walter Noble Burns, "The Last Stand of the Buffalo," *Saturday Evening Post*, March 23, 1912.

39. Harry Maule to Walter Noble Burns, August 20, 1926, and January 7, 1927, Walter Noble Burns Collection, Box 7, University of Arizona Special Collections, Tucson.

40. Wyatt Earp to Hart, September 6, 1926, Earp Family Papers, Arizona Historical Society.

41. Hart to Wyatt Earp, September 9, 1926, Earp Family Papers, Arizona Historical Society.

42. Maule to Burns, July 1, 1927, Burns Collection, Box 7, University of Arizona Special Collections.

43. Burns to Maule, June 15, 1927, Burns Collection, Box 7, University of Arizona Special Collections.

44. See Maule to Burns, May 26, 1927; Maule to Burns, May 31, 1927; Burns to Maule, June 2, 1927; Burns to Maule, June 15, 1927; Warwick Carpenter to Maule, June 16, 1927; Maule to Carpenter, June 17, 1927; Earp to Maule, June 25, 1927; Maule to Wyatt Earp, July 7, 1927; Maule to Burns, July 8, 1927; Burns Collection, Box 7, University of Arizona Special Collections.

45. Walter Noble Burns, *Tombstone: An Iliad of the Southwest* (New York: Doubleday, 1927), 26, 258.

46. "Billy Sunday: A Man's Christian," *Chicago Inter-Ocean*, March 30, 1910.

47. Wyatt Earp to Maule, May 24, 1927, Earp Family Papers, Arizona Historical Society; and Burns Collection, Box 7, University of Arizona Special Collections.

48. Wyatt Earp to J. H. Hammond, May 21, 1925, Lake Papers, Box 3, Huntington Library.

49. Wyatt Earp to Hart, November 18, 1924, Earp Family Papers, Arizona Historical Society.

50. "They Lived in Tombstone," undated typescript, Francis C. Lockwood Papers, Box 5, Arizona Historical Society.

51. Frank C. Lockwood, *Pioneer Days in Arizona, from the Spanish Occupation to Statehood* (New York: Macmillan, 1932).

52. "They Lived in Tombstone," Lockwood Papers, Box 5, Arizona Historical Society.

53. Wyatt Earp to Lake, November 9, 1928, Lake Papers, Box 3, Huntington Library. See also Wyatt Earp to Lake, March 6, 1928, Lake Papers, Box 3, Huntington Library.

54. Lake to Wyatt Earp, December 25, 1927, Lake Papers, Box 6; Wyatt Earp to Lake, January 16, 1928, Lake Papers, Box 3, Huntington Library.

55. For the preparedness campaign, see Theodore Roosevelt, *Fear God and Take Your Own Part* (New York: George H. Doran, 1916), 15–58; David M. Kennedy, *Over Here: The First World War and American Society* (New York: Oxford University Press, 1979), 3–44.

56. For Lake, see Alfred Jacoby, "The Life and Legend of Stuart Lake," *San Diego Union*, October 30, 1960; Lake's author's questionnaire for Houghton Mifflin, 1931, Lake Papers, Box 7; Lake to Warren G. Harding, June 8, 1922; Lake's brief autobiography in his application for a Guggenheim Fellowship, March 27, 1932, Lake Papers, Box 6, Huntington Library.

57. Lake to Leon Fraser, October 16, 1921; Maynard C. Harding to Veterans Bureau, November 28, 1921; Lake to Charles R. Forbes, December 31, 1921, Lake Papers, Box 9; Melvin S. Henderson to S. Kudish, May 7, 1924; Henderson to Lake, May 3, 1926, Lake Papers, Box 10, Huntington Library. "Stuart Lake, Biographer of Wyatt Earp, Dies," *Los Angeles Times*, January 28, 1964; "Stuart Lake, Wrote Wyatt Earp Story," *New York Times*, January 28, 1964.

58. Loren Palmer to Lake, July 8, 1921; Roger William Riis to Lake, September 6, 1921; Trell Yocum to Lake, February 16, 1924; Thoreau Cronyn to Lake, May 6, 1924; William Chenery to Lake, November 6, 1925; James Young to Lake, November 30, 1926; Young to Lake, May 12, 1927; Young to Lake, February 14, 1928; Lake Papers, Box 2, Huntington Library.

59. Ella King Adams to Lake, October 20, 1927; Adams to Lake, November 28, 1927; Grace Thack to Lake, November 1, 1927; Lake Papers, Box 3, Huntington Library.

60. Wyatt Earp to Lake, November 2, 1928, Lake Papers, Box 3, Huntington Library.

61. Wyatt Earp to Hart, July 4, 1928, Earp Family Papers, Arizona Historical Society.

62. Stuart Lake, *Wyatt Earp: Frontier Marshal* (Boston: Houghton Mifflin, 1931), 66, 89.

63. Ira Rich Kent to Lake, August 30, 1929; April 5, 1930; August 9, 1930; Lake Papers, Box 4. Lake to Kent, September 3, 1929, Lake Papers, Box 7, Huntington Library.

64. Wyatt Earp to Lake, January 10, 1929, Lake Papers, Box 3, Huntington Library.

65. "Tamer of Wild West Dies," *Los Angeles Times*, January 14, 1929; "Famous Frontier Gunman Is Dead at Hollywood," *Chicago Tribune*, January 14, 1929; "Noted Gun Gunfighter of Old West Dead," *New York Times*, January 14, 1929; "Wyatt Earp, Noted Gunman of Old Frontier Days, Dies," *Washington Post*, January 14, 1929.

66. Kent to Lake, October 14, 1931, citing a letter to the *New York Herald Tribune* from George S. Lewy critical of the newspaper's positive review of Lake's biography of Earp, Lake Papers, Box 4, Huntington Library.

67. Kent to Lake, October 15, 1931; January 7, 1932; February 28, 1942; April 29, 1944; Lake Papers, Box 4, Huntington Library.

68. Eric Hobsbawm and Terence Ranger, eds., *The Invention of Tradition* (Cambridge, UK: Cambridge University Press, 1983); David Blight, *Race and Reunion: The Civil War in American Memory* (Cambridge, MA: Harvard University Press, 2001).

69. Walter Benjamin, "The Work of Art in the Age of Mechanical Reproduction," in Hannah Arendt, ed., *Illuminations*, trans. Henry Zahn (New York: Harcourt, Brace, 1968).

SELECT BIBLIOGRAPHY

MANUSCRIPT COLLECTIONS

ABRAHAM LINCOLN PRESIDENTIAL LIBRARY,
SPRINGFIELD, ILLINOIS
Irvine, Esther Lillian, Data on the Earp Family, c. 1958.

ARIZONA HISTORICAL SOCIETY, TUCSON
Cason, Mabel Earp, Papers.
Cochise County Collection.
Earp, Josephine Sarah Marcus, Collection.
Earp Family Manuscript Collection.
Goodfellow, George Emory, Papers.
Gray, John Pleasant, "When All Roads Led to Tombstone," c. 1940.
Hancock, James Covington, Reminiscences.
Lockwood, Frank C., Papers.
Medigovich, Sam V., Manuscript Collection.

BANCROFT LIBRARY, UNIVERSITY OF CALIFORNIA, BERKELEY
Earp Brothers Dictations.
Waterman Family Papers.

CENTRAL COLLEGE ARCHIVES, PELLA, IOWA
Curtis Family Papers.
Earp Family Papers.
Nossaman Family Papers.

FORD COUNTY HISTORICAL SOCIETY, DODGE CITY, KANSAS
Cason, Mabel Earp, and Vinnolia Earp Ackerman Manuscript, c. 1937.
Earp, Louisa Houston, Letters, 1880–82.
Flood, John Henry, "Wyatt Earp," c. 1925.

HUNTINGTON LIBRARY, SAN MARINO, CALIFORNIA
Lake, Stuart N., Papers.

KANSAS HERITAGE CENTER, DODGE CITY
Early Dodge City Letters.

KANSAS STATE HISTORICAL SOCIETY, TOPEKA
Baker, Marion Jane, Letters.
Glick, Gov. George, Correspondence, 1883.
Hand, Julia, Diary, 1872–73.
Masterson Collection.
Purdy, Wilson, Journals 1874–79.
Wichita City Records, 1871–81.
Wilson, Wentin A., Diary, 1876.

MISSOURI STATE ARCHIVES, JEFFERSON CITY
Barton County Circuit Court Records, 1866–69.
Barton County Circuit Court Records, 1870–73.
Barton County Execution Docket, 1870–75.
Barton County Marriages, 1866–81.

**NATIONAL ARCHIVES, SOUTHWEST REGION,
FORT WORTH, TEXAS**
Record Group 21, Larceny Jacket Number 59, U.S. District Court for the Fort Smith
    Division of the Western District of Arkansas.

**PEORIA HISTORICAL SOCIETY, SPECIAL COLLECTIONS CENTER,
BRADLEY UNIVERSITY, PEORIA, ILLINOIS**
Police Docket, January 27, 1871–March 26, 1872.

**SOUTHWEST MUSEUM/AUTRY NATIONAL CENTER,
LOS ANGELES, CALIFORNIA**
Chafin, Earl, Manuscript Collection.
Hooker, Forrestine C., "An Arizona Vendetta: The Truth About Wyatt Earp and Some
    Others," c. 1918.

UNIVERSITY OF ARIZONA SPECIAL COLLECTIONS, TUCSON
Behan Family Papers.
Burns, Walter Noble, Papers.
Clum, John Philip, Collection.
Dake, C. P., Correspondence.
Hand, George O., Diary.
Minutes of the Tombstone Common Council.

PUBLISHED PRIMARY SOURCES

Bailey, Lynn R., ed. *A Tenderfoot in Tombstone: The Private Journal of George Whitwell Parsons*. Tucson: Westernlore Press, 1996.

———, ed. *Tombstone from a Woman's Point of View: The Correspondence of Clara Spalding Brown*. Tucson: Westernlore Press, 2003.

Beattie, George W., ed. "Rousseau Diary: Across the Desert to California from Salt Lake City to San Bernardino in 1864." *San Bernardino County Museum Association* 6 (Winter 1958): 1–17.

Breakenridge, William. *Helldorado: Bringing Law to the Mesquite*. Boston: Houghton Mifflin, 1928.

Carmony, Neil B., ed. *Apache Days and Tombstone Nights: John Clum's Autobiography*. Silver City, NM: High Lonesome Books, 1997.

Chafin, Earl, ed. *The Rousseau Diary*. Riverside, CA: Earl Chafin Press, 2002.

Chaput, Don. *The Earp Papers*. Encampment, WY: Affiliated Writers of America, 1994.

Cilch, Kenneth R., and Kenneth R. Cilch, Jr. *Wyatt Earp, the Missing Years: San Diego in the 1880s*. San Diego: Gaslamp Books, 1998.

Clum, John. *It All Happened in Tombstone*. 1929. Reprint, Flagstaff, AZ: Northland Press, 1965.

Devol, George. *Forty Years a Gambler on the Mississippi*. 1892. Reprint, New York: Johnson Reprint Company, 1988.

Earp, Wyatt. "How I Routed a Gang of Arizona Outlaws." *San Francisco Examiner*, August 2, 1896.

Gatto, Steve. *The Real Wyatt Earp: A Documentary Biography*. Edited by Neil B. Carmony. Silver City, NM: High Lonesome Books, 2000.

Hand, George O. *One Hundred Days on the San Pedro: The Contention City, A.T. Diary of George O. Hand, March 23–July 1, 1882*. Tombstone, AZ: Cochise Classics, 1988.

Hart, William S. *My Life East and West*. Boston: Houghton Mifflin, 1929.

Hooker, Forrestine C. *Child of the Fighting Tenth: On the Frontier with the Buffalo Soldiers*. New York: Oxford University Press, 2011.

Masterson, William Barclay. "Famous Gun Fighters of the Western Frontier, Second Article: Wyatt Earp." *Human Life*, February 1907.

McIntire, Jim. *Early Days in Texas: A Trip to Hell and Heaven*. 1902. Reprint, Norman: University of Oklahoma Press, 1992.

The Past and Present of Warren County, Illinois. Chicago: H. F. Kett, 1877.

Reidhead, S. J., ed. *A Church for Helldorado*. Roswell, NM: Jinglebob Press, 2006.

Tucson and Tombstone General and Business Directory for 1883 and 1884, Containing a Complete List of All the Inhabitants, with Their Occupations and Places of Residence; the Public Officers, Secret Societies and Churches, Together with Other Useful Information Concerning Both Cities. Tucson, AZ: Cobler & Co., 1883.

Van Dyke, Theodore S. *Millionaires of a Day: An Inside History of the Great Southern California "Boom."* New York: Fords, Howard, and Hulbert, 1890.

Walsh, Raoul. *Each Man in His Time*. New York: Farrar, Straus and Giroux, 1974.

Wright, Robert M. *Dodge City: The Cowboy Capital*. Wichita, KS: 1913.

SECONDARY SOURCES

Ahlstrom, Sydney E. *A Religious History of the American People*. New Haven, CT: Yale University Press, 1972.

Anderson, Douglas Firth. "Protestantism, Progress, and Prosperity: John P. Clum and 'Civilizing' the U.S. Southwest, 1871–1886." *Western Historical Quarterly* 33 (Autumn 2002): 315–35.

Ashburn, Frank Davis. *Peabody of Groton: A Portrait*. New York: Coward McCann, 1944.

Atack, Jeremy. "Tenants and Yeomen in the Nineteenth Century," *Agricultural History* 62 (Summer 1998): 6–32.

Ball, Larry D. "Before the Hanging Judge: The Origins of the United States District Court for the Western District of Arkansas." *Arkansas Historical Quarterly* 49 (Autumn 1990): 199–213.

———. *The United States Marshals of New Mexico and Arizona Territories, 1846–1912*. Albuquerque: University of New Mexico Press, 1978.

Barra, Allen. *Inventing Wyatt Earp: His Life and Many Legends*. Edison, NJ: Avalon, 2005.

Bartholomew, Ed Ellsworth. *Wyatt Earp, 1848 to 1880*. Toyahvale, TX: Frontier Book Co., 1963.

Bederman, Gail. *Manliness and Civilization: A Cultural History of Gender and Race in the United States, 1880–1917*. Chicago: University of Chicago Press, 1995.

Beezley, William H. *Judas at the Jockey Club, and Other Episodes of Porfirian Mexico*. Lincoln: University of Nebraska Press, 1987.

Benton-Cohen, Katherine. *Borderline Americans: Racial Division and Labor War in the Arizona Borderlands*. Cambridge, MA: Harvard University Press, 2011.

Boag, Peter G. *Environment and Experience: Settlement Culture in Nineteenth-Century Oregon*. Berkeley: University of California Press, 1992.

————. *Same-Sex Affairs: Constructing and Controlling Homosexuality in the Pacific Northwest*. Berkeley: University of California Press, 2003.

Bodenhamer, David J. "Law and Disorder on the Early Frontier: Marion County, Indiana, 1823–1850." *Western Historical Quarterly* 10 (July 1979): 323–36.

Boessenecker, John. *Lawman: The Life and Times of Harry Morse, 1835–1912*. Norman: University of Oklahoma Press, 1998.

Booth, Larry, Roger Olmsted, and Richard F. Pourade. "Portrait of a Boom Town: San Diego in the 1880s." *California Historical Quarterly* 50 (December 1971): 363–94.

Bray, Alan. "Homosexuality and the Signs of Male Friendship in Elizabethan England." In *Queering the Renaissance*, edited by Jonathan Goldberg, 40–61. Durham, NC: Duke University Press, 1994.

Breen, T. H. "Horses and Gentlemen: The Cultural Significance of Gambling Among the Gentry of Virginia." *William and Mary Quarterly*, 3rd ser., 34 (April 1977): 239–57.

Brown, Richard Maxwell. *No Duty to Retreat: Violence and Values in American History and Society*. Norman: University of Oklahoma Press, 1994.

Burg, B. R. "Officers, Gentlemen, 'Man-Talk,' and Group Sex in the 'Old Navy,' 1870–1873." *Journal of the History of Sexuality* 11 (July 2002): 439–56.

Burns, Walter Noble. *Tombstone: An Iliad of the Southwest*. New York: Doubleday, 1927.

Butler, Anne M. *Daughters of Joy, Sisters of Misery: Prostitutes in the American West, 1865–1890*. Urbana: University of Illinois Press, 1985.

Colwell-Chanthaphonh, Chip. *Massacre at Camp Grant: Forgetting and Remembering Apache History*. Tucson: University of Arizona Press, 2007.

Conzen, Kathleen Neils. "A Saga of Families." In Clyde A. Milner II, Carol A. O'Connor, and Martha Sandweiss, eds., *The Oxford History of the American West*. New York: Oxford University Press, 1994.

Corkin, Stanley. *Cowboys as Cold Warriors: The Western and U.S. History*. Philadelphia: Temple University Press, 2004.

Cott, Nancy F. *Public Vows: A History of Marriage and the Nation*. Cambridge, MA: Harvard University Press, 2000.

Cronon, William. *Nature's Metropolis: Chicago and the Great West*. New York: Norton, 1991.

Cunningham, Gary L. "Gambling in the Kansas Cattle Towns: A Prominent and Somewhat Honorable Profession." *Kansas History* 5 (Spring 1982): 2–22.

Danhof, Clarence H. "Economic Validity of the Safety-Valve Doctrine." *The Tasks of Economic History*, supplement to *Journal of Economic History* 1 (December 1941): 96–106.

DeLay, Brian. *War of a Thousand Deserts: Indian Raids and the U.S.-Mexican War*. New Haven, CT: Yale University Press, 2008.

D'Emilio, John, and Estelle Freedman. *Intimate Matters: A History of Sexuality in America*. New York: Harper and Row, 1988.

Deverell, William. *Railroad Crossing: Californians and the Railroad, 1850–1910*. Berkeley: University of California Press, 1996.

———. "To Loosen the Safety Valve: Eastern Workers and Western Lands." *Western Historical Quarterly* 19 (August 1988): 269–85.

Dick, Everett. *The Sod-House Frontier, 1854–1890: A Social History of the Northern Plains from the Creation of Kansas and Nebraska to the Admission of the Dakotas*. Lincoln, NE: Johnsen, 1954. First published 1937 by D. Appleton-Century.

Diggs, Marylynne. "Romantic Friends or a 'Different Race of Creatures'? The Representations of Lesbian Pathology in Nineteenth-Century America." *Feminist Studies* 21 (Summer 1995): 317–40.

Doyle, Don Harrison. *The Social Order of a Frontier Community: Jacksonville, Illinois, 1825–70*. Urbana: University of Illinois Press, 1978.

Dykstra, Robert. "Body Counts and Murder Rates: The Contested Statistics of Western Violence." *Reviews in American History* 31 (December 2003): 554–63.

———. *The Cattle Towns*. New York: A. A. Knopf, 1968.

———. "Field Notes: Overdosing on Dodge City." *Western Historical Quarterly* 27 (Winter 1996): 505–14.

———. "Violence, Gender, and Methodology in the 'New' Western History." *Reviews in American History* 27 (March 1999): 79–86.

Fabian, Ann. *Card Sharps, Dream Books, and Bucket Shops: Gambling in Nineteenth-Century America*. Ithaca, NY: Cornell University Press, 1990.

Faragher, John M. *Sugar Creek: Life on the Illinois Prairie*. New Haven, CT: Yale University Press, 1986.

———. "The Tale of Wyatt Earp." In Mark Carnes, ed., *Past Imperfect: History According to the Movies*, 154–61. New York: Holt, 1995.

———. *Women and Men on the Overland Trail*. New Haven, CT: Yale University Press, 1979.

Feller, Daniel. *The Public Lands in Jacksonian Politics*. Madison: University of Wisconsin Press, 1984.

Fields, Armond. *James J. Corbett: A Biography of the Heavyweight Boxing Champion and Popular Theater Headliner*. Jefferson, NC: McFarland, 2001.

Findlay, John M. *People of Chance: Gambling in American Society from Jamestown to Las Vegas*. New York: Oxford University Press, 1986.

Foner, Eric. *Free Soil, Free Labor, Free Men: The Ideology of the Republican Party Before the Civil War*. New York: Oxford University Press, 1970.

———. *Reconstruction: America's Unfinished Revolution, 1863–1877*. New York: Harper and Row, 1988.

Foos, Paul. *A Short, Offhand Killing Affair: Soldiers and Social Conflict During the Mexican-American War*. Chapel Hill: University of North Carolina Press, 2002.

Fredrickson, George M. *The Inner Civil War: Northern Intellectuals and the Crisis of the Union*. Urbana: University of Illinois Press, 1993.

Freedman, Estelle. "Sexuality in Nineteenth-Century America: Behavior, Ideology, and Politics." *Reviews in American History* 10 (December 1982): 196–215.

Galenson, David W., and Clayne L. Pope. "Economic and Geographical Mobility on the Farming Frontier: Evidence from Appanoose County, Iowa, 1850–1870." *Journal of Economic History* 49 (September 1989): 635–55.

Gates, Paul Wallace. *The Farmer's Age: Agriculture, 1815–1860.* New York: Holt, Rinehart and Winston, 1960.

———. *Landlords and Tenants on the Prairie Frontier.* Ithaca, NY: Cornell University Press, 1973.

———. "Land Policy and Tenancy in the Prairie States." *Journal of Economic History* 1 (May 1941): 60–82.

———. "Large-Scale Farming in Illinois, 1850–1870." *Agricultural History* 6 (January 1932): 14–25.

———. "Tenants of the Log Cabin." *Mississippi Valley Historical Review* 49 (June 1962): 3–31.

Geertz, Clifford. *The Interpretation of Cultures: Selected Essays.* New York: Basic Books, 1973.

Gerth, H. H., and C. Wright Mills, eds. *From Max Weber: Essays in Sociology.* New York: Oxford University Press, 1958.

Goldman, Marion S. *Gold Diggers and Silver Miners: Prostitution and Social Life on the Comstock Lode.* Ann Arbor: University of Michigan Press, 1981.

Gorn, Elliott J. "'Gouge and Bite, Pull Hair and Scratch': The Social Significance of Fighting in the Southern Backcountry." *American Historical Review* 90 (February 1985): 18–43.

———. *The Manly Art: Bare-Knuckle Prize Fighting in America.* Ithaca, NY: Cornell University Press, 1986.

Graybill, Andrew R. *Policing the Great Plains: Rangers, Mounties, and the North American Frontier, 1875–1910.* Lincoln: University of Nebraska Press, 2007.

———. "Rural Police and the Defense of the Cattleman's Empire in Texas and Alberta, 1875–1900." *Agricultural History* 79 (Summer 2005): 253–80.

Gregson, Mary Eschelbach. "Population Dynamics in Rural Missouri, 1860–1880." *Social Science History* 21 (Spring 1997): 85–110.

Hahn, Stephen. *The Roots of Southern Populism: Yeoman Farmers and the Transformation of the Georgia Upcountry, 1850–1890.* New York: Oxford University Press, 1983.

Halttunen, Karen. *Confidence Men and Painted Women: A Study of Middle-Class Culture in America, 1830–1870.* New Haven, CT: Yale University Press, 1982.

Hanson, Stephen, and Patricia Hanson. "The Last Days of Wyatt Earp." *Retrospect,* March 1985.

Harring, Sidney. *Crow Dog's Case: American Indian Sovereignty, Tribal Law, and United States Law in the Nineteenth Century.* New York: Cambridge University Press, 1994.

———. "The Development of the Police Institution in the United States." *Crime and Social Justice* 5 (Spring–Summer 1976): 54–59.

Hatch, Nathan O. *The Democratization of American Christianity*. New Haven, CT: Yale University Press, 1989.

Haywood, C. Robert. *Victorian West: Class and Culture in Kansas Cattle Towns*. Lawrence: University Press of Kansas, 1991.

Higham, John. "The Reorientation of American Culture in the 1890's." In *Writing American History: Essays on Modern Scholarship*, 73–102. Bloomington: Indiana University Press, 1970.

Hobsbawm, Eric J. *Bandits*. New York: Pelican, 1972.

———. *Primitive Rebels: Studies in Archaic Forms of Social Movements in the 19th and 20th Centuries*. New York: Norton, 1959.

Holliday, J. S. *Rush for Riches: Gold Fever and the Making of California*. Berkeley: University of California Press, 1999.

Holt, Michael F. *The Rise and Fall of the American Whig Party: Jacksonian Politics and the Onset of the Civil War*. New York: Oxford University Press, 1999.

Hornung, Chuck, and Gary L. Roberts. "The Split." *True West* 48 (November–December 2001): 58–61.

Howe, Daniel Walker. *Making the American Self: Jonathan Edwards to Abraham Lincoln*. New York: Oxford University Press, 2009.

Hurt, R. Douglas. *Agriculture and Slavery in Missouri's Little Dixie*. Columbia: University of Missouri Press, 1992.

Hurtado, Albert L. *Intimate Frontiers: Sex and Gender in Old California*. Albuquerque: University of New Mexico Press, 1999.

Hutchinson, W. H. *Oil, Land, and Politics: The California Career of Thomas Robert Bard*. Norman: University of Oklahoma Press, 1965.

Hutton, Paul Andrew. "Showdown at the Hollywood Corral: Wyatt Earp and the Movies." *Montana: The Magazine of Western History* 45 (Summer 1995): 2–31.

Igler, David. *Industrial Cowboys: Miller & Lux and the Transformation of the Far West, 1850–1920*. Berkeley: University of California Press, 2001.

Isenberg, Andrew C. "The Code of the West: Sexuality, Homosociality, and Wyatt Earp." *Western Historical Quarterly* 40 (Summer 2009): 139–57.

———. *The Destruction of the Bison: An Environmental History, 1750–1920*. New York: Cambridge University Press, 2000.

———. *Mining California: An Ecological History*. New York: Hill and Wang, 2005.

Jacoby, Karl. *Shadows at Dawn: An Apache Massacre and the Violence of History*. New York: Penguin, 2008.

Jay, Roger. "The Gamblers' War in Tombstone." *Wild West*, October 2004, 38–45.

———. "Wyatt Earp's Lost Year," *Wild West*, August 2003, 46–52.

Johnson, David A. "Vigilance and the Law: The Moral Authority of Popular Justice in the Far West." *American Quarterly* 33 (Winter 1981): 558–86.

Johnson, Paul E. *A Shopkeeper's Millennium: Society and Revivals in Rochester, New York, 1815–1837*. New York: Hill and Wang, 1978.

Johnson, Susan. *Roaring Camp: The Social World of the California Gold Rush*. New York: Norton, 2000.

Jordan, Terry G. *North American Cattle-Ranching Frontiers: Origins, Diffusion, and Differentiation*. Albuquerque: University of New Mexico Press, 1993.

Kammen, Michael. *Mystic Chords of Memory: The Transformation of Tradition in American Culture*. New York: A. A. Knopf, 1991.

Kimmel, Michael. *Manhood in America: A Cultural History*. New York: Free Press, 1996.

King, Ros. *The Works of Richard Edwards: Politics, Poetry, and Performance in Sixteenth-Century England*. Manchester, UK, and New York: Manchester University Press, 2001.

Lake, Stuart N. *Wyatt Earp: Frontier Marshal*. Boston: Houghton Mifflin, 1931.

Lamar, Howard. *The Far Southwest, 1846–1912: A Territorial History*. New York: Norton, 1970.

Lang, Arne K. *Prizefighting: An American History*. Jefferson, NC: McFarland, 2008.

Lender, Mark Edward, and James Kirby Martin. *Drinking in America: A History*. New York: Free Press, 1982.

Leonard, Carol, and Isidor Wallimann. "Prostitution and Changing Morality in the Frontier Cattle Towns of Kansas." *Kansas History* 2 (Spring 1979): 34–53.

Levine, Peter. "Draft Evasion in the North During the Civil War, 1863–1865." *Journal of American History* 67 (March 1981): 816–34.

Liebman, Robert, and Michael Polen. "Perspectives on Policing in Nineteenth-Century America." *Social Science History* 2 (Spring 1978): 346–60.

Lockwood, Frank C. *Pioneer Days in Arizona, from the Spanish Occupation to Statehood*. New York: Macmillan, 1932.

Lopez, David. "Cowboy Strikes and Unions." *Labor History* 18 (Summer 1977): 325–40.

Lubet, Steven. *Murder in Tombstone: The Forgotten Trial of Wyatt Earp*. New Haven, CT: Yale University Press, 2004.

Mahoney, Timothy R. "Urban History in a Regional Context: River Towns on the Upper Mississippi, 1840–1860." *Journal of American History* 72 (September 1985): 318–39.

Martin, Edgar W. *The Standard of Living in 1860: American Consumption Levels on the Eve of the Civil War*. Chicago: University of Chicago Press, 1942.

Maurer, David W. "The Argot of the Faro Bank." *American Speech* 18 (February 1943): 3–11.

May, Dean. *Three Frontiers: Family, Land, and Society in the American West, 1850–1900*. New York: Cambridge University Press, 1994.

McGrath, Roger D. *Gunfighters, Highwaymen, and Vigilantes: Violence on the Frontier*. Berkeley: University of California Press, 1984.

McKanna, Clare V., Jr. "Alcohol, Handguns, and Homicide in the American West: A Tale of Three Counties, 1880–1920." *Western Historical Quarterly* 26 (Winter 1995): 455–82.

———. *Homicide, Race, and Justice in the American West, 1880–1920*. Tucson: University of Arizona Press, 1997.

McLoughlin, William G. *After the Trail of Tears: The Cherokees' Struggle for Sovereignty, 1839–1880*. Chapel Hill: University of North Carolina Press, 1993.

McPherson, James M. *Ordeal by Fire: The Civil War and Reconstruction*. 2nd ed. New York: McGraw-Hill, 1992.

Mercer, Lloyd J. *Railroads and Land Grant Policy: A Study in Government Intervention*. New York: Academic Press, 1982.

Mitchell, Lee Clark. *Westerns: Making the Man in Fiction and Film*. Chicago: University of Chicago Press, 1996.

Murray, John F. "Generation(s) of Human Capital: Literacy in American Families, 1830–1875." *Journal of Interdisciplinary History* 27 (Winter 1997): 413–35.

Nissenbaum, Stephen. *Sex, Diet, and Debility in Jacksonian America: Sylvester Graham and Health Reform*. Westport, CT: Greenwood, 1980.

Oakes, James. *Slavery and Freedom: An Interpretation of the Old South*. New York: A. A. Knopf, 1990.

Oberly, James W. "Westward Who? Estimates of Native White Interstate Migration After the War of 1812." *Journal of Economic History* 46 (June 1986): 431–40.

Odd, Gilbert. *The Fighting Blacksmith*. London: Pelham, 1976.

Opie, John. *The Law of the Land: Two Hundred Years of American Farmland Policy*. Lincoln: University of Nebraska Press, 1994.

Orsi, Robert J. *Sunset Limited: The Southern Pacific Railroad and the Development of the American West, 1850–1930*. Berkeley: University of California Press, 2005.

Packard, Chris. *Queer Cowboys and Other Erotic Male Friendships in Nineteenth-Century American Literature*. New York: Palgrave Macmillan, 2005.

Parrish, William E. *Missouri Under Radical Rule, 1865–1870*. Columbia: University of Missouri Press, 1965.

Peck, Gunther. "Manly Gambles: The Politics of Risk on the Comstock Lode, 1860–1880." *Journal of Social History* 26 (Summer 1993): 701–23.

Peiss, Kathy. *Cheap Amusements: Working Women and Leisure in Turn-of-the-Century New York*. Philadelphia: Temple University Press, 1986.

Perkins, Elizabeth A. "The Consumer Frontier: Household Consumption in Early Kentucky." *Journal of American History* 78 (September 1991): 486–510.

Pessen, Edward. "The Egalitarian Myth and American Social Reality: Wealth, Mobility, and Equality in the 'Era of the Common Man.'" *American Historical Review* 76 (October 1971): 989–1034.

Peterson, Richard H. "In San Diego, Wyatt Earp Was All-Business—and Business Was Booming for a While." *Wild West*, October 2004, 66–69.

Pleck, Elizabeth. "Two Worlds in One: Work and Family." *Journal of Social History* 10 (Winter 1976): 178–95.

Potter, Claire Bond. *War on Crime: Bandits, G-Men, and the Politics of Mass Culture*. New Brunswick, NJ: Rutgers University Press, 1998.

Powers, Richard Gid. "J. Edgar Hoover and the Detective Hero." *Journal of Popular Culture* 9 (Fall 1975): 257–78.

Prescott, Cynthia Culver. "'Why she didn't marry him': Love, Power, and Marital Choice on the Far Western Frontier." *Western Historical Quarterly* 38 (Spring 2007): 25–46.

Putney, Clifford. *Muscular Christianity: Manhood and Sports in Protestant America, 1880–1920*. Cambridge, MA: Harvard University Press, 2001.

Riess, Steven A. *Sport in Industrial America, 1850–1920*. Wheeling, IL: Harlan Davidson, 1995.

Roberts, Gary L. *Doc Holliday: The Life and Legend*. Hoboken, NJ: Wiley, 2006.

Robinson, Cyril D., and Richard Scaglion. "The Origin and Evolution of the Police Function in Society: Notes Toward a Theory." *Law and Society Review* 21 (1987): 109–54.

Rohrbough, Malcolm. *Days of Gold: The California Gold Rush and the American Nation*. Berkeley: University of California Press, 1997.

Rorabaugh, W. J. *The Alcoholic Republic: An American Tradition*. New York: Oxford University Press, 1979.

Roth, Randolph, Michael D. Maltz, and Douglas L. Eckberg. "Homicide Rates in the Old West." *Western Historical Quarterly* 42 (Summer 2011): 173–95.

Rotundo, E. Anthony. *American Manhood: Transformations of Masculinity from the Revolution to the Modern Era*. New York: Basic Books, 1994.

———. "Body and Soul: Changing Ideals of American Middle-Class Manhood, 1770–1920." *Journal of Social History* 16 (Summer 1983): 23–38.

Ruth, David. *Inventing the Public Enemy: The Gangster in American Culture, 1918–1934*. Chicago: University of Chicago Press, 1996.

Salas, Miguel Tinker. *In the Shadow of the Eagles: Sonora and the Transformation of the Border During the Porfiriato*. Berkeley: University of California Press, 1997.

Schob, David E. *Hired Hands and Plowboys: Farm Labor in the Midwest, 1815–1860*. Urbana: University of Illinois Press, 1975.

Schwantes, Carlos. "Protest in a Promised Land: Unemployment, Disinheritance, and the Origin of Labor Militancy in the Pacific Northwest, 1885–1886." *Western Historical Quarterly* 13 (October 1982): 373–90.

Sellers, Charles. *The Market Revolution: Jacksonian America, 1815–1846*. New York: Oxford University Press, 1991.

———. "Who Were the Southern Whigs?" *American Historical Review* 59 (January 1954): 335–46.

Shannon, Fred A. "A Post-Mortem on the Labor-Safety-Valve Theory." *Agricultural History* 19 (January 1945): 31–37.

Shillingberg, William B. *Tombstone, A.T.: A History of Early Mining, Milling, and Mayhem*. Spokane, WA: Arthur H. Clark, 1999.

———. "Wyatt Earp and the 'Buntline Special' Myth." *Kansas Historical Quarterly* 42 (Summer 1976): 113–52.

Slotkin, Richard. *Gunfighter Nation: The Myth of the Frontier in Twentieth-Century America*. New York: HarperCollins, 1992.

Smith, Daniel Scott. "Family Limitation, Sexual Control, and Domestic Feminism in Victorian America." *Feminist Studies* 1 (Winter–Spring 1973): 40–57.

Smith, Michael T. "The Beast Unleashed: Benjamin F. Butler and Conceptions of Masculinity in the Civil War North." *New England Quarterly* 79 (June 2006): 248–76.

Smith-Rosenberg, Carroll. "The Female World of Love and Ritual: Relations Between Women in Nineteenth-Century America." *Signs* 1 (Autumn 1975): 1–29.

Stampp, Kenneth. *America in 1857: A Nation on the Brink*. New York: Oxford University Press, 1990.

Steckel, Richard H. "The Health and Mortality of Women and Children, 1850–1860." *Journal of Economic History* 48 (June 1988): 333–45.

Stewart, Alan. *Close Readers: Humanism and Sodomy in Early Modern England*. Princeton, NJ: Princeton University Press, 1997.

Stoll, Steven. *Larding the Lean Earth: Soil and Society in Nineteenth-Century America*. New York: Hill and Wang, 2002.

Tanner, Karen Holliday. *Doc Holliday: A Family Portrait*. Norman: University of Oklahoma Press, 1998.

Tefertiler, Casey. *Wyatt Earp: The Life Behind the Legend*. New York: Wiley, 1997.

Thernstrom, Stephen. *Poverty and Progress: Social Mobility in a Nineteenth-Century City*. Cambridge, MA: Harvard University Press, 1964.

Truett, Samuel. *Fugitive Landscapes: The Forgotten History of the U.S.-Mexico Border*. New Haven, CT: Yale University Press, 2006.

Tyrrell, Ian R. *Sobering Up: From Temperance to Prohibition in Antebellum America, 1800–1860*. Westport, CT: Greenwood Press, 1979.

Unruh, John D. *The Plains Across: The Overland Emigrants and the Trans-Mississippi West, 1840–60*. Urbana: University of Illinois Press, 1979.

Urban, William. "Nicholas Earp's Iowa Lands." Unpublished manuscript.

———. "The People Versus Nicholas Earp." *Illinois Historical Journal* 90 (Autumn 1997): 173–90.

———. "Wyatt Earp's Father." *True West*, May 1984.

———. "Wyatt Earp Was Born Here: Monmouth and the Earps, 1845–1859." *Western Illinois Regional Studies* 3 (Fall 1980): 154–67.

Vanderwood, Paul J. *Disorder and Progress: Bandits, Police, and Mexican Development*. Lincoln: University of Nebraska Press, 1981.

Vangilder, Marvin. *The Story of Barton County: A Complete History, 1855–1972*. Lamar, MO: Reiley, 1972.

Wade, Richard. *The Urban Frontier: The Rise of Western Cities, 1790–1830*. Cambridge, MA: Harvard University Press, 1959.

Walker, Henry P. "Arizona Land Fraud Model 1880: The Tombstone Townsite Company." *Arizona and the West* 21 (Spring 1979): 5–36.

Walker, Richard. "From Settlement to Fordism: The Agro-Industrial Revolution in the American Midwest." *Economic Geography* 67 (October 1991): 281–315.

Walsh, Margaret. "From Pork Merchant to Meat Packer: The Midwestern Meat Industry in the Mid-Nineteenth Century." *Agricultural History* 56 (January 1982): 127–37.

———. "Pork Packing as a Leading Edge of Midwestern Industry, 1835–1875." *Agricultural History* 51 (October 1977): 702–17.

Walters, Ronald G. *American Reformers, 1815–1860.* New York: Hill and Wang, 1978.

Warren, Louis S. *Buffalo Bill's America: William Cody and the Wild West Show.* New York: A. A. Knopf, 2005.

Weber, David J. *The Spanish Frontier in North America.* New Haven, CT: Yale University Press, 1992.

Wells, Jonathan Daniel. *The Origins of the Southern Middle Class, 1800–1861.* Chapel Hill: University of North Carolina Press, 2004.

West, Elliott. *The Contested Plains: Indians, Goldseekers, and the Rush to Colorado.* Lawrence: University Press of Kansas, 1998.

———. *The Saloon on the Rocky Mountain Mining Frontier.* Lincoln: University of Nebraska Press, 1979.

———. *The Way to the West: Essays on the Central Plains.* Albuquerque: University of New Mexico Press, 1995.

White, Richard. "Information, Markets, and Corruption: Transcontinental Railroads in the Gilded Age." *Journal of American History* 90 (June 2003): 19–43.

———. *Railroaded: The Transcontinentals and the Making of Modern America.* New York: Norton, 2011.

Wiebe, Robert. *The Search for Order, 1877–1920.* New York: Hill and Wang, 1967.

Wiley, Bell Irvin. *The Life of Billy Yank: The Common Soldier of the Union.* Indianapolis: Bobbs-Merrill, 1951.

Winter, Thomas. *Making Men, Making Class: The YMCA and the Workingman, 1877–1920.* Chicago: University of Chicago Press, 2002.

Winther, Oscar Osburn. *The Transportation Frontier: Trans-Mississippi West, 1865–1890.* New York: Holt, Rinehart and Winston, 1964.

Wright, Gavin. *The Political Economy of the Cotton South: Households, Markets, and Wealth in the Nineteenth Century.* New York: Norton, 1978.

Wright, Louis B. "The Male-Friendship Cult in Thomas Heywood's Plays." *Modern Language Notes* 42 (December 1927): 510–14.

Wyatt-Brown, Bertram. *Southern Honor: Ethics and Behavior in the Old South.* New York: Oxford University Press, 1982.

Wyman, Mark. *Hoboes: Bindlestiffs, Fruit Tramps, and the Harvesting of the West.* New York: Hill and Wang, 2010.

Zeikowitz, Richard E. *Homoeroticism and Chivalry: Discourses of Male Same-Sex Desire in the Fourteenth Century.* New York: Palgrave Macmillan, 2003.

Zornow, William Frank. *Kansas: A History of the Jayhawk State.* Norman: University of Oklahoma Press, 1957.

ACKNOWLEDGMENTS

Uncovering the story of a man who lived most of his life in the shadows has been the central task I faced in writing this book. This humbling process left me with great respect for biographers generally and biographers of Wyatt Earp in particular. I have doubtless made many mistakes in trying to puzzle out the details of Earp's life. I would have made many more without the help I received. I am grateful to the librarians and archivists, notably Peter Blodgett, David Murray, and the incomparable George Laughead, who helped me find some of Earp's scattered letters and memoirs. I owe an enormous debt to the many scholars, including Lynn Baily, Allen Barra, Bob Boze Bell, Neil Carmony, Earl Chafin, Kenneth Cilch and Kenneth Cilch, Jr., Steve Gatto, Chuck Hornung, Roger Jay, Steven Lubet, Robert G. McCubbin, Richard Peterson, S. J. Reidhead, Gary Roberts, William Shillingberg, Casey Tefertiler, and William Urban, who have devoted years to the pursuit of documentary information about the Earp family. They have uncovered important evidence that has substantively contributed to our understanding of this elusive man. Though some of them may disagree with some of my conclusions, I would not have been able to write this book without their many years of dedicated work.

I began the research for this project with a grant from the National Endowment for the Humanities to participate in a five-week summer seminar at the Huntington Library in California. My thanks to Bill Deverell for organizing the NEH seminar and for his faith in this project. Research funds from Temple University allowed me to travel to archives in Arizona, Kansas, Illinois, and Iowa. During my research, I had the help of two doctoral students in history at Temple, Bob Deal and Alex Elkins. My thanks to them both. A sabbatical from Temple gave me time to finish writing. Rob Rapley and Katie Lord helped me track down images of Earp.

I am grateful to Irwin Balik for his keen interest; he listened to me talk about Earp while I was working out my understanding of him. I wrote this book as a member of the History Department at Temple University, which has proved to be an exceptionally nurturing place for research and writing. I had numerous conversations with colleagues about Earp; I am deeply grateful to them, including Michael Alexander, Beth Bailey, Barbara Day-Hickman, Bob Deal, Ryan Edgington, David Farber, Travis Glasson, Petra Goedde, Peter Gran, Mark Haller, Will Hitchcock, Richard Immerman, Larry Kessler, Jay Lockenour, Harvey Neptune, Art Schmidt, Todd Shepard, Bryant Simon, Howard Spodek, Ben Talton, Heather Thompson, Liz Varon, David Watt, Jon Wells, and Vlad Zubok.

At Farrar, Straus and Giroux, Thomas LeBien was an early supporter of this project. Ileene Smith gave me indispensable advice and saw the book through to conclusion. Dan Gerstle was helpful and supportive throughout. I am grateful to Mike Angell, Beth Bailey, David Farber, Andy Graybill, Nick Guyatt, David Rich Lewis, Joel Schorn, and Louis Warren for reading all or part of the manuscript and giving me valuable criticisms.

I wrote this book for family: my mother, Joan; my sister, Kim, and brother, Eric; my children, Kai, Elena, and Noah; and my wife, Petra, whose love, support, and encouragement made this book and many other things possible.

INDEX